SPECIAL FORCES PRINCIPLES **BOOK ONE**

THE GREEN BERET WAY

Leading Elite Teams
Under Extreme Conditions

LTC ROBERT W SCHAEFER (Ret.)

Copyright © 2026 by Robert Schaefer

Published in the United States of America
by First Redwood Publishing

All rights reserved. No part of this book may be used or reproduced in any manner whatsoever without written permission except in the case of brief quotations embodied in critical articles and reviews.
Available at special discounts for bulk purchases. Special book excerpts or customized printings can also be created for specific needs.

FIRST EDITION

Cover and interior design by Gwyn Flowers,
GKS Creative, Nashville, TN.

Library of Congress Cataloging-in-Publication Data has been applied for.

ISBN: 978-0-9802395-7-7 (Paperback)
ISBN: 978-0-9802395-6-0 (eBook)
ISBN: 978-0-9802395-8-4 (Audiobook)

Printed in the United States of America

For media inquiries, contact: AK@AKLiterary.com

For more information on keynotes, consulting, coaching, courses, books, and more, go to:
TheGreenBeretWay.com/info and RobertWSchaefer.com

Contents

A Few Clarifications Before We Begin: SF vs. SOF v

Preface vii

Introduction: The Road To Leadership 1

Chapter One: Basic Training 13

Chapter Two: SFAS 51

Chapter Three: The Q-Course 77

Chapter Four: Language School 147

Chapter Five: Airborne and SERE................... 209

Acknowledgements................................. 303

A FEW CLARIFICATIONS
BEFORE WE BEGIN

SF vs. SOF

The official title of the Green Berets is U.S. Army Special Forces, usually abbreviated as "SF." This should not be confused with the U.S. Air Force Security Forces, which is often referred to as "SF" within the Air Force. Air Force Security Forces wear blue berets and Army Special Forces wear green ones - hence the name. With the addition of the new U.S. Space Force, we can expect that they will be referred to as "SF" at some point in the future as well. Anytime the abbreviation "SF" is used in this book it refers to Army Special Forces and is used interchangeably with the term "Green Berets."

Special Operations Forces (SOF) is a very broad term that encompasses all of the special operations units in the U.S. Military. It runs the gamut from Tier-1 counterterrorism forces to familiar names like Green Berets, Rangers, SEALs, Pararescue as well as all the units that support the missions including Military Intelligence, Psychological Operations (PSYOPS), sustainment brigades, aviation brigades, SEAL Delivery Boat teams, schools, maintenance units, and supply units.

SF is part of SOF, but "SF" and "SOF" are not used interchangeably.

There are multiple references to military ranks in the book, and unless otherwise noted, the ranks mentioned in this book are U.S. Army - which are very similar to the Air Force and Marines. The US Navy uses a different rank system, which may cause confusion with the ranks of other services. Therefore, any mention of navy ranks in this book will include the corresponding Army ranks in parentheses.

Non-Commissioned Officers (NCOs) is the official term for sergeants and petty officers (Navy). The term "NCOs" is used interchangeably with "sergeants" and/or "petty officers."

Preface

For almost 40 years I've had the opportunity to work closely with truly outstanding people on some truly amazing teams. While I've had the pleasure of serving with some incredible leaders, I've experienced some horrible ones, too. They've all had something to teach me.

I'm pretty confident that I don't belong in either of those two groups. Rather, like all U.S. military officers and NCOs, I am a product of a highly effective system that takes regular people and turns them into competent leaders. And as part of Army Special Forces, I was brought into a very different leadership system, one that is responsible for taking those same competent leaders and making them capable of leading elite teams that routinely achieve the (seemingly) impossible.

This is an important point because there's a perception that average people can't do what special operations personnel do. That's not true. And this book is about the fact that almost everyone can learn how to lead like Green Berets because almost all special operations personnel start off as normal people who get put into extraordinary systems. This book lays out one of those systems.

This is not a book about my leadership philosophy. If anything it's a chronicle of my failures, lessons learned, and examples of how my leaders did it right. This isn't a book about anyone in particular; rather, it is an explanation of the characteristics and culture of Special Forces leadership from which all Green Berets are created and later charged with being the standard bearers to model and train each new generation.

Why hasn't this book been written before? Probably because most Green Berets don't realize that they've been brought up in a different system until you point out some of its traits: like the no-salute rule in a Green Beret compound, or the fact that officers on A-Teams are referred to by their first names instead of "sir," or the relaxed grooming standards on some missions that allow for full beards. Some might say those are simply cultural aspects, and they're right. But culture flows from leadership; it's not a separate thing.

There are other leadership books written by military personnel from specialized units (Navy SEALs, fighter pilots, etc.), and they all have something to offer. But I haven't found them as relevant to what most businesses do because their missions usually are much shorter and don't require developing long-term relationships with people from different cultures (with very different values and ways of thinking) to accomplish difficult things in unforgiving environments. Green Berets are different from other special operations forces because their two primary missions depend on motivating and working *with* other people instead of fighting them.

Over the past ten years I've analyzed the characteristics of Special Forces leadership because I've been teaching them to businesses, and at some point I needed to be sure that what I was teaching was based on something tangible. I needed to be able to clearly explain how Special Forces (SF) leadership is different from the conventional military leadership model (and even other special operations forces). Green Berets are responsible for accomplishing no-fail strategic missions of national importance in denied territories under the harshest and demanding of conditions. I wanted to deconstruct how ordinary people get trained to do that.

I was a student of leadership even before I entered the military and have read and studied every classic text and most (if not all) of the highly-regarded contemporary ones. Additionally, I was an enlisted soldier who became a sergeant who then became an officer, so I had the rare opportunity to attend more leadership schools than most in the military - and see the entire system from the bottom to (almost) the very top. I'm certified in and teach some well-regarded civilian leadership programs which has allowed me to see where military themes have been adopted. And I've been privileged to work with some legendary leaders who allowed me to read their unpublished personal notes, speak with them for hours about their thoughts on leadership, and even help to develop their ideas into programs from which others could learn.

I began teaching leadership programs while I was still in the military but never thought much of it until I was asked by a friend to teach a course to his company. At the time I thought to myself "I don't know anything at all about business leadership, so I'm not sure I have much to offer," but I agreed to help my friend. So as not to embarrass myself (or my friend), I did a lot of preparation and added extra material so that I could talk to them about the high-level leadership topics in which I thought they'd be interested.

Within the first 5 minutes of my presentation I realized that something was wrong. I stopped and asked the audience to raise their hands if they'd ever had any leadership training before. Only the CEO raised his hand, saying he'd done a program 20 years earlier while working on his MBA. Up until that point I'd been worried that I wouldn't have anything to teach this group and instead I found that almost everything I'd prepared was too advanced for that group and that we needed to start with the basics, the stuff that privates and seamen are taught when they first go through boot camp.

I was expecting that we'd need to discuss vision statements, company culture, and corporate governance. Instead, I passed on simple things like "what gets checked gets done" and "inspect what you expect" and *that's* what they found helpful. After the course, I worked with the managers one on one to help them become proficient with their new skills, and that's when I saw first-hand how the principles of Special Forces leadership could have profound effects in the corporate world, too.

As I worked with more and more companies, I soon noticed a distinct pattern. The vast majority of managers get a leadership position because they are good at their job (one that they had been trained in), but they had never gotten any training or tools for their new job, being a leader.

Company after company, the pattern continued. The entrepreneurs who started great companies with great employees would come to a standstill because they didn't have a leadership team with the skills, tools, or mindsets required to become truly successful. They had started off with a great team, but they didn't have the ability to scale and create more great teams.

Using the principles of Special Forces leadership, they were able to transform their businesses in very short order.

Once we'd worked on leadership issues, I was asked to develop solutions to some of their other systemic problems.

I'd look at their current methods and be surprised that they weren't as effective as what we used in the military or Special Forces. So, I took the tools and procedures that I knew worked, modified them for each particular company, and helped them implement the solutions.

At some point I realized that if I was going to continue recommending these solutions, I'd better figure out exactly why they worked and what they were based on. I initially looked at conventional military systems, which are already exceptionally good because they are based on best practices and constantly re-evaluated and updated by professional cadres to stay relevant. But while those solutions were good, what really helped these companies was when I modified something that we'd used in Special Forces.

It all came into sharp focus when I was helping a manager develop some goals for her team which, according to accepted practice, should be "SMART" goals. But I found myself telling her to take additional steps if she wanted to ensure success (things we did in SF). At which point I asked myself, "How smart are SMART goals if they need an addendum?" So I researched and analyzed SMART goals and realized that, while they work, they're not the *best* way because well-defined goals also need to answer the questions "why?" and "is it worthwhile (what's the ROI)?" And ultimately, these are the most important questions because many people will stop working towards a goal once they realize what the cost is. But you can't begin to calculate ROI until you've got a firm grasp of "the why."

Also the action plan must be built in. We can't simply ask if they're actionable or achievable - or, whatever the "A" is supposed to mean. So I analyzed how we achieved goals (missions) in Special Forces and then designed MAPPED goals (Metrics, Actions, Purpose (why), Profitable (worthwhile), Exact, Deadlines) so that my clients would be more successful in achieving their objectives, and they were.

SMART goals are good, but being "good" is not "good enough" in Special Forces. In the world of Special Ops, there is the "best" (the standard), and the rest (unacceptable). There is a higher standard for everything because "impossible" only happens consistently through "exceptional."

Green Berets do quite a few things differently than the regular Army, and even within the special operations community. And while the conventional military's system of leadership training is already outstanding, what happens in Special Forces has the potential to take everyone to another level entirely.

In the regular army, 24 year-old sergeants are responsible for leading groups of 8 - 15 soldiers. But in Special Forces 24-year-old Green Beret sergeants are routinely assigned to train, advise, equip, influence, and lead a foreign military force of 40 to 50 soldiers, often in another language. In a regular army infantry unit, a captain would command 120 soldiers whereas a Special Forces captain is trained to advise, influence, and lead units like a Lieutenant Colonel would, with hundreds or even thousands of fighters. And when I say "influence" I mean using the art of graduate-level leadership, which is getting people to do what you want them to do *because they want to do it*.

Think about how much more difficult it is to lead someone when you're not in a position to force them to do what you want them to do, when they're not motivated by threats of getting fired, demoted, punished, or not getting a raise for failing to carry out your directives.

This is a different type of leadership than what is practiced in the conventional military - a traditional pyramidal structure based on "command" which is a top-down approach that's proven to be effective for thousands of years. It's also the basis for most commercial and charitable organizations as well.

However, the business environment has changed dramatically in the past 20 years and what was considered to be good before isn't always producing the best results today. And the "regular" way is definitely not what the most cutting-edge, the most creative, and the most successful companies are doing.

Yes, the "perfect" is the enemy of the "good," but think of perfection as a direction, not an end state, and know that the "best" is always worth striving for.

In an ever-increasingly complex and changing business environment we have seen dramatic shifts in the workforce. The newer generations aren't motivated by the same things that motivated their parents, and prefer shorter workweeks and wellness programs to more pay. In just the past few years we're had "the great resignation," "the great retraining," "quiet quitting," the rise of the hybrid remote employee, DEI (Diversity, Equity, and Inclusion) initiatives, and more.

You can use the standard command style of leadership in these situations and you may get good results and you might even change some of their behaviors, but not their attitude or mindset. Sure, you could fire someone. But how quickly can you get a replacement? How long will it take to train them? What if the person you want to fire is highly skilled and your company really needs them? What is the cost of turnover?

But forget about addressing problems - what's most important is how to get the best out of all your people all the time. You can't threaten someone to improve their performance from "good to great"; they'll find another job. And how do we keep our superstars? They can go anywhere they want so they're looking for a good paycheck *and* a good work environment, and they know they can get it. Use a stick with them and they're gone. But don't use enough carrots or the right kind of carrots and they'll leave as well.

These are the types of challenges I began helping clients overcome. And once I'd deconstructed how we did things in Special Forces, I also began researching how highly successful companies work with their teams. And what I found astounded me. Whether or not they arrived at their practices on their own, had consultants from the SPECOPS community, or outright lifted some of the elements directly from our Special Forces playbook (which has been around since WWII and the OSS and Jedburgh teams), the most successful companies have adopted practices that are strikingly similar (in some cases identical) to how Green Berets operate, make decisions, and empower their "lowest" elements in the pyramid.

I could now offer "SF" solutions with far greater confidence knowing that they came from our unique tradition and culture *and* had been vetted in the modern workplace. And the more I looked the more I discovered that "The Green Beret Way" was highly applicable in today's competitive and rapidly-shifting business environment. All I had to do was to "translate" the concepts from "SPECOPS to business" and create tools to support them. This all coalesced into a comprehensive program which is explained in detail in this book.

INTRODUCTION

The Road To Leadership

Why Special Forces Leadership?
The official designation of Special Forces teams that conduct missions is "Operational Detachment-Alpha" (ODA), otherwise known as the "A-Team."

It's amusing that the term A-Team, while universally recognizable, is usually not associated with the Green Berets. In everyday conversations we talk about "sending in the A-Team," being "on the A-Team," "bringing your A-game," and others. Those terms became fashionable largely because of the popular 1980's TV show *The A-Team* starring Mr. T and George Peppard and the 2010 movie with Liam Neeson and Bradley Cooper. What most people don't realize is that the term A-Team is the basic unit of Army Special Forces and the source of every other reference to "A-Team" in popular culture.

It's referred to as an A-Team because it is the primary unit of action and employment. Multiple A-Teams are supported by a B-Team, and multiple B-Teams are supported by a C-Team. You might more readily recognize a B-Team as a "company" (commanded by a major instead of a captain) and a C-Team as a "battalion," (commanded by a lieutenant colonel) because that is officially what they are. A Special

Forces Group (5th Group, 10th Group, etc) is a brigade-level organization commanded by a colonel and has multiple battalions and companies underneath it in the organizational pyramid, resembling most businesses with senior management at the top.

This is important to understand because, while it looks the same on paper, a critical difference between SF and traditional leadership is that the usual military pyramid is turned upside down in terms of operational importance, priority, and allocation of resources. As we'll discuss in detail later in the book, a vitally important principle of Special Forces leadership is that the higher your rank, the more your job is to support those who are "below" you in the pyramid.

There's another reason they call it an "A" team: it's full of A-Type personalities. Each operator is an incredibly talented "Alpha lion" that would be the boss in any other organization and lead their own team. The WWII recruiting pitch for the Office of Strategic Services (OSS, which later split into the CIA and the Green Berets) was that it needed "PhD's that can win a bar fight."

Think about what it would be like to be put in charge of 30 brilliant scientists from different fields to solve a big problem in half an hour. You'd spend the first 25 minutes just trying to get them in order and come to an agreement on how to attack the problem. We often refer to those situations as "herding cats." But what if all those cats were bigger, badder, stronger, faster, meaner, smarter, more experienced, more talented, more competent (and generally better-looking) than you. That would be like herding lions, Alpha lions, the lion that leads a pride or group.

That's what a Special Forces A-Team is: a group of Alpha lions that, when properly coordinated and motivated, routinely achieve what others believe to be impossible. But as you can imagine, working with lions is not easy. First of all, it can be terrifying to surround yourself with team members that are all better than you in just about everything. It essentially makes you superfluous. Secondly, lions have options. So getting them to agree to work with you (and the other lions) means creating a team where they feel like they can be successful and have the freedom to operate at their fullest potential. To be "the best."

But when you *do* create that magic, when you successfully create a team of lions that are all working towards the same vitally important objective...well, you'd better stand back. [1]

To say that Special Forces teams have "outsized results" relative to their size is an understatement. Each SF team (12 Green Berets) is considered to be a strategic national asset because their missions often change the geopolitical landscape. In just over a month, in 2001, a group of 100 Green Berets (assisted by some CIA personnel) liberated Afghanistan from the Taliban, an *entire country* that multiple Soviet Armies with more than 100,000 troops with tanks, helicopters, artillery and rockets couldn't take during their 10 year war with the Afghans. One of those teams' exploits were immortalized in the movie *12 Strong*. Another of those teams worked with Hamid Kharzai, who would be the first president of Afghanistan after the Taliban.

---

[1] All analogies break down under too much scrutiny. While there are both similarities and discrepancies in the lion pride analogy, there is nothing to be gained in going down that rabbit hole.

Ironically, but not surprisingly, it was also small teams of Green Berets that were instrumental in stopping the Soviet Union from overtaking Afghanistan from 1979 - 1989.

In 1999, when Russian airborne troops rolled through NATO lines into Kosovo and seized the Pristina Airport in a bid to insert themselves into the multinational coalition following the end of the Kosovo War, NATO Supreme Allied Commander General Wesley Clark ordered British Lieutenant-General Sir Michael Jackson to take back the airport from the Russians, by force if necessary. The world was on edge; it was the closest that NATO and post-Soviet Russia had come to war and Jackson famously responded to Clark "I won't start WWIII for you." So instead of WWIII, *one* SF team was sent to deal with an entire Russian airborne brigade and tasked with stopping the killing on both sides. That team made historic achievements with the Russians and, according to the official Special Operations Command's history book, "helped to better US-Russian relations." Relatively low-ranking Army guys improved diplomatic relations between the world's opposing superpowers; that just doesn't happen outside of SF.

SF Teams *routinely* change the course of history. These 12-man teams consistently achieve what others believe to be impossible. And this is why SF Teams are the first forces sent to any conflict area where the U.S. will deploy forces. And because of their expertise, SF Teams are sent under the radar to numerous countries throughout the world every year with little to no fanfare to advise and assist U.S. allies in order to *prevent* wars and conflicts from occurring in the first place.

These outsized results are so legendary that not-so-friendly countries have what appear to be ridiculous instructions on what to do if Green Berets are nearby. During the Cold War, official written Soviet Army doctrine was to flatten an *entire square kilometer* with rockets and artillery and then send in an infantry battalion (500 soldiers) into any area in which they suspected an SF team might be operating. After the fall of the Soviet Union, Russian Airborne and SPETSNAZ troops got a chance to work with Green Berets up close and assess their prowess for themselves, and current Russian doctrine still reflects the old Soviet one.

Keep in mind that a 3-man recon team from ODA-534 held off over 100 Iraqi soldiers for more than 6 hours during the First Gulf War. You didn't hear about that mission because those results are routine, and many of those missions were classified and therefore kept secret. But a quick google search will show you multiple stories of Green Berets taking on impossible odds and winning.

In 2008 a team of 12 Green Berets was ambushed in the most impenetrable valley in Afghanistan by *hundreds* of mujahadeen. Many hours later, the SF Team was finally evacuated - wounded, but with no deaths - leaving behind over 150 dead mujahadeen. Hundreds more mujahadeen had already retreated, taking hundreds more of their wounded with them. During their 10-year war with Afghanistan, the Soviets never even tried to enter the Shok Valley, despite their overwhelming numbers.

That is the power of elite teams, revered by allies and feared by enemies, which is why you want to harness this capability for yourself. So that *you* will be able to routinely achieve what others think is impossible and bring in outsized results quarter after quarter and year after year. And because

Green Berets are made and not born, and because the tenets of SF leadership are learned, *you can build that kind of team, too* - if you are willing to pay the price. It takes a special kind of leadership to lead lions, to build elite teams that routinely achieve the impossible.

This book is designed to help you do that; to guide you down your own path to becoming a truly great leader who can build elite teams that routinely achieve "impossible" results. The principles in these chapters are fundamental to the kind of leadership required in Special Forces, but they aren't restricted to SF or even the military. Many of them are already being used by some of today's best companies and organizations and giving them the edge that makes them truly great.

EPIC Leadership
Leaders get people to do what they want them to do in support of common or organizational goals; great leaders practice the *art* of leadership; and then there is a special kind of leadership that we've heard about, seen in movies, or read about in books - the kind of leadership that inspires a team to confidently charge into the jaws of hell.

There have been plenty of attempts to label this particular kind of leadership, but existing terms are insufficient; they capture some aspects of leadership but don't embody what's needed for great leadership, much less EPIC leadership.

For instance, I hate the term 'servant leadership' due to its inherent contradiction. Although I wholeheartedly agree that leaders must support their subordinates in accomplishing their tasks, *no one follows a servant anywhere* unless they are escorting you to your hotel room. It's not in the job description. It's like saying "Jumbo Shrimp." The definition of a servant includes "domestic service; public service; or one who expresses submission, recognizance, or debt to another."

Not very inspiring, is it? It doesn't make me jump up and yell "I'll follow her anywhere!"

Empathetic Leadership is a better term, but that model doesn't go far enough either. Empathy gets us headed down the right path, but it's not the entire package; it lacks several crucial elements such as mission accomplishment, character, purposefulness, and motivation.

If I hear that someone is an empathetic leader, I'm apt to think to myself "sounds like she'd be good to work for." But it still doesn't inspire me to jump up and shout: "I'd follow her anywhere."

Servant and Empathetic leadership are great starting points. They are necessary, *but not sufficient*. Neither of them are enough to take you to the next-level because, well, frankly, they weren't designed to.

To lead Elite teams, you must be more than just an empathetic leader. You have to add the extra three aspects and be the kind of leader that people are clamoring to work for: the kind that inspires *fierce* trust; the kind that team members are willing to pass up better-paying jobs for; the kind that makes people say, "I'd follow her anywhere." Elite teams require **EPIC** leadership - Empathetic, Purposeful, Inspirational, with impeccable Character.

How do you become an EPIC leader? That's what the rest of this book is about - giving you the purpose, direction, motivation, and resources to create and lead extraordinary teams that achieve the impossible. Routinely.

How Green Berets are Made

Individual Training and Qualification

All Green Berets go through **Basic Training** and then work for years before they ever make it to a team. Even so, all candidates train extra hard for at least a year before they get to the first phase, **SFAS** (Special Forces Assessment and Selection) and most of them have already graduated Airborne School (one of the best "fear-conquering" courses available - discussed in Chapter 5). All that pre-training is necessary to get through SFAS, an arduous 21-day sleep and food-deprived, body-breaking pain fest involving jog-marching with an 80-pound rucksack for 25 miles a day.

If selected, candidates are required to rest and recover at least one month before they attend the **Q-Course** (Special Forces Qualification Course). SFAS isn't designed to teach you anything, but you learn the true extent of your intestinal fortitude and mental commitment. The Q-Course is where future Green Berets learn all the basic skills needed to be on an A-Team, all while being constantly assessed. If you pass the Q-Course, you are awarded your Green Beret (provisionally), but you're still not ready for a team. During my active service, only 10% of the soldiers that applied to Special Forces made it this far.

It's imperative to know how to communicate so all Green Berets attend **Language School** and are required to speak at least one foreign language spoken in their Area of Operations. You can still fail or get kicked out during this phase. And finally, there is Level 3 **SERE** School (Survival, Evasion, Resistance, and Escape). Generally it takes about 2 full years to get through the training pipeline, and you can fail out anywhere along the way.

Team Qualification and Training

But even when a Green Beret finally gets to their first A-Team, the training never stops. Most teams have a primary mode of employment or infiltration (HALO, SCUBA, Direct Action, etc.) that requires a new team member to learn at least one specialty skill as well as all the team Standard Operating Procedures (SOPs) and battle drills.

However, the primary responsibility of any SF team is meticulously **Planning and Executing** missions. Not just any missions, but no-fail missions of strategic importance in denied territories under arduous conditions with little-to-no support, the kinds of things that only elite teams can achieve.

When a new Green Beret finally earns a spot on the team, they become responsible for maintaining and improving the team and its culture, a responsibility which can vary wildly between teams. Every great team is responsible for **Building the Legend** and the greatest teams always have Green Berets eagerly vying for vacant positions when a team member transitions to a new job (often kicking and screaming as they're dragged away). Legendary teams achieve legendary results, and everyone wants to be a part of that.

Your Own Personal Q-Course

If you decide that you want to be a leader of a legendary team, your path will also be arduous because excellence never happens by accident. You'll be going through your own personal training pipeline that will be difficult, time-consuming, and sometimes painful. It's okay if you decide this isn't for you; not everyone wants to put in the time and effort required to become an EPIC leader. But remember, Green Berets are made, not born. Other people have successfully become great leaders, so you can, too. Just follow the program.

And to make it easier, you'll come right along with us. Your training will follow the same path that all Green Berets take, and you will learn the same important leadership lessons that they do throughout each phase of Special Forces training. And just like the training pipeline for Green Berets, the phases for your Q-Course will be done in the same order because each skill builds upon the previous. So the chapters in these books are arranged as follows:

Book 1 - Individual Training and Qualification
- Chapter 1: Basic Training
- Chapter 2: SFAS: Personal Assessment
- Chapter 3: Q-Course: Training and Qualification
- Chapter 4: Language School: Effective Communication
- Chapter 5: Airborne & SERE: Conquer Your Fear

Book 2 - Team Qualification and Training
- Chapter 6: The Team - Leading Lions
- Chapter 7: Missions: Planning & Execution
- Chapter 8: Building the Legend: Create Amazing Team Cultures

After you read Chapter Two, you'll need to decide if you're ready to commit to the work outlined in the following chapters. While some people prefer to tackle tasks immediately, I recommend reading the entire book first, then going back to complete the exercises. It's like reading through the full set of instructions before assembling something complicated. I don't want you to get bogged down and miss out on the valuable insights that you can start using right away. One of my favorite phrases is, "Don't be smarter than the instructions." So, don't try to outsmart the process. Read through all the instructions before assembly.

So grab your duffle bag, hop on the bus, and hang on. It's going to get interesting.

CHAPTER ONE

Basic Training

Before a soldier tackles the Special Forces Qualification Course, they have to go through basic training and learn the fundamentals of leadership: What leadership is, what it comprises, how it differs from management and, most importantly, what separates great leaders from merely competent ones. That involves understanding your own Leadership Operating System and understanding how to establish Active Trust. The trouble is, as with most practices, a little knowledge can make you think you're already an expert.

After my 11 weeks of basic training, I certainly thought I knew a lot more than I did. And what I did know hadn't really set in yet because I hadn't put it into practice. The problem only worsened over the next two years as I went to more army schools and was often given positions that were "leadership" in name only. They didn't have any real responsibility or authority, and I never got to use any of the lessons I'd learned. Sure, I looked good "on paper." I looked good to myself, but my skills were hollow. My training for the Special Forces rapidly exposed my deficiencies.

I'm admitting to this up front because you may also imagine you've learned to be a leader in your civilian versions of basic training: while getting a business degree, from reading books on leadership or memoirs by leaders, or in an ad hoc way as part of your job. Until you've been deliberately trained and tested, however, you too may be leaders in title only. Being a VP, doesn't make you a leader. In fact, I would bet you've received no real training at all. During my speaking engagements to rooms full of executives, I ask who has undergone formal leadership training, and often it's only the CEO who raises their hand. And then they admit that their training was 30 years earlier, which might as well be the Dark Ages, the demands of means of leadership have changed so much. Their leadership operating system might as well be quotes written on Post-it notes and stuck around their monitor. So, in this chapter I'll take you through the basics so we're speaking the same language.

The first thing to learn, as I was fortunate enough to be told early on, is that your people come first.

Leaders Eat Last

Special Forces Assessment and Selection (SFAS) is designed to assess a prospective Green Beret's knowledge, skills, abilities, and character under acute stress. It applies extreme duress for extended periods of time so that candidates show their true colors, what they are genuinely made of. SFAS is designed to assess everything about you. And even though the focus seems to be on physical strength and stamina, what the evaluators are really looking for is to see who you are, your character. One of the ways they evaluate that is by placing everyone in a leadership role a few times to see what they do under stress.

I went to SFAS as a Specialist E-4, which is the rank between Private First Class and Sergeant. Even though I hadn't yet attended any of the Army's leadership schools, it didn't matter; everyone has to show leadership ability and potential. To ensure that everyone is evaluated, leadership positions rotate every day. At some point it became my day to be the platoon sergeant. The platoon sergeant position was simple: form up the platoon (4 four squads of 6-10 candidates) prior to any movement; check with the squad leaders to ensure everyone was present; call the platoon to attention (or put them "at ease"); march them to where we needed to go; and repeat the process once an event was complete.

It was all super easy because all the rest of the candidates were being evaluated as "followers," so they weren't going to screw up. They didn't want to look bad in front of the evaluators so they weren't going to be late for a formation, show up without their gear, have dirty boots, or do anything that would make a platoon sergeant look like they weren't doing their job properly.

The only hard part of the leadership position was sacrificing your precious time to ensure that you were always in formation a few minutes ahead of everyone else to take charge. You were also always the last to do anything because the entire platoon filed out before you left formation. And you took up time planning and remembering what needed to be checked, where you were going, or which platoon was going first. While that coordination time didn't take more than 30 minutes total a day, that was 30 minutes of sleep lost. And when you're already only getting about 3.5 hours of sleep a day for 3 solid weeks, jog-marching an 80# rucksack for 25 miles a day AND doing a timed 3, 5, or 10-mile run a few times a week, that extra 30 minutes of sleep is incredibly important.

My turn as platoon sergeant had gone smoothly all day, and as we came back into our training compound that evening I was looking forward to finally relaxing a bit knowing that I'd probably passed my evaluation.

We had a few minutes to store our gear before we headed off to our only "real" meal of the day, the highlight of everyone's day because we needed every calorie we could get and usually there was something hot, one of our few comforts. Like everyone else, I rushed to stow my gear and then raced back outside to form up the platoon and head to chow.

The area where they served the meal was small and could only accommodate about 20 people at a time. Groups were staggered so as one squad was leaving, another was coming in. They rotated who got to go first to chow every day because every minute was precious. The sooner you got done eating, the sooner you could start working on your gear, and maybe you'd get an extra 15 minutes of sleep that night. Not only did the platoons rotate, but each squad within the platoon would rotate, as well. If you were ever lucky enough to be the first squad of the first platoon to go to chow, it was like winning the lottery.

The day I was the platoon leader, 4th squad, the squad I was assigned to was slated to go first. Jackpot! I was excited because I'd already lost quite a bit of time that day conducting platoon sergeant duties, and I was thinking about how I could use the extra time I'd get back by getting to chow at the head of the line. When it was time for the platoon to go eat, I gave the order for the 4th squad to move out, told the 1st, 2nd, and 3rd Squad Leaders to leave in order but wait for five minutes before following the squad ahead of it (standard practice), took my place in my usual squad, and headed off to eat. Our evaluator looked at me a bit funny, but at SFAS, they never tell you anything. They only ever say, "Do your best, candidate."

You never talk when you're in formation marching someplace, but as soon as we got to the chow line, the guy in front of me turned around and whispered, "What are you doing?" I said, "It's our turn to go first tonight, so I got in line like normal." He was a sergeant and had been in the Army a lot longer than me and said, "No. You have to go back. You're in charge and so you have to make sure that everyone else gets here and then you go last."

Deep down, I already knew this. Even though I hadn't been in the Army very long, I knew it was the right thing to do. But I was ravenously hungry and I was desperate to try and catch up a bit on my sleep. So instead of doing what I knew was right, I tried to "get over." But after the sergeant pointed out my mistake, I inwardly cursed and sadly walked back to the platoon area and sent out the rest of the squads one-by-one, the way it's supposed to be done.

Once back, the Evaluator came up to me and asked what I was doing back so soon. I told him that I came back because I was the Platoon Sergeant and it was my job to make sure everyone else got fed before I did. He didn't say a word, but a few minutes later I saw him writing in the little book that all the evaluators had with them to take notes.

I'm convinced that the only reason I ever became a Green Beret was because my fellow candidate was kind enough to let me know how badly I was messing up. Leaders eat last. Leaders focus on the team, not themselves. Leaders always prioritize the needs of the team above their own. Yeah, there are some perks that come with the job, but being a leader means you'll work longer, have more responsibilities, more headaches, more meetings – more of everything.

Notice how I keep using the word "leader" and not manager. That's intentional. They shouldn't be confused because leadership and management are not the same thing.

Leadership and Management Are Not the Same Thing
But in the business world we rarely stop to think about the difference. Why should we? Most supervisors are called "managers" and not "leaders;" all the books are about "best management practices;" and one day we all hope to join the ranks of "senior management."

However, if you're in a leadership position in the military and someone refers to you as a manager, it's almost always an insult, and a pretty big one at that. Being referred to as a manager implies a negative perception of your leadership skills, suggesting that you lack the ability to be effective, and that you rely on others to handle challenging tasks.

Leadership is getting people to do things you want them to do.

Leadership in organizations means getting a group of people to achieve missions or goals that benefit the organization. Military officers and NCOs *manage* systems, processes, and inventories but their primary role is to *lead* people.

There may be some management roles in the civilian world where people aren't involved, but if you are working exclusively with systems, then your title is probably "engineer," "dispatcher," or something similar. There are some pure management positions where you are responsible for inventories, fleets of vehicles, spare parts, or other equipment. Almost all jobs that have the word "manager" in the title require motivating at least one other person to accomplish tasks. Management is complementary to Leadership, but does not take its place.

The higher they go in an organization, the more management skills leaders need. They'll need to understand policies, procedures, and regulations to achieve efficiencies and comply with the law to ensure their organization functions properly as part of a larger organization. But regardless of how high you go, you will still be a leader first.

Every leader depends on an operator. Behind every system, program, and project there is a person operating it. If you've led the operator properly and something goes wrong, the operator is much more likely to be able to fix the problem on their own. Moreover, you will have confidence that they can and will take care of any issues so you can continue to focus on the mission.

Good leaders empower their team members to take initiative and lead themselves, enabling them to operate effectively and efficiently, often exceeding expectations. While their role may be operating the system, your role is to lead the operator.

So, if you supervise *anyone,* you must begin to think of yourself as a *leader* instead of a manager. Although you may have additional responsibilities related to management, it's important to recognize that first and foremost, you are a leader, regardless of personal preference. Managers get their teams to the chow line on time and in the right order; leaders ensure their people actually get fed by making sure everyone else goes before them. To build great teams, it is crucial to understand, embrace, and fully commit to your role as a leader.

Regardless of your title, it is leaders, not managers, who build great teams.

People First, Systems Second
Thinking of yourself as a leader first is critical because when you properly realign yourself as a Leader (of people) and then a Manager (of systems), it naturally follows that People are first and Systems come second. And that principle "People First, Systems Second" or "People, then Systems" is paramount if you want to build truly great teams. And if you can simply do those two things – always think of yourself as a leader first and then always act in accordance with the principle of "People First, Systems Second" – there is a pretty good chance you'll be an adequate leader even if you get everything else wrong.

This simple idea: "People First, Systems Second" is *so* important that it is the very first of the Special Forces Truths. Notice it's not referred to as a "principle." We have the "principles of war," "principles of joint operations," "special operations imperatives," "core values," "mission criteria," and plenty of other important concepts with a name that conveys their significance. However, the idea of "people first, systems second" is so crucial and fundamental to successful special operations that it's considered to be a *fact*. It is a truth, akin to gravity. It is not a theory but is considered a fundamental law. Special Forces is the sole U.S. military organization that incorporates 'truths' as official military doctrine, with five SF Truths in total.[2] The first and therefore most important one is: *"Humans are more important than hardware,"* or, People First, Systems Second. [3]

Lead, then manage.

Seems simple, doesn't it?

Take a minute to really think about what that means for you. Because, while the concept may appear simple, the commitment required to genuinely practice and embody it is anything but. Because when 10 different urgent things all hit your desk at the same time while five different clients are on the phone, and you're already overworked and understaffed, and multiple urgent tasks must be completed within the hour, it is easy to forget that we are leaders, to forget our mission, to lose our courage, to let our commitment slip, and just take the easy way out.

Managers *check off things* on their to-do lists; leaders *check in on their people.* Managers complete projects; leaders create progress. Managers focus on outputs; leaders focus on outcomes.

---

[2] They are now referred to as Army SOF (Special Operations Forces) Truths because the rest of the Army's Special Operations Forces adopted them from SF.

[3] Software development startups are considered to have some of the most successful teams in the business world today and who wouldn't want to mimic their success? All of the processes used to create the most successful software use the AGILE framework (developed in 1981 as the AGILE Manifesto) of which the first tenet is: "Individuals and interactions over processes and tools."

Components of Leadership: Be, Know, Do

People First and Systems Second refers to the methodology of achieving those goals. It's not an end unto itself. It's not about prioritizing people over the mission, as in servant or empathetic leadership. If you can't accomplish the mission, you're ineffective and you won't be a leader for long. Think *people first, systems second, mission essential.*

In a world where executives are often incentivized to prioritize short-term gains over long-term integrity to boost the stock prices upon which their compensation is based, leading first is a revolutionary act. In an amoral economy driven by quarterly earnings and stock prices, the true measure of a leader isn't just in the immediate profits generated but in developing their people to achieve and exceed long-term company goals. Great leaders ensure their actions reflect their core values, even under pressure, because BE'ing is the most important component of leadership.

Leadership has three components: what you know; what you do; and who you are (Know, Do, Be). But the military uses a different order: Be, Know, Do - because great leadership starts with who you are. I can teach you numerous leadership techniques and you can learn leadership tasks like problem solving by reading about techniques (Know). You can become proficient by using them through repetition and practice (Do). However, the most critical part of leadership is the part that you can't learn in books – the "Be" – that is, who you are. There's no Drill Sergeant or Master Training anywhere in the world that can make us proficient in integrity or moral courage. We are the only ones who can change our character, which is *by far* the most important aspect of great leadership.

Our character is critical because we will always default to – and act in accordance with – our true nature, especially when under stress and things are at their worst. As leaders, who we are is far more important than what we know or how well we can do something.

Leaders aren't born. Leaders are made. But *great* leaders make themselves by becoming the leaders they want to be.

It doesn't matter how much leadership stuff you read in a book. Even in the military, with its highly effective system for developing competent leaders, it's not solely about reading. It's the "being" and the "doing" through practical application. It's about having the courage to try something, knowing you'll likely make mistakes, and possessing the humility to accept advice on how to do better next time. And then doing it over and over again until you get it right.

So while you're not going to become a great leader by reading this book, you can become a great leader by DOing the things in this book. And the first thing you need to DO is BEcome a person that personifies the most important leadership traits so that they manifest naturally and authentically in every situation, especially under stress.

You become that person through tremendous effort, by doing the hard stuff until it becomes a part of who you are, your BEing.

Once you do something repeatedly, whether it's good or bad, it becomes ingrained in you. Practice doesn't necessarily make perfect because if you repeatedly practice doing something incorrectly, you will learn to do it poorly, and it will become your default approach – which is not the desired outcome. Therefore, a better way to conceptualize it is 'Perfect

Practice Makes Perfect' or, even better: Perfect (or Best) Practices Practiced Perfectly Makes Perfect. This is our ultimate goal.

But before we embark on our perfect practice, we need to understand what the most effective practices entail and determine how many, if any, are already integrated into our authentic leadership style. The unfortunate reality is that most people fail to utilize best practices due to a lack of proper leadership training, which results in a limited understanding of what 'right' looks like. Most of us need to update our Leadership Operating System (LOS) – if we have one at all.

Leadership is getting people to do **what** you want them to do. But **how** we get them to do it is our "leadership style" - and what's truly important is not the "what," but the "how."

Our Leadership Operating System (LOS)
How we react in a given situation and, therefore, how we lead, is shaped by our experiences, our beliefs, our worldview, our frames of reference, and many other influences operating silently in the background.

Consider worldview as the internal dynamics of a successful startup. Here's an example: **Ethan (one of my clients)**, is a passionate entrepreneur who founded an AI-driven customer service startup with a small, dedicated team. In the early days, everyone wore multiple hats and made quick decisions based on a shared vision, which shaped Ethan's initial perspective on leadership and collaboration. As the company grew, formal processes like project management tools and hierarchical decision-making were introduced to manage complexity. These changes gave structure to Ethan's worldview but also placed limitations on how to think about things, much like windows and doors in a house shape your view and movement.

In addition to our worldview, we possess a complex web of emotions, perceptions, assumptions, experiences, unexamined patterns of behavior, social conditioning, prejudices, morals, and all kinds of other "programming" known as frames of reference.

Ethan's belief in tight supervision created a micromanagement culture, reflecting his frames of reference – the underlying assumptions and patterns of behavior he brought to his leadership role. This approach initially seemed necessary to maintain productivity but eventually stifled innovation. When top developers began leaving due to the stifling micromanagement culture, it highlighted how these frames of reference were limiting the company's potential.

Our worldview and frames of reference inform and dictate how we see the world and how we act. But because they are hidden, we don't see them operating, and therefore we can't determine if they are useful unless we explore them.

All of this together composes our "leader's mindset" or our "Leadership Operating System" (LOS). However, just like any computer operating system that hasn't been updated or cleaned up in many years, our own LOS may not always be operating in the most effective manner. Chances are, unless you've spent some time examining and updating it, you'll find that it's corrupted and out of date.

This is important because who we are dictates our natural default behaviors, and while we can try to act in a manner inconsistent with our default or use a different leadership style when things are good and we aren't under stress, we will immediately switch to our default mode once thinking stops and "doing" begins.

For instance, if you've come to believe that people are basically lazy, then your LOS will always be geared towards close supervision of those you lead. You'll want to control everything as much as possible and may even be a micromanager. You'll likely want everyone in the office so you can see they're working, not trusting them to get their jobs done out of your sight. You feel justified in the way you currently operate because you feel like it has worked in the past.

However, elite teams never materialize spontaneously or organically in an atmosphere where the leader intuitively believes that everyone is lazy, because elite teams are comprised of highly motivated people that chafe under close supervision and micromanagement. Moreover, the fastest way to destroy an existing great team is to start closely supervising its members as this undermines their autonomy, stifles creativity, and erodes trust. Treating highly talented people as anything less than professionals will cause them to stop acting like professionals, leading to a loss of short-term productivity and drive them to seek employment elsewhere, stripping away any hope of long-term team effectiveness.

The problem is that we are not very good at seeing the inner workings of our own operating system. Just like with our computer's OS, we rarely (if ever) check to see if there are any underlying issues or conduct preventative maintenance until it crashes. Back before operating systems automatically updated themselves, many of us would go for years without updating to the newest software. We didn't see a need if we didn't notice any problems. And even if we did see a problem, we tried to ignore it or find a work-around because if we did try to examine the OS, most of us wouldn't understand it anyway.

Imagine having to manually update your smartphone. Would anyone check every month to find out which apps have gotten updates and then go into each and every one to manually update it?

It's exactly the same with our LOS; numerous studies have shown that we are excellent at identifying hypocrisy in others and terrible at seeing it in ourselves. We all know at least one senior leader who is constantly talking about how important it is to "live the company values" but isn't following them herself – yet she ardently believes in her heart that she is the visible standard of them.

The same goes for all the other lines of hidden code (frames of reference) that determine how our Leadership OS does its job. Paradoxically, *while it is the engine that powers us to do our jobs and live our lives, it is also the governor (limiter) that hinders our ability for greater performance.*

Ethan's startup initially thrived on the versatility and quick decision-making of a small, talented team. This setup worked well initially, much like a normal car engine gets you from point A to point B. However, as the company grew, the initial processes and management style began to limit its performance. Ethan realized that to achieve outstanding performance, he needed to make deliberate changes to his leadership approach.

In order to upgrade his engine, Ethan decided to overhaul his management practices. He invested in advanced project management tools, leadership training, and focused on creating a culture of trust and autonomy. This transformation required significant effort and resources, much like the upgrading of a car's engine for superior performance. By making these deliberate improvements, Ethan's company was able to boost productivity, retain top talent, and achieve exceptional results. Superior performance - in anything - doesn't happen by accident - it's a deliberate process with a significant cost.

Let's continue with our previous example: if your LOS includes the widely held belief that "most people are lazy," and you read a leadership book or go to a management course where you are told that micromanaging is counterproductive, you'll say to yourself, "Okay, instead of micromanaging, I'm going to do xxx instead," (whatever that particular book or course told you to do) and when the opportunity arises you'll exert some self-discipline to try it with the "new" approach.

The problem is that you still believe that people are inherently lazy and so no matter how hard you try not to micromanage, you will eventually "default" and act in accordance with your true beliefs, the current version of your Leadership OS. While discipline and willpower can help you resist the urge to micromanage in the short term, the first time something really important and stressful comes along, you will freak out and revert back to what you "know" works and start micromanaging again. You can't change innate beliefs by going to a course or reading a book; only you can change you. True, lasting change requires a fundamental shift in your underlying beliefs and purpose.

Modern neuroscience backs this up. In his book *Thinking, Fast and Slow*, Nobel Prize-winning psychologist Daniel

Kahneman describes two systems of human decision-making. System 1 is fast, automatic, emotional — it takes over in moments of stress or threat. System 2 is slower, deliberate, and logical — but it requires conscious energy and attention.

Kahneman's research shows that when pressure hits, most people don't choose how to respond. Their System 1 takes over, running whatever beliefs and instincts are already baked into their Leadership OS. That's why reading a book or attending a course rarely creates lasting change. Unless you rewire what System 1 has to work with, you'll keep defaulting to the same patterns.[4]

And that's just *one* line of code in your LOS! This is why I say that you need to make a conscious decision on what kind of leader you want to be, if your personal mission requires it, and decide if it's a price you're willing to pay. Because to lead elite teams you need to examine all of your paradigms to determine which are effective and determine those that need updates or changes. Purpose – the BE – is what gets you past defaulting back to old habits. It provides us with the conviction to stay the course when our discipline fades.

The good news is that we aren't stuck with our current default for the rest of our lives. Just as you are able to change the "default browser" on your computer so that the information that you see is presented and grouped in a different way, you can change or update your LOS, too.

This is important because a different browser (a window/how you see the world/information) also affects how your operating system works. Some browsers work better than

---

[4] Daniel Kahneman, Thinking, Fast and Slow (New York: Farrar, Straus and Giroux, 2011).

others and some work better with specific operating systems. And while it's not as easy as changing your default browser on your computer, you can also change the window through which you see, organize, and interpret the world. And once we change that default, we will naturally act differently because it becomes who we are, our way of BEing.

Like most things worth doing, changing our LOS is difficult and there's a cost. We'll cover some ways to do that in the next chapter. But now, it's time to talk about next-level leadership, which can only manifest when a leader has *an effective internal LOS that is authentically reflected externally*. This alignment is what distinguishes truly great leaders—they inspire and motivate not just through their actions, but through a deep-seated authenticity that resonates with their teams.

We cannot practice the "art of leadership" until we have the internal strength and confidence to build active trust with our teams, inspiring and motivating them effectively.

The Art of Leadership
Leaders get people to do what they want them to do. But *great* leaders practice the *art* of leadership.

The **Art of Leadership** is getting people to do things you want them to do *because **they** want to do them*. Elite teams require the latter and that is what we'll focus on. The Art of Leadership is focused on the "how." How do you get people to do what you want them to do because they want to do it?

Well, it's not by doing all the things you normally associate with leadership and management.

When you picture leadership, what comes to mind? Probably the usual checklist: planning, organizing, delegating, problem-solving, personnel evaluations, setting goals, managing budgets. That's what most people think leadership is. But those aren't leadership. Those are just tools—means to an end. They help, sure, but they don't define what great leaders actually do. You can do all those things and still fail as a leader if you haven't provided what your people really need.

Before we talk about tools or activities, we have to be clear about the job itself. What leaders are actually supposed to do is simple: just two things. First, provide PDMR—Purpose, Direction, Motivation, and Resources. Second, build an atmosphere of Fierce Trust, which only comes through the 4 C's: Character, Communication, Consideration, and Coaching.

That's the real job: provide PDMR and build Fierce Trust through the 4 C's. Everything else—planning, delegating, goal setting, budgeting—still matters. But none of it works the way it's supposed to unless those two things are in place. The tools and activities don't lead people - you do. And you lead best when every action you take is powered by purpose, delivered with character, and built on trust.

Think of it like this: PDMR and the 4 C's are the engine. The tools are the transmission. The better your engine runs, the more power you can send through the system. Without that engine, even the best tools just spin.

Let's break it all down.
Leadership Art is built upon PDMR and Active Trust developed through the 4 C's. All effective leaders must be able to provide Purpose, Direction, Motivation, and Resources (PDMR) in varying degrees depending on the organizational level while fostering Active Trust through the demonstration

of Character, Communication, Coaching, and Consideration (referred to as the 4C's).[5]

Purpose, Direction, and Motivation (PDM) is a core Army leadership concept that is introduced to basic trainees on day two of bootcamp – it's that fundamental. The Purpose is critical and that's why it's listed first. Purpose is the "why" and often if the "why" is strong enough, it provides all the direction and motivation needed. Direction refers to the guidance and instructions on what needs to be done, any guardrails or constraints, and what the metrics for success are. Motivation refers to the methods and strategies used to get the best efforts from the team. While this is considered basic leadership, it's surprising to see that it's not more common in the business world.

In the military, virtually everything is imbued with PDM. From your first formation in the morning to going to sleep, it's all about PDM. Let's look at a typical morning:

> 06:00: Physical Training to get stronger and fitter: (P) be more effective in combat; (D) push-ups, sit-ups, 5 mile run along a specific route; (M) follow me and quit lagging behind!
>
> 07:00 – 09:00: Personal hygiene and breakfast: (P) be prepared for the day's activities; (D) shower, shave,

---

[5] The Army has its own set of leadership 4C's: Candor, Commitment, Courage, and Competence. They also discuss the "how" of leadership. Those work just fine in the Army because servicemen and women have already self-selected multiple times and have chosen to stay in the military and its culture. You can use those as well if you want. But what I want to emphasize is the need for absolute trust when leading elite teams, so the 4C's I'm referring to is what's required to develop an atmosphere of Fierce or Active Trust. Moreover, in the modern business world I believe that real communication, consideration, an attitude of 'coaching' rather than 'directing', and having a strong character are critical to succeeding and that perhaps the Army's 4C's could use a refresh.

prep your uniform; (M) the platoon sergeant will tear you a new one if your boots aren't shined or your uniform is dirty.

09-11:00: Preventive Maintenance Checks and Services (PMCS) on selected equipment: (P) all equipment is 100% ready to go at all times; (D) conduct level 2 maintenance on all the squad's night vision equipment and update the maintenance log; (M) the platoon sergeant is going to check it during an inspection to make sure it was done – and done right.

I could go on and on - whether it's maintenance, training, meetings, or combat operations, every task and activity has PDM. To civilians, the motivation aspect may not be obvious, but that is why leaders in fighting units are up front with the troops and why "follow me" is the motto of the infantry.

You've seen good leaders in all walks of life use PDM. For instance, a mid-level manager might gather their team for a briefing on an upcoming product launch aimed at capturing a new market segment. But instead of simply telling everyone what to do, she explains the company wants to drive growth and establish a strong foothold in an emerging market (purpose). The manager should provide detailed *directions*, outlining the marketing strategy, timelines, key deliverables, and each team member's specific roles. To *motivate* the team, the manager might share success stories from previous launches, but she might also hint that the division hasn't been doing so well for the past year and the team needs a successful launch for everyone to keep their jobs. People are often motivated more from a fear of loss than of gain.[6]

The Army doesn't include "Resources" (time, money, food, equipment, aircraft, etc.) in its PDM model, and here we see our first instance of where the Green Beret leadership model differs from the conventional army. Special Forces are highly dependent upon resources and even though it is never explicitly expressed as such, providing resources to the A-Teams is a primary function of Special Forces leadership. In the regular Army there are units specifically tasked with providing "beans, bullets, and bandages" (as well as fuel, spare parts, etc.) to the line units. And while those units also exist within a Special Forces Group (a Brigade-sized organization), it is the commander's responsibility (as well as his task) to ensure A-Teams have what they need, especially because those requests are often non-standard and unavailable through normal supply channels.

A deployed A-Team may ask for a shipment of pack mule harnesses to be parachuted to them 350 miles behind enemy lines at 3 am. Pack mule harnesses aren't available through normal supply chains, so it requires a lot of extra work to get them, put them on pallets, and parachute those pallets behind the lines to the correct place at the right time. Commanders in regular units would laugh at such a request. However, those harnesses could be crucial in establishing rapport and fostering a positive working relationship with the local guerrilla fighters as it demonstrates the strength and strategic capabilities of the U.S. So getting teams what they need, no matter

---

6 Napoleon famously said "Men are moved by two levers only: fear and self-interest." Chapter five is entirely devoted to the power of fear.

how weird it sounds, is a critical component of leadership in special operations.

In the corporate world, don't ever assume that resources will magically appear, so the PDMR model is what we all should be using. Ensure your people have everything they need to accomplish the task or you're setting them up for failure. Think of PDMR as the compass points you'll need to successfully navigate your journey towards great leadership.

Active / Fierce Trust
You simply cannot build amazing teams without an atmosphere of Active Trust. Active Trust is different because it's not passive ('Of course I trust her'); rather it's active. It motivates and fosters forward momentum ('That sounds scary as hell, but let's go boss, we're with you all the way!') Trust is the foundation that holds everything together and enables us to be effective in our leadership tasks. All leaders must foster some passive trust to get anything done, but the ability to forge Active Trust is where we begin to see the difference between "good" and "great" leaders. That's why the leadership model we'll use depicts Active Trust surrounding all the leader tasks.

Active Trust is built from the 4 C's: **C**haracter, **C**ommunication. **C**onsideration, and **C**oaching.[7] It doesn't take very long to establish basic trust, but developing Active Trust requires time and continuous effort and it can be shattered in an instant. Trust is *so* important it has its own list of requirements. As you review the list below, you'll notice that each item corresponds to one or more of the 4 C's. In general, the following list emphasizes your Character because, as a leader, who you are matters more than what you know.

1. Integrity. Integrity is the opposite of hypocrisy; it is the soul of trust and it can really be distilled down to two ideas: "Your word is your bond" and "Your actions match your words."

The term 'integrity' originates from the Latin word 'integer,' which means whole or complete. In this context, integrity refers to the consistency of your character and honesty with yourself. Integrity is the glue that holds everything together in a consistent and effective whole. If your beautiful home collapses, it's because it's lost its "structural integrity;" its strength comes from what's inside – all the stuff that you can't see like the foundation and the rebar – not the pretty stuff that makes others say your home is beautiful.

According to cutting-edge leadership research, integrity shouldn't be considered a virtue but rather a state of being that is essential for exceptional performance. The idea is that the more broken, tainted, or compromised something is, the less potential it has to operate at its fullest capability. It makes perfect sense when discussing a building or a

---

[7] This 4C framework is part of the Endogenous Leadership™ model – where you set the conditions that people can successfully lead themselves. The 4C's form a "Ring of Trust" that surrounds all the leadership tasks.

steel beam; we've seen how things fail when they are made incorrectly or with improper materials and they've lost their "structural integrity" – and if you think about it, it's the same for human beings as well. [8]

Most experts say that ethics is the backbone of good leadership. I think they're wrong. It's integrity. Let me explain. Ethics are external, a set of moral principles or values that prescribe an individual's behavior or conduct. Ethics, usually someone else's idea of what's right and wrong, is often codified into a formal system or set of rules which can be applied in various contexts, including personal, professional, and social environments. It serves as a guide for making choices that are not only legally acceptable but also morally commendable. Ethics can be considered the "what" of moral action – what we ought to do and why. But ethics are malleable. Ethical codes vary greatly between different cultures, societies, and organizations. What really matters is if we adopt a particular ethical code.

Our personal values are just as important as ethics. Personal values are the core beliefs and principles that guide our behaviors and decisions. They reflect what we consider most important and serve as the foundation for our character and actions. Sometimes our personal values don't align with a set of ethics. The company work ethic might be to be at your desk every day from 9 am to 6 pm. But if you value performance over time clocks, you will probably let really high

---

[8] "Integrity: A Positive Model that Incorporates the Normative Phenomenon of Morality, Ethics, and Legality". Werner Erhard, Michael C. Jensen, Steve Zaffron. Pg 17. The logical outcome of their argument is that when integrity isn't viewed as necessary for the highest levels of performance, people and organizations will often (paradoxically) sacrifice integrity in the name of performance.

performers take off early on occasion if they've gotten everything done. A specific set of ethics isn't particularly important unless we adopt them as our personal values.

Integrity is the quality that allows us to navigate these diverse landscapes with consistency and moral clarity. Integrity is the alignment between an individual's values, actions, and words. It means being truthful and consistent in one's principles, both in public and private. It's our integrity core that becomes the basis for our leadership and it takes center stage in the leadership model we'll see over and over again.

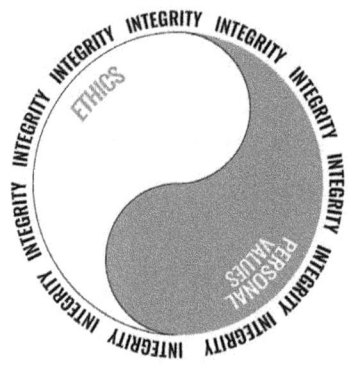

Ethics provides the moral framework that establishes what is right and wrong, but integrity is the manifestation of following that moral framework consistently. Ethics is *prescriptive*, outlining specific moral principles and rules, integrity is *personal*, involving the internalization and consistent application of these principles.

Ethics are a passive set of rules that exist 'on paper,' whereas integrity is the *active* engagement with and practice of those rules. Without integrity, ethical principles may remain abstract; integrity is what brings them to life through action. Ethics are the standards against which integrity is measured; integrity reflects alignment to ethical standards.

There's nothing passive about leadership; action is crucial. And what really matters is consistency in those actions. You might not believe in your boss' personal values or the company ethics but as long as the boss demonstrates integrity and consistently applies those ethics and values to themselves and the rest of the team, even when faced with challenges or opportunities for personal gain, then it's not particularly important if we believe in the company ethics or the boss' values. We can all play by the rules as long as they're crystal clear and apply to everyone all the time.

Our leadership is based upon and flows naturally out from our integrity.

2. Authenticity and Integrity go hand in hand. While integrity refers to being complete and uncorrupted, authenticity is the quality of being genuine and true to the original. Whereas integrity means "your word is your bond", authenticity means "your words = your actions = your truth." "It accurately reflects aspects of the leader's inner self, so it can't be an act;" it's what the Harvard Business Review calls "the attribute that uniquely defines Great Leaders."[9] Fortunately, authenticity is not determined by ourselves. Rather it's defined by how others perceive us so it's a quality that can be developed and enhanced.

Authenticity is significant because if we fail to align our actions with our words (which ideally reflect our true selves), people will eventually feel deceived and lose respect for us. Without their respect, we're done and we might as well pack our bags.

Paradoxically, authenticity is what we do when no one is watching, yet it only registers as authentic if someone else sees it.

The LOS encompasses both Integrity and Authenticity. Integrity represents our internal core (our level of integrity), while Authenticity serves as the GUI (Graphic User Interface) through which others engage with us. So when there is a problem with either one, it readily becomes apparent to everyone.

There are some additional character traits or activities besides the 4C's that help us build Active Trust which we'll discuss in later chapters, but the necessity of "character" should now be self-evident.

Great teams operate in an environment of Active Trust, so it's helpful to think of Trust as an arena, ring, halo, or even an orbit where the 4C's constantly create the conditions for good leadership to thrive.

---

9   Managing Authenticity: The Paradox of Great Leadership, by Rob Goffee and Gareth Jones, Harvard Business Review, December 2005

Basic Training

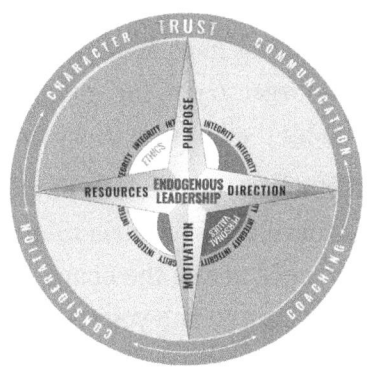

Real Leadership Activities

So far we've talked about what leadership is and some of the most important elements of "how" we should lead. But now it's time to discuss what leaders do and what they're responsible for. This is where we put it all together.

Bring it in for a moment and take a knee. We've covered a lot so far and I'm going to give you some pretty comprehensive lists here in a moment. You don't need to memorize everything because there is an infographic that lays it all out. *Don't worry* if you think that you can't do something yet. We're going to cover every area in this book, and none of it is beyond your abilities. Remember, Green Berets are created through a system, and that system will work for you, too.

As I said before, most leaders are made, not born. But *all great leaders make themselves* by **KNOWING** how to effectively:

- **Organize** the work and the effort, structuring tasks and resources efficiently to maximize productivity. A well-organized team knows exactly what needs to be done and has the tools and strategy to do it.

- **Set goals** and create action plans, defining clear objectives and outlining steps to achieve them. Goals give your team a target to aim for, and a solid action plan ensures you hit the bullseye every time.

- **Establish metrics** for success at all levels and for all actions, developing criteria to measure progress and performance across the board. Metrics are your compass, guiding you and your team toward continuous improvement and excellence.

- **Prioritize**, determining the most important tasks to focus on for optimal results. Knowing what to tackle first keeps your team from getting bogged down in less critical work and drives momentum.

- **Delegate** and follow up to ensure it's done properly (what gets inspected gets done), assigning tasks to others and monitoring progress to ensure completion. Effective delegation empowers your team, but consistent follow-up ensures accountability and success.

- **Train/Teach/Coach**, educating and guiding team members to enhance their skills and performance. Investing in your team's development turns good employees into great ones and builds a culture of continuous improvement.

- **Communicate**, conveying information clearly and effectively to ensure understanding and collaboration. Great leaders are great communicators; they listen, articulate, and foster an environment where ideas flow freely.

- **Resolve conflicts**, addressing and managing disagreements to maintain a harmonious work environment. Conflict is inevitable, but how you handle it can make or break your team's cohesion and morale.

- **Solve problems**, identify issues and find effective solutions promptly. Being a leader means being a problem solver; tackle issues head-on with a proactive and strategic approach.

- **Make decisions**, choosing the best course of action confidently and efficiently. Indecision is the enemy of progress. Make informed decisions swiftly to keep your team moving forward.

- **Manage time effectively,** organizing both personal and team time to prioritize essential tasks and responsibilities. By prioritizing correctly, you can maximize impact and make the most out of every hour for yourself and your team without burning out.

- **Perform your job competently**, executing your duties with skill and proficiency to set a strong example. Competence breeds confidence; when you excel in your role, you inspire your team to follow suit and strive for excellence.

Note that each element on the list is a combination of PDMR. For instance, delegating involves ensuring the person doing the work understands the Purpose; gets Direction or guidance on the standard of success; has the Resources required to do the task; and gets the proper Motivation so it's done well and on time. If you ensure that all of your leadership actions consider PDMR, you're well on your way to becoming a decent leader.

The good news is that there are tools available that can help even the most junior leader effectively do the tasks on the list above. If you don't have an innate or previously trained ability to perform these tasks, you can quickly develop competency by using effective tools. As such, we don't need to spend much time assessing them, especially as we discuss effective methods in later chapters. For now, all you need to do is to do a quick mental inventory to ensure you have effective tools for everything mentioned above and, if not, actively seek them out and become proficient in their use. If you've gotten consistent feedback from others that you need to improve on the skills above, then find better tools and master them.

There isn't a tool for everything; nonetheless, all leaders must routinely **DO** the following tasks:

- Get Results/Execute
- Lead by example and effectively manage oneself first
- Build, support, and sustain effective teams
- Establish and maintain an atmosphere of active trust, which is necessary and sufficient to create positive working environments
- Improve individual and team performance
- Advance the entire organization's goals
- Be proactive in addressing problems, improving performance, systems, and so on

I've inundated you with things to do: PDMR; build trust through the 4C's; know how to do a lot of tasks; and more. Don't try to memorize all of it. Instead just look at the leadership model below. It takes everything we've discussed so far – including all the leadership tasks listed above – and puts it all together in a way that shows how each task is influenced by the major elements.

All the things leaders need to "know" and "do" are listed around the inside perimeter of the Trust Ring. But more importantly, you can see how every task is arranged in relation to PDMR and the 4C's. Find "defining what's important" at the 1 o'clock position in the blue circle. This task is most closely aligned with "purpose" so it's closest to the "purpose" compass point (north), but it's also about providing "direction"

(so it's both "purpose" and "direction"). And in order to build trust within our team, it's important to communicate "what's important" to our team in order to provide that direction, so it's in the "communication" quadrant in the Trust Ring.

E*very* task that leaders do is listed in the blue circle, and they have been placed so they are aligned with PDMR and the 4C's. Look at "training" at the 5 o'clock position. Training your people gives them Direction, it Motivates them, and you do it through Coaching. While the model isn't 100% exact, it still puts all leader tasks in perspective and allows us to see how everything works together.

I know this seems like a busy graphic, but trust me, we use it all the time with all our clients and students and everyone loves it once they understand it. They say it makes leadership easier to understand and they'd rather have this picture than a bunch of lists and things to memorize.

Back to Be

But ultimately great leadership is not just about ensuring that things get done, it's about *how* you ensure they get done. And because the following are primarily personality traits, they are the elements that we focus on in the EPIC Leadership Assessment that we'll discuss in chapter two.

I developed the EPIC Leadership Assessment because I was frustrated with standard personality tests that seem to equate "leadership" with "wanting to be in charge" rather than assessing someone's ability to be a good leader. There are other leadership assessments out there, but they are expensive. Most people never get the chance to get good leadership training, but everyone deserves the opportunity to become a better leader, so I worked for years with a talented psychometrician and programmer to make a professional, normed, validated, and *free* assessment for everyone.

Don't try to memorize the lists. Just take the assessment at: thegreenberetway.com/epic so you can understand how you, and those who know and work with you, see you in terms of **BE**ing:

- Trustworthy (so important that it has its own list below)
- Confident, secure and self-assured, which should be reflected in one's professional demeanor
- Decisive
- Resilient
- Empathetic
- Self-Disciplined
- Humble
- Caring, receptive, friendly, warm, and encouraging (people must want to be around you - or at least not actively trying to get away)
- Curious and inquisitive
- Adaptable
- Proactive (self-starter, full of initiative)
- Resourceful
- Committed
- Focused
- Fair (although it's part of trustworthiness, it is listed separately due to its importance)

- Versatile
- Self-Controlled (with appropriate demeanor and grace)

In addition to the above, **truly** great leaders must have high levels of, or **BE** exceptionally:

- Courageous (not to be confused with bravery, unless there is a physical threat), as it is a prerequisite for developing an abundance mentality
- Abundance Mentality, which also requires a deep sense of self-worth and self-confidence
- Virtuous, in the classic sense, not "morals"
- Willing to assume the best in others' intentions
- Creative
- Continuous Self-Improvement
- Personal Balance
- Mental Agility

Again, *don't worry* about the lists – or that it seems like I'm asking you to drink from a firehose at the very beginning of the book. By the time we get to chapter three it will all make perfect sense and it will seem like you've understood this your entire life.

But before we delve into those concepts, we have to discover our big "why." Why do we want to be a leader in the first place and how much are we willing to work towards becoming a great leader? We dig deep into this question in the next chapter, so let's be sure we take away the most important concepts from this one first.

Conclusion
- ◊ Leadership and Management are not the same thing. Be a leader, then manage. People first, systems second. People are more important than hardware.

- ◊ Be, Know, and Do. The order is intentional because who you are is more important than what you know. What you Know and Do can be taught and supplemented with tools, but your Character (Be) is something that takes a lot of work, has a high cost, and requires you to assess where you're really at before you even attempt to go to the next phase – training.

- ◊ There's leadership, the art of leadership, and EPIC leadership. It's not enough to be a "servant" or "empathetic" leader. Leading elite teams requires EPIC leadership: Empathetic, Purposeful, Inspirational, and Character-based.

- ◊ It's imperative to review and assess our own Leadership Operating System so we can understand why we think and do the things we do. We can update our LOS to ensure we are utilizing the most effective and up-to-date algorithms.

- ◊ Leading elite teams requires more than conventional leadership. It entails consistently providing PDMR: Purpose, Direction, Motivation, and Resources, within an atmosphere of Active/Fierce Trust, achieved through the Four C's: Character, Consideration, Communication, and Coaching.

CHAPTER TWO

SFAS

Personal Assessment

There is a high cost associated with being a leader of great teams – whether in SF or in business. And you must pay it because leading great teams and retaining the best talent requires more than "good"; it must go beyond the basics of "conventional" leadership. Many people aren't ready to lead because they've never done the work to build the proper skills and gain the necessary attributes – but they don't know it because they've never really assessed themselves. There are no shortcuts. Personal self-assessment is painful and there is no guarantee of success because even after all the work, there is a good chance we'll find out that we're not ready, and some will decide that it's simply not worth the price.

This chapter dives deep into understanding our motivation and personal skill sets. To do that, we must start with an assessment. In Special Operations, assessments are designed to push candidates to their limits to ensure only the best make it through, saving time and resources for those truly committed. Similarly, before we embark on our own leadership journey, we must evaluate ourselves to determine if it's worth the cost and if we're willing to invest the necessary time and resources. Just as Special Forces Assessment and Selection (SFAS) weeds out those who aren't ready, we must do the same to ensure our commitment to becoming exceptional leaders. To illustrate this point, let me walk you through what SFAS is like for aspiring Green Berets.

Special Forces Assessment and Selection (SFAS)
As I mentioned in the first chapter, SFAS evaluates potential Green Berets on their knowledge, skills, abilities, and character under intense stress. This process applies extreme pressure over extended periods in order to break self-discipline and bravado, revealing candidates' true natures and resilience. While SFAS may seem to prioritize physical strength and endurance, its true focus is on assessing character.

The assessment is achieved through a number of different techniques, all done concurrently, so that the effects of each stressor are compounded. These techniques include extreme physical activity, sleep deprivation, food deprivation, constant pain, extensive mental and psychological testing when exhausted, extremely high (but secret) standards for all events, no feedback of any kind — ever, assigning impossible tasks and expecting them to be accomplished, no chance for recovery, limited time for all tasks, no free time, no contact with the outside world, and no comforts.

That is all just a nice way of saying that SFAS is designed to break you – both physically and mentally. It is 21 days long, so the cumulative effects are compounded and most candidates who complete all 21 days have stress fractures in one or both of their feet upon completion. Many candidates sustain injuries and are unable to pass selection. You can easily spot recent candidates in garrison because instead of wearing boots, they're wearing running shoes and doing the "SFAS Shuffle" because of the stress fractures in their feet. Most candidates also lose at least 20 pounds of body weight. But as challenging as the physical aspects may be, the mental strain is often even more daunting.

Individual Phase

There are two phases to SFAS: individual phase and team phase. A typical day during the individual phase would start around 4 am with a long foot movement to a training area with an 80-pound rucksack.[10] Then we'd be told to drop our rucks, put on our running shoes, line up and then to "go." They didn't tell you how far you had to run. It could be 5 miles, 10 miles, 15 miles. The distance was unknown. And you also knew there was a very high time standard to meet, but, because it was secret, you couldn't maximize your potential. You either had to go at maximum speed the entire time (in case it was a short distance), or go at a slightly slower pace in case it was a longer distance.

---

10 Technically, the standard was/is only 60 pounds, but that doesn't include water or personal equipment. Rucksacks were weighed multiple times per day (often in the middle of an event) to ensure no one was cheating, so everyone added an extra 5 pounds for a margin of error. And because you never knew when you'd have a chance to refill your water, you always carried 2 hip canteens (1 quart each) and at least two 2-quart canteens in your rucksack to refill the smaller ones on your hip. 6 quarts of water = 13 pounds. In addition to your rucksack, you also wore your Load Bearing Equipment - which was another few pounds and then your rifle (7.5 pounds). So, in reality, you were carrying between 75 - 85 pounds at all times.

One of my buddies remembers receiving instructions before his first run. The Cadre said, "Candidates, when I tell you to start running, you run, and when I tell you to stop running, you stop, what are your questions?" One Candidate raised his hand and asked, "How far is the run?" The Cadre's response was, "Candidates, when I tell you to start running, you run, and when I tell you to stop running, you stop, what are your questions? Needless to say, there were no more questions after that.

So even as you begin running, you're already totally stressed out because you don't know if you've made the correct decision to pace yourself or go all out. And while you're running you watch the others and think that maybe they know something that you don't and so you start to second-guess yourself and change your pace. It is a complete and total psychic ambush, which is the intention.

No one tells you your time when you cross the finish, which is usually around a bend in the road, so you can't try to "kick it in" for the last few hundred meters. No one tells you whether you passed or failed. You wait for everyone else to finish, and then the evaluator asks if anyone wants to go home. He asks in a very nice way, as if he already knows you haven't passed and is kindly giving you the opportunity not to waste any more of your time. Some raise their hands and move off to another area. Then the truck with all your gear arrives, you put it back on, and march off to the next event.

So before 7 am you've already marched 5+ miles, run a multi-mile sprint, and are already worried that you didn't make the cut. And as you hump to your next event, the voice in your head starts doubting because if you didn't correctly guess the length of the run and conserved a bit of energy, you were probably one of the last to finish. So maybe you've already failed an event and might not get selected no matter what you do. Do you stay in the course and go through another two weeks of pain if you've already eliminated yourself? Or do you commit to staying even if it is a huge waste of time at this point?

You can see how this would totally mess with your head, especially when it happens day after day. Many Candidates just say "screw this", and leave.

The next part of a typical "individual phase" day is long-distance navigation for time. Everyone gets map coordinates for a different point on the map and then is told to "begin." Once you get to the next point, they give you another one, but no additional information. Once again, you know there's a very high standard for completing the movements and because you don't have any information about what is going to happen, you have to give your maximum effort at all times, something which is impossible to do indefinitely, especially as you already smoked your legs during the morning run.

During these long movements the doubts creep in because it's hours and hours under a ruck with no one to talk to and nothing to keep you distracted. As such, you are a prisoner of your fears and doubts, constantly struggling with the voice that asks "Is this really worth it? And if you can't say "yes", if you don't have a compelling reason to be there, you quickly give up. This is when all self-discipline fails. And as much as I love the oft-quoted phrase "discipline equals freedom," it falls short because *discipline dies without purpose.*

Those that have purpose motivate themselves by playing games in their head to find the tallest tree in the distance and say to themselves "I'll just keep going until that tree." And once you reach that particular tree you find the next one and just keep going. And going. And going. However, after days and days of this isolation compounded by the ever-growing fatigue, that "tree" starts to get closer and closer until finally you're just trying to convince yourself to make it to the next tree. And then the next. At one point, my world became so small that all I could do was continuously chant in my head "one more step" for hours at a time.

But it wasn't just the monotony and the mental hurdles to get over. There was also the pain. While we'd all gotten used to carrying heavy rucksacks in order to get ready for SFAS, and while we'd meticulously broken in our boots to ensure they were comfortable and always wore two pairs of socks (thin polypropylene underneath regular socks) to prevent blisters, nothing prepares you for 25 miles a day, every day. The blisters we got during that first week were the size of silver dollars and a ¼ inch thick, and there were usually a few of them on each foot. Imagine spending the last part of a timed event nursing those blisters and still moving as fast as you could, praying that your feet would just go numb.

During the first week, most of us visited the medics every day to have them drain the blisters and squirt tincture of benzoin underneath the blister flap. This did three things: it sterilized the blister so it wouldn't get infected; it's sticky, so it literally glued down the blister flap and helped to create a callous; and it burned like hell. Tincture of benzoin is usually used to adhere bandages to skin, and in this case, the bandage was our own blister skin flap adhering to the raw, tender, bleeding tissue underneath. But after a few days of the blisters/benzoin routine, we all had nice hard calluses on our feet and as long as we continued to take good care of our boots every day, we avoided the really bad blisters for the duration of the course.

After we returned to "camp" and visited the medics, we'd get about seven minutes to eat a meal. We might get 30 minutes total to do maintenance on our gear (especially our boots) and prep it for the next day and then they would march us off to a comfortable air-conditioned classroom (not to be nice, but to make us fall asleep and fail) and we would take math and logic tests until late into the night.

In truth, they were probably simple tests, but I remember them being some of the most difficult I had ever taken because after slogging through 25 miles and being sleep-deprived, it is almost impossible to stay awake, much less complete a math test. You fight to stay awake and finish the tests, but your brain is so fried that it takes you five minutes to do a simple addition problem.

We'd go outside to "go to the bathroom" in the heavily-used and violently-fragrant porta-potties, lock the door, and snag 5 minutes of sleep whenever we could. But the evaluators knew this trick and would come around every so often and knock on all the doors and make you get out and go back inside. Something is very wrong when you realize that the only thing you have to look forward to (besides your one hot meal) is catching five minutes of shut-eye in a disgusting, overused porta-potty.

Finally, we would be released to get a few hours of sleep. They say you get 4 hours a night. That's a lie. They might allow four hours for sleep, but by the time you ensure your stuff is ready to go for the next day, get to your rack (metal bunk beds without mattresses), and get everyone else to stop moving, no one ever got more than three and a half hours on the best of days.

And it's like that every day until Team Phase, which is even worse.

Team Phase
During "Individual Phase," you're completely responsible for your own success or failure and you only have to contend with the voice in your head. But during "Team Phase" you work with your squad which gets multiple "impossible" missions per day. If you're put in charge of one of those missions and your team fails to accomplish it, it's your responsibility – and there are no mitigating factors. And if you fail a mission, there is a good chance you will not get selected. Most Candidates lead two missions during Team Phase and if they fail at both, they automatically fail the course. It doesn't matter if your team sucks; it doesn't matter if someone breaks a leg en route; if it's your mission, the success or failure falls on you alone.

Squads start with ten candidates, but injuries and voluntary drops whittle that number down as the days go by. Every loss is a blow to the team; the missions are impossible to begin with— even more so when you have fewer people.

We're not supposed to talk about the events at SFAS so that future Candidates won't have any "G-2" (intel) and have an easier go of it. Although at this point the original "missions" have probably all been replaced because word gets around after a while. The ones that do not change are the ones where it doesn't matter if you know what's going to happen or not. The "Sandman Event" is the "Sandman" and you're not going to think of any better way to handle that mission by knowing about it ahead of time.[11]

They "say" that all the missions can be completed, but when I went through SFAS, it was only the second time it had been conducted (before all the events were ironed out and before any of us could get intel on the course), so it was a literal shock to our psyches every time they told us what they wanted us to do because they were impossible. We were lucky to complete even a few missions during Team Phase. One of our missions was to move a jeep to a location 12 miles away, up and down hills, through deep sand within five hours. However, the mission was impossible because the jeep was out of gas, missing all four wheels, and "contaminated by chemical weapons" so we couldn't touch it. I'm sure later classes already had enough intel so that at least one candidate knew how to figure out the puzzle (which is why they have to keep changing the missions), but for us, we just kind of looked at the evaluator like he was a space alien and said "What????? You want us to do what?" And in a complete monotone, the Evaluator would deadpan "do your best."

That's when things got ugly.

---

11 The "Sandman" is pretty straightforward. Each team gets two "downed pilots" - (flight suits filled with 400 pounds of sand) that need to be transported to a safe medevac location about 10 miles away. Because the sandmen are so much heavier than human beings, you have to use metal poles (weighing 40 pounds apiece) instead of wooden ones for the stretcher - but you can only get 4 Candidates on each stretcher at once. You very quickly learn that there is no way to carry a stretcher weighing that much with your hands - especially as you're still carrying your 80 pound ruck, rifle and the rest of your gear. Even the strongest hands will give out after carrying that much for a few hundred meters. So you end up hoisting the stretcher 6' off the ground and laying it across the top of four Candidates' rucksacks who then must jog-march in unison so the stretcher doesn't slip off. Oh - and that 10 miles is a deep sandy, hilly path. If your team has 10 Candidates you're lucky because two can rest and rotate in and out with the rest of the team. If you only have eight Candidates -- it sucks to be you.

It's hard enough to lead highly motivated people who are used to being in charge. It's another thing altogether when no one actually knows what to do. The impossible situations are designed to put the Candidates in just such a position because there are multiple options and all of them suck. So how the leader (and the rest of the team) conduct themselves in such utter ambiguity speaks volumes about their character.

The clock is already ticking so some team members advocate for immediate action and urge the team to start without further delay. Others, however, emphasize the importance of taking a few minutes to think and come up with a better plan than just muscling through it because doing so will save time and effort in the long run.

Those that "must do something" head into the treeline to find any downed trees that could be used as levers or to construct a conveyance and "fortunately" find two wheels and some long metal poles[12], and while this is good news, now another argument erupts: "let's just throw it all together and GO! The clock is ticking!" Others argue for investing additional time to securely lash the poles to the vehicle, ensuring they remain intact and stable throughout the mission. The more often you have to stop to fix the "rig," the longer the mission will take. A well-thought-out plan allows the greatest number of candidates to push and pull at the same time, maximizing both speed and power.

In the end, the Candidate chosen to lead that particular mission has the responsibility of unifying the group and choosing a decisive course of action. Additionally, the leader also

---

12 Yes, it can be done with only two wheels, long metal poles, sufficient lashing material, and leverage.

has to decide when to take breaks and for how long, ensuring that everyone is doing their part, and assessing the weakest members to ensure they don't succumb to heat exhaustion. Because, while individual injuries suck for the Candidate who gets sent home, it also seriously jeopardizes mission completion because every person is required to get the job done.

So before you even get selected to attend the Q-Course, before you get *any* SF training at all, you are assessed on your ability to lead people in "impossible" missions in hostile conditions, with no information, no sleep, little food, extreme stress, multiple injuries, and sheer exhaustion. SFAS is a leadership crucible, where those who don't possess the necessary qualities are swiftly eliminated or succumb to burnout.

There are two such missions per day during Team Phase making it far worse than "just" jog-marching 25 miles in sandy terrain every day. It means spending at least six hours per day carrying an additional 50 - 100 pounds, resulting in a total weight of at least 150 pounds. Many people can't lift 150 pounds to begin with, let alone carry it while traversing hilly terrain for extended periods. And no matter how strong you are or how hard you've trained, your body starts to break down in those conditions because human beings are simply not designed to carry that much weight for an extended time.[13]

Pain is your only constant companion throughout SFAS, and we took so many 800mg Motrin tablets a day that we began calling them 'Vitamin M.' Many of us gave ourselves

---

[13] Science says that people shouldn't carry more than $1/3$ of their body weight over long distances. Most Candidates weigh around 180 pounds when they start SFAS so max ruck weight should be 60 pounds. Since most Candidates lose at least 20 pounds during SFAS, the effects of Team Phase are even worse.

liver damage during those 21 days that we still deal with. Some Candidates quit just to stop the pain.

The Navy SEALs have "Hell Week," often regarded as one of the most challenging selection programs in the world because they only get one hour of sleep per day and the other 23 hours are non-stop physical hell. Nonetheless, I think Hell Week is a better program because the Navy designed their course to preserve the Candidates' physical well-being by limiting it to one continuous week and giving candidates six weeks to prepare for it at the beginning of their training. It's hell, but at least your body doesn't get destroyed.

How hard is SFAS? In my class a Candidate fractured his leg the day before the final road march, which is ridiculously long and with a very challenging time. You simply cannot pass the road march unless you run most of it with that heavy rucksack. The guy couldn't walk without crutches, much less run, but he didn't go to the medics because they would have immediately pulled him from the course. The Evaluators were aware of his broken leg but, in line with their usual approach, remained silent. The following day, on crutches, he lined up with the rest of us for the final ruck run in the sand. Despite his injury, he did 12 miles before the evaluators took mercy on him and pulled him from the course and took him straight to the medics who promptly diagnosed his leg fracture and put him in a cast.

However, *he was prepared to do all xx miles[14] on crutches* because (as he told us) the only thing worse than doing a "ruck

---

14   While not classified, the length of the final ruck is considered "information OPSEC (operational security)" so we don't divulge that. But that event makes a marathon look like a "recovery day."

race" with a broken leg on crutches would be to do SFAS all over again. It wasn't so much that he was *hardcore*, as much as he wasn't stupid (and yes, he got selected). But the biggest reason that he – and the rest of us – were all willing to do whatever it took to become Green Berets was because we had already answered the why: why am I *really* here? Why do I *really* want to become a Green Beret? Because if you just want to be cool and say "I'm in Special Forces" then you won't make it.

You need to have a deeply-held and very clearly defined reason – a personal mission – to be willing to put yourself through so much misery. And if you show up to SFAS without knowing your personal mission, you either figure it out fast, or you quit. All the "internal" work is critical because although SFAS appears to be a physical course, it is primarily psychological; it's all about what happens *after* you've reached physical exhaustion, constant pain, and zero morale.

Lessons Learned From SFAS

- There is a **high price** to pay just to try out, with no guarantee of success.

- Many candidates **eliminate themselves** if they can't answer the "Why."

- Many candidates are **not ready** and therefore not selected.

- No one makes it through the course on discipline alone. Discipline fades quickly without a burning purpose to sustain it. We talked about this in the last chapter—how our best intentions and discipline can fail when things get really tough, and we default to our "normal" selves.

- The experience transforms you, instilling strength, confidence, and resilience. It is a crucible that burns out weaknesses and imperfections so that you can be forged into a Green Beret in the next phase.
- A few individuals who are ready and get selected have typically invested significant effort beforehand and paid a high price to develop the necessary skills and qualities.

Keep these lessons in mind because they will also apply to you when you go through your own personal SFAS – laid out at the end of this chapter. It will also be a rigorous journey designed to test your leadership abilities and skills. Just as SFAS weeds out those who aren't ready, you must assess your motivations and capabilities to ensure you're prepared for the challenges ahead and determine if facing those challenges is worth it. Undergoing your own assessment to understand your strengths and weaknesses is necessary because each chapter that follows will help you build and develop the skills and attributes necessary for EPIC leadership.

The Big Why

Most of the dropouts in SFAS weren't for injuries; they were voluntary drops because they didn't have a clear mission. They couldn't answer "the why" because they hadn't done a proper assessment of themselves ahead of time to know if SFAS was even worth it for them. Or if they did know "the why", they didn't want it enough to endure the suckfest. Understanding "the Why" is critical because *you can't determine ROI (is this worth it?) until you've established "the Why."*

Even if a candidate makes it to the end, they could still be a "non-select" if their assessment doesn't indicate sufficient integrity, confidence, resiliency, self-discipline, humility, teamwork, adaptability, resourcefulness, proactivity, commitment, creativity, versatility, mental agility, and self-control. Candidates must also demonstrate leadership skills (or potential) by communicating effectively, getting results, resolving conflicts, taking care of their team, making decisions, organizing, prioritizing, delegating, and providing purpose, direction, motivation, and resources to the team while leading by example.

It is no coincidence that the above list also just happens to be a subset of what *you* need to be an outstanding leader. And, just like Green Beret Candidates, *you* must know your own "why" because you will also need to pay a price to be evaluated. Authentic assessments involve confronting one's weaknesses with personal courage and a genuine commitment to self-improvement.

So how do you gain the education, training, and experience required to become a great leader? There are some established paths that are consistently effective but regardless of the route you take, the first step must always be an assessment of your skills, attributes, and knowledge.

YOUR Personal Leadership Assessment and Selection

Have you ever thought about the facets of your personality that make you unique? If you don't know your own strengths and developmental needs (areas for improvement) and you step in front of a pack of lions and expect to lead them, they will eat you on the spot. Because if you can't even articulate what, if any, value you bring to the team then there is no way you'll know how to employ *their* strengths in an effective manner.

Leaders of great teams *must* know how to put the skills and talents of all their team members to their best use. However, if a leader has never taken the time to understand herself, how could she possibly have the knowledge, experience, or desire to understand and fully utilize team strengths and mitigate team weaknesses?

At a more basic level, what we're talking about is "Life 101." It is far more difficult (and far less likely) to have a fulfilling life, to achieve your goals and become the person that you want to be, if you have never undergone a proper assessment because chances are good you'll end up in the wrong job in the wrong company in the wrong industry. Really understanding ourselves allows us to play to our strengths rather than our weaknesses, like knowing when to delegate a task to someone else who can do it better and who actually likes doing it! A leader who knows their strengths and the areas in which they don't excel will also know the type of people to bring to the team to fill the gaps. Most importantly, it highlights areas for improvement so that you can become the best version of yourself and *earn* the right to lead. Passing Life 101 is a prerequisite for Elite Leadership 450.

Passing Life 101 is more than just knowing your preferences and strengths: understanding your weaknesses actually makes you stronger. Why? Because it allows you to stop wasting time on tasks you're not proficient at, delegate them to others, and focus your energy on areas where you truly excel.

This way, you no longer need to pretend you're good at everything and can instead hone the skills that set you apart.

Focus on Strengths

A Special Forces team is made up of experts in different areas with built in redundancy. There are junior and senior sergeants in Weapons, Engineering / Demolitions, Medical, and Communications. Leadership consists of the team leader and the executive officer (XO) as well as the Team Sergeant and the Intel Sergeant (assistant Team Sergeant). Everyone is good at the basics, but the commo sergeants will never build improvised explosives as well as the demo sergeants, and vice versa. Even the Team Sergeant or the XO (who've spent most of their careers in SF) are fully cross-trained on only three of the six specialties of a team. No one expects a Green Beret to be an expert on everything.

So why do so many managers in today's workforce pretend that they already know everything or that they don't have any areas where they can still grow? Was Einstein a great basketball player? Is Michael Jordan a great physicist? Does anybody care? *Real* experts are always happy to tell you what they're *not* good at and what they don't know because they have confidence in the areas where they excel.

If you go to football tryouts and the coach asks, "what position do you play" and you answer: "I'm good at everything," you are wasting everybody's time. If *you* don't know what you're good at and where you should *not* be played, you're no good to anyone. You can always say:, "I'm pretty good at linebacker, but I really want to play cornerback, and I've been working hard at it so I'd appreciate a shot at that as well."

> Think about your own circumstances. Are you trying to be good at everything, or have you thought about what is truly important and focused on those few things? Of course, if we don't feel like we've mastered something significant, we don't like to admit it. If we're not good at something, we're afraid of what others will think about us. But learning to tame our fears, something required to lead great teams, starts with this step. Don't worry if you're not there yet—we go deep into this topic in chapter five, so help is on the way.

How much more likely are you to succeed as a new leader if you say to your team on your first day "My brain works very analytically and I'm not very touchy-feely so I'll need your help to make sure that our decisions take into account the impact on our customers. Also, sometimes I might come across as a little standoffish. I don't want to be that way, so I'd appreciate it if you'd let me know if I'm coming across too strong." Those are the words of a self-confident leader who is completely up front about areas that they need their team to help them out with. As long as you really are strong in the areas you claim to be, everyone will appreciate your humility and be glad to help. People *want* to follow leaders like that.

Unfortunately, many people are not willing to make the effort of critically examining themselves and accepting the truth. Just like SFAS, most of it's not difficult (in terms of complexity), but it's hard to do and there's no guarantee of success.

360° Assessments

By assessments, I'm not talking about taking personality tests, which are usually pretty benign or even fun. They have their use in determining your strengths and preferences. I'm talking about a candid and comprehensive 360° leadership assessment from a large group of people with whom you interact often to identify your strengths and areas for improvement, especially those you've been reluctant to recognize. It's called "360 degree" because it gathers feedback from all directions – peers, subordinates, supervisors, friends, family, and the individuals themselves – providing a complete, all-around view of a person's performance and behavior. Finding out what's actually true is hard because it's often painful confronting honest feedback, but *great leaders know that the truth is more important than looking good or feeling good about themselves.*

Some personality or strengths assessments are available for free, although they may not provide in-depth explanations or improvement strategies. Reputable leadership assessments are another story. You'll have to pay and the same restrictions apply – a limited report on what the results mean. Assessment companies state that only basic results are provided because only certified facilitators or coaches are trained well enough to be able to understand the nuances of your profile, provide you with an accurate picture, and suggest action plans for improvement.

But the biggest problem I have with most "leadership" assessments is that they only measure your willingness and desire to be in charge; they don't dig into the personality traits that make you a good leader. So, it's common that someone scores high in leadership when they're not actually well equipped for it. Just wanting to lead doesn't make you a good leader. Leadership success depends on *why* you want to be a leader.

Many people want to get into "management" because it means more money, a title, a promotion, the next step in their career, or because they think they have enough seniority and it's their turn to move up. Some leaders are very passive. They didn't necessarily want to be put into a leadership position, but now that they're in charge they just want to take care of people and aren't focused on the team's potential. A third group of people want to be in charge because they believe that they can do better than the person currently in that role and are frustrated by being held back. Maybe they see the untapped potential in the team; maybe they are just tired of their leader missing opportunities and being ineffective. Maybe they dislike the current culture of disregarding others or managers who frequently repeat phrases like "Don't bring me problems, bring me solutions!"

Those are very different motivators. And as you can imagine, these three types of people will operate differently as managers.

The first group lacks intrinsic motivation beyond personal gain. Their focus is primarily on themselves; they believe that they must be successful regardless of what it means for the team - and that the team is there to make them successful. They don't always keep their promises; they often don't hold themselves to the same standards they expect of everyone else; and they listen with the intent of moving you along as quickly as possible.

They are "top-down" driven. If you're reading this book, chances are you don't belong to this group. Individuals in this group typically lack interest in improving their leadership skills as they genuinely believe they are already exceptional leaders. Instead, they're focused on what they need to do for their next promotion, what will make them look good, what kinds of advantages or perks they can get, or getting people to like them.

The third type of person willingly attends leadership courses and is constantly seeking opportunities for improvement. They focus on individual team members to ensure they deliver their best work so the team achieves outstanding results. In essence, their primary focus is the team. Most importantly, in their hearts they believe that the team must be successful in order for them to be successful.

Unfortunately, both groups one and three score high on the leadership trait on most personality assessments, which is not a true reading of someone's basic leadership abilities, much less those required for great leadership.

I'm certified to administer and interpret results for a few assessments, but I've found that none of them are specific enough or measure the things required to BE a leader. Previously, I administered multiple assessments to obtain a consistent "basic" picture, extrapolated specific character traits, and then integrated direct input from my clients' peers, bosses, and subordinates to develop a more accurate profile. However, that approach is excessively cumbersome and time-consuming, prompting me to develop my own 360°.

The EPIC Leadership Assessment is available for free at thegreenberetway.com/epic.[15] There are instructions on how

---

15 The EPIC Leadership Assessment is completely science-based with all scales and items validated and normed through the International Personality Item Pool (IPIP). The Cronbach Reliability Estimates for all items are above .78 and validated through IPIP.

to take the assessment and how to send it to other people. There is also a guide on interpreting basic results. And unlike other assessments, I explain in the next chapter (and the accompanying workbook) how to utilize the assessment results to formulate a personal action plan for improvement in each area of the assessment.

Why do I advocate a 360° leadership assessment as the appropriate method? And why assess your integrity as a measure of your leadership ability instead of how proficient you are in written communications or problem solving or prioritizing or delegating?

As we discussed in the last chapter, leadership has the three components of Be, Know, and Do. I can teach you how to use tools for problem solving and you can become proficient by reading about techniques (Know) and then practicing them (Do). However, the most critical part of leadership is the part that you can't learn in books, the "Be". That is, who you are. Great leadership comes from within because we will always default to and act in accordance with our true nature – who we are – especially when under stress and things are at their worst.

Most leaders aren't born; they're made. But even born leaders have work to do to become great leaders. And regardless of whether or not you're a born leader, *all great leaders make themselves* by becoming the leader they want to be. And that's why the EPIC Assessment focuses on the things required to be a great leader.

Finally, we use a 360° assessment because it compares what you think about yourself to what others think to get to the truth. So the more people you can convince to assess you, the more accurate the results. The EPIC Assessment is anonymous so that people can give their honest opinions without fear or worry. While you might worry that some people will take this as an opportunity to "sandbag" you, it's been our experience that it rarely happens, and the program alerts us to outliers.

The results will surprise you. Yes, there will be some areas where you don't score as high as you think you should. That's good feedback and you should accept it and work to improve those areas. But what affects most people most profoundly is when everyone else rates them much higher on something than they rate themselves. This is always cause for deep introspection and can dramatically change the way you think and operate.

One person who took the assessment was dumbfounded by the fact that everyone else rated his creativity at 99% while he only put himself at 70%. He considered "creative" people to be artists, musicians, and poets while his peers recognized that he was always coming up with new and inventive ways to attack problems. He'd written professional peer-reviewed articles and contributed to edited volumes. He played the piano and even wrote his own music. But he felt he didn't meet the threshold for "real" creatives.

Before he took the assessment he shied away from participating in problem-solving or decision-making efforts because he thought he didn't have anything to offer. After confronting his own self-imposed limitations and finally seeing what was perfectly clear to all his peers, he started participating and subsequently helped the company both save money and increase sales.

The link has all the instructions for the others you ask to participate. It also has cut-and-paste verbiage to put in your email requests. We've made it easy for you so there's no excuse not to take it!

Decision Time

So now it's your turn. Remember the lessons learned from earlier because they apply towards your process as well. Just like SFAS, your own personal assessment will be hard and there are no shortcuts. Each step is crucial for your growth, so don't skip any. Embrace the process below with the same intensity and commitment as a Special Forces candidate and you're on your way towards making yourself into the great leader you want to be.

1. Determine if being a leader is worthwhile (the Why) and decide if you truly want to do it. If you decide against it, that's fine. There is no shame in being honest with yourself and deciding that you don't want that path. There are plenty of people who have said they're happy doing what they're doing and don't want the added stress and responsibility.

2. If you answered "yes" in step one, then it's time for you to go through your own SFAS. Take the EPIC Leadership Assessment (or other highly-rated 360° leadership assessment that evaluates the SFAS traits mentioned above) and get 10 people to take the assessment about you (at least 7 for accurate results; more is better). Choose a broad and diverse group of individuals, including supervisors, peers, and subordinates.

This may be difficult for you, but remember, there is a high cost associated with true assessments.

3. Review and accept the assessment results, being brutally honest with yourself. This can be very difficult for some people because examining and challenging weaknesses (or unacknowledged strengths) is threatening. However, the courageous will dive straight into the deep end without attempting to fool themselves and do one of the following:

   a. Acknowledge that you're not prepared and/or unwilling to put in the necessary effort. That's a personal decision and there's no shame in this. Leadership, like Special Forces, isn't for everyone.

   b. Realize you're not ready and commit yourself to gaining the skills and traits required for great leadership. Not everyone is ready for leadership at this level, so you must be prepared for some disappointment and be willing to do the work necessary to earn the right to lead elite teams despite the fact that there is no guarantee.

   c. Recognize your readiness for further advancement and go straight to the next phase of training.

I'm guessing this book is not what you were expecting. It doesn't sound fun, does it? Sounds like a lot of work, right? "Elite" doesn't happen by itself; it's always the result of a specific objective and a lot of hard work. Nobody gets a Green Beret just because they want one. Exceptional is earned.

If you want to run with the Big Dogs, you first have to make yourself into a Big Dog. And if you want to *lead* the Big Dogs, then you must make yourself into one of the best. No one follows the slow and weak.

But you want more, right? You want to go to the highest level and lead lions. Then make yourself into a lion that others will follow. *Great leaders make themselves.* But before you embark on any long, arduous journey you must have a clear destination in mind and a precise understanding of your current position to plan an efficient route towards your goal.

Are you ready? Are you willing to pay the price?

CHAPTER THREE

The Q-Course

Training and Qualification
The last easy day was yesterday. If you thought the assessment was tough, get ready. Training and qualification is even harder. Moreover, you don't get any credit for having done well so far and you can (and probably will) fail at any time. The good news is that training and qualification is doable. People less intelligent and talented than you have successfully passed, so you can, too. Additionally, you can get the training you need in multiple ways, but all of them require lots of "field exercises" in order to get truly qualified.

The Q Course
The majority of the candidates that complete SFAS and get selected to attend the SF Qualification Course celebrate loudly and enthusiastically. Not me. I was very subdued, so much so that several of my friends thought that I hadn't been selected. I made it but I didn't want to celebrate because I was afraid that the cadre would notice and realize they'd made a mistake. I was humbled and grateful because I knew that I had probably just barely passed – and then only because

of the intervention of one of my squad mates who taught me a valuable leadership lesson.

If you pass SFAS, you must wait at least 30 days before you can attend the Special Forces Qualification Course, otherwise known as the Q-Course or simply, "the Q." A 30-day waiting period is required for your stress fractures to heal properly and because the hard stuff has just begun and assessment never ends. In the Q-Course, the rucksacks get even heavier, the time under those rucks gets longer, there's now an academic requirement in addition to the physical one, and you can still get tossed from the course at any time during the long training pipeline.

The Q-Course is presently conducted in 5 phases: Basic SF training (Phase 1); Individual Specialty Training (2); SF Team Training (3); Language School and combatives (4); and Survival, Evasion, Resistance and Escape (SERE) Level 3 Course (5). It is hard to keep the order of these phases straight because someone is always messing with the pipeline and the current configuration of the course combines Phase 1 and SERE and moves language school before the team training. [16]

Phase 1 is about 2 months long; the MOS schools (Phase 2) can last between 3 months to a year; Phase 3 is about a month; language school (Phase 4) can be anywhere from 2–4 months, depending on the language; and SERE is a month. There is always a short break between phases, constant administrivia, and the occasional holiday. The

---

16 Don't hold me to this. The phases and the order of the phases change every few years because someone gets a good idea and needs to put their personal "stamp" on the course, but these five are the building blocks of every SF soldier's training.

shortest training pipeline, a Bravo (weapons sergeant) learning Spanish, takes a full year. The longest training pipeline is almost two full years.

However, it's never that straightforward because plenty of students drop or fail out, get pushed back to the following class (all students get one chance to recycle, if they fail), and some students might even get a new specialty and start all over. For instance, the Delta (medic) course is notoriously difficult and has a high fail rate because it's like a mini medical school. However, not making the cut to be a Delta doesn't mean you can't excel as a Bravo (weapons).

Prior to the start of Phase 1, every student is assigned a provisional Special Forces MOS (Military Occupational Specialty) based on their scores, general aptitude, and all those late-night tests during SFAS. The Career Management Field for Special Forces is '18,' so any SF MOS will start with "18" and then be given a letter code to indicate their specialty. All Army officers, regardless of their branch, have the letter identifier A (Alphas), and in SF the Weapons Sergeants code is "B" (Bravos), Engineering and Demolitions Sergeants are Cs (Charlies), Medical Sergeants are Ds (Deltas), and Communications is E (Echoes). There are other MOSs on a team, but those are given to experienced SF soldiers that get special training and serve in special jobs. [17] However, to become a Green Beret one must follow one of the five basic routes: Alpha, Bravo, Charlie, Delta, or Echo.

---

17 All First Sergeants/Team Sergeants in the Army are "Z" (Zulus), so an SF Team Sergeant is 18Z, the assistant commander is a warrant officer and is an 180A, Intel Sergeants / Assistant Team Sergeants are 18F.

Phase 1

Everyone gets assigned the provisional MOS during Phase 1 so students can be divided into teams of 12 just like operational A-Teams. Generally, no one knows how to do anything associated with their 18-series MOS, but the idea is that you'll go through Phase 1 like a "normal" team.

Having a "team" for Phase 1 is necessary because a significant portion of the phase is spent in the woods learning how to conduct small unit tactics and specialized SF team tactics. This includes patrolling, security operations, patrol base operations, raids, ambushes, recons, and leadership. And then multiple teams come together to learn how to operate as a platoon and company in attack, defense, and more. The manual I received during my first time as an 18C was over an inch thick. The course is even longer now.

Even though we trained until we could execute all the missions and tasks at a higher standard than required by the regular army, it was still just the most basic of SF skills. It was like learning multiplication and division as prerequisites to studying algebra or trigonometry; it establishes a common language and foundation on which other skills are built. For students who had spent a lot of time in the infantry, as scouts, or attended Ranger School prior to joining SF, it was pretty easy; for everyone else, it was a steep learning curve. And while the number of students leaving, recycling, or failing was lower than SFAS, we always lost a few students in every phase.

I was "fortunate" enough to get to go through the entire Q-Course twice, first as a sergeant and 10 years later as an officer. Despite having successfully earned my Green Beret as an 18C, serving on an SF Team during the first Gulf War (giving me the privilege of wearing an SF Combat Patch) and being on a special projects team doing super cool classified stuff, they said I still needed to take the entire Q-Course all over again once I became an officer.

At the time I thought it was complete BS. I thought I already knew everything I needed to know about leadership, and I wanted to get back to a team as quickly as possible, not spend another year in school! But the SF Training Command emphasized that *leading* an A Team was an entirely different job and that I wasn't just learning a new "hard skill" (guys on teams who learn a new SF MOS only attend Phase 2 – what I wanted) and I needed to do the whole thing over again.

> This is a profoundly important point that we're going to see repeatedly in this book - just because you know how to "do" things doesn't mean you've learned how to be a leader. To become an effective leader means learning a completely different skill set and experiencing a completely different set of challenges. Even though I'd been commissioned and gone through basic and advanced officer courses and had multiple leadership positions as a lieutenant, if I hadn't been forced to go through the entire course again, I would have never had the confidence to lead a *Special Forces* team later.

That sucked. I was 10 years older than when I first went through as an 18C, and I felt every day of those 10 years during every hour of the Q-Course. But in the end, as much as I hated it, they were right. As much as I thought I knew, I still didn't know nearly enough to take on the job of leading lions. It was one thing to be *on* an A-Team, but there was an even hotter crucible that I needed to survive if they were going to allow me to *lead* an A-Team - and my instructors made sure I was well aware of it. They were all senior sergeants, and in their eyes, I was a traitor. I'd gone to the "dark side" when I became an officer, and some made it their personal mission to ensure I failed.

The Q-Course was tough physically, but for me and another SF "mustang" [18] doing the Q a second time as officers was a complete mind-fuck. Sorry, there's not a less profane way to say it. It was an intentional attempt to destabilize, confuse, and manipulate us to quit. Dave, the other mustang I started with was an 18D (medic), and he was a true stud. Dave was the epitome of a Special Forces soldier from any branch in any country. He was bigger, badder, stronger, faster, smarter, and way better looking than everyone around him. Dave was everything I'd ever wanted to be as a Green Beret, and he intimidated the hell out of me despite the fact that we belonged to our own special group of SF mustangs. Dave had gone to all the cool schools like High Altitude Low Opening (HALO) parachuting and Special Forces SCUBA school (probably the toughest school in the Army) and obviously knew his stuff. He'd been commissioned as a medical corps officer and, like me, as soon as he reached the rank of 1st Lieutenant, he applied to return to SF.

---

18 A "mustang" is military slang for an NCO who becomes an officer -- someone who has "bucked the system." In my experience, mustangs were either some of the finest officers I ever saw -- or some of the absolute worst. If sergeants become officers because they just want the higher pay, to get saluted, the higher retirement, and to have all the trappings associated with being officers, they become terrible officers who only care about their career. However, the ones who became officers because they wanted to do "more" often became truly outstanding leaders that we all would have followed anywhere.

The Q-Course

We were both surprised to see another SF mustang in the course because it's pretty rare to see one at all, much less have two in the same Q-Course class. I was relieved because I thought I'd have a buddy for the duration of the course, someone with whom I could commiserate and keep me motivated. But he didn't last. He was upset about all the bullshit they were putting us through; he couldn't understand it and kept saying: "That's not what it's like on a team and they know it!"

He was absolutely right, but it didn't matter. Life on an SF Team is very, very good and being an SF Medic gives you an even greater measure of respect because it's so difficult to become a Delta and there are so few of them. Moreover, because he was such a stud he'd been on SCUBA teams, which is where almost everyone wants to be because they are generally held in greater esteem than the regular teams. So being treated like a private in basic training, constantly being yelled at and being generally considered "less than" drove him crazy because arguably, he *was* far more qualified, more knowledgeable, and more experienced than every member of our cadre; he could have (and probably should have) been teaching them!

I tried to convince him to stay. I kept saying that it was temporary and we'd get through it and once we got back on to a team it would all be okay. But despite the fact that everyone knew he could have easily made it through if he wanted to, he couldn't answer the "why" anymore. In the end, he decided that he'd have a very successful career in the medical corps where being a former Green Beret would be highly valued by the others around him. He said "I don't need this shit!" And he didn't. So he left. I'm sure he was very successful.

Dave's departure deeply affected me. He was a far superior Green Beret in every way, but the idea that I was still in the course and he wasn't completely messed with my head. For the first time I had serious doubts about whether I could make it all the way through, because if Dave couldn't do it, then what chance did I have? I had to think hard about why I was there a second time when I'd already gotten my Green Beret. In the end, it was about the job. I didn't want to be in the regular army. I wanted to lead lions! I had something to prove both to myself and to the world. I didn't have a plan B because I never wanted a plan B. I was all-in and I would either make it or crash and burn.

That doesn't mean there weren't plenty of times I wanted to quit. I was under constant intense scrutiny and I had to watch every step. So even though I was already a "long tabber" with an SF Combat Patch, I took them off my uniform to let the cadre know that I understood that *what I did or earned before didn't matter and I still needed to prove myself every day.* But all the instructors knew everything about me. There was no escaping the Eye of Sauron; they saw everything and ensured I didn't get anything the easy way.

A Special Forces Tab is a double-edged sword. On the one hand, you are immediately afforded a measure of respect and almost everyone assumes that you have a very high degree of professionalism and knowledge. The downside is that everyone assumes that you have a very high degree of knowledge and so your performance can never, *ever* be anything less than outstanding. In the regular Army, scoring a 290 out of 300 on the Physical Training (PT) test earned you a badge to wear on your PT uniform. However, if a Green Beret scored a 290, he was letting down the regiment and all of his brothers, especially in front of regular army troops. We used the "extended" scale. which means that you only started accumulating points after you "maxed out" the PT test at 300.

So they didn't need to make it any harder for me because I felt immense pressure to always do better than everyone else. So when I screwed up or didn't perform well, I was ashamed. After all, I'd done the Q-Course once already, and much of the material in Phase 1 and 3 was the same.

Although there is some classroom instruction, much of the Q-Course and most exams take place in the field. And, just like in SFAS, Land Nav is one of the skills in which you must demonstrate extremely high proficiency. The good news is that once you're in the actual Q-Course, you get real instruction. The bad news is the movements are significantly more challenging than SFAS and the "Star Exam" is widely known as one of the toughest in the world for its physical and mental difficulty. It's called "The Star" because the legs of each movement are very long (5 - 12 miles each) so they cross each other despite being conducted in a huge training area. There are at least five long movements so when you're done, your routes roughly resemble a star. There is also a large swamp in the middle of the training area which creates a mountain of trouble.

There were a lot of things we learned in Phase 1, but I'm going to spend a little time on Land Nav because it exemplifies the skills required for effective leadership and serves as a strong metaphor for many of the pitfalls leaders often fall into. First of all, no one will follow you until you can learn to lead yourself; if you can't figure out where you are and how to best get to where you want to go with the equipment you've got on-hand, you've got no business navigating (or setting goals) for anyone else. Land Nav is all about planning, bypassing obstacles, and constantly moving towards the objective even if it looks like you're going sideways or backwards.

It's an individual skill, but it's critical for leading a team because without it, no matter how well you plot your path to success, you won't make it. It's one thing to have the ability to plan on paper, but another thing entirely to do it on real terrain where all kinds of unexpected obstacles jump up in your path and force you to find ways around them. While conducting combat patrols, the leader has many responsibilities and so someone is always designated as "primary compass" to ensure the team stays on the right path. But the leader *never* gives up the responsibility to ensure that the team gets to the objective on time, so the leader must constantly check their compass, too.

Finally, The Star is the best reminder that performance that was good enough before, (during SFAS), doesn't cut it when conditions are harder and the stakes are higher. Even if you meticulously follow the planned path, success isn't guaranteed as the actual conditions on the ground may be completely different from what the map says and the *only* certainty is that things will not go as planned.

Traversing the Mirkwood

Working with a map and compass seems straightforward: plot your course on the map, set the azimuth on your compass, and start moving in the right direction. However, to pass The Star, you must run through the woods as much as possible (at night, with at least 80 pounds of full gear and your rifle) because you won't pass if you just walk, even at a fast pace, because you've only got 12 hours to complete about 25 miles.

While going over the top of a large hill may look like the fastest and most direct route when planning, when you arrive at the actual hill and find every inch of it covered in vines and branches so dense that you have to crawl underneath them to squeeze through, your original plan flies out the window. Conversely, the map might show a low area that appears to be dry (because it's not depicted as water or marshland), but when you get there you sink down to your waist in the mucky bog because it rained hard the night before. So if you don't run every chance you get, you're almost guaranteed to fail.

But the problem with running through the woods at night is that, well, you're running through the woods at night! You can't see, so you're going to trip over things, get smacked in the face, run a stick through your eye, or step into a sinkhole. There are plenty of students who end up breaking a leg or spraining an ankle and get recycled when running The Star.

Then there are the Wolf Spiders.

Wolf Spiders are big (up to three inches), with a nasty bite. Wolf Spiders earned their name due to their predatory behavior of chasing down and pouncing on their prey while injecting venom with their fangs. Wolf Spiders spin their webs between trees about six feet off the ground, and I've encountered webs reaching up to five feet in diameter. Just imagine running through one of those massive spider webs in the middle of the night and having your face stuck in the center. Of course you immediately stop, as running through it would cause the web to cling to you and trail behind, meaning you'd probably have a giant Wolf Spider stuck to your rucksack ready to jump down your collar at the worst possible moment. So, you don't run through them; you slam on the brakes, try to back out of the web and hope that none of the web sticks to you, or that a Wolf Spider hasn't already jumped onto you or your gear.

Once you back out of the web, you look to see if there isn't a way around it. But there's never just one web. In some areas the Wolf Spiders are so thick that entire sections of the forest are covered in webs, like a big white wall. I'm pretty sure that J.R.R. Tolkien got his inspiration for the giant spiders in The Mirkwood Forest from spending time in the North Carolina woods avoiding Wolf Spiders. Unfortunately, when an entire section of the forest is blanketed in webs, you can't go around every one of them because there are just too many. Therefore, each person develops a strategy to deal with Wolf Spiders. I'd break off a long, thin, flexible branch (what they used to call a switch) and keep the end swirling about four feet in front of me when running through especially dark sections. The switch would break the web, and the swirling motion gathered it around the stick and prevented it from getting in my face.

Of course, this meant that more often than not, there was a Wolf Spider in that webby glob at the end of the stick, so once I got clear of their hunting grounds, I'd drag the stick behind me in the dirt to pull the web off the stick and start the process all over again. While this sounds like a great idea, it had its risks because if we were caught using any kind of "spider stick" we'd have gotten in trouble because we were supposed to be carrying our rifles in both hands like we would on a real patrol instead of carrying it in one hand with a spider stick in the other.

But Wolf Spiders, sinkholes, and even bears were really just distractions from the real challenges of navigating at night. The real issue was the terrain and the fact that the "truth" (in this case an official US Geological Survey map that gets updated every five years) was rarely so straightforward.

The key to Land Nav isn't your actual skill. It's controlling your mind and not getting discouraged every time you run into an unplanned obstacle or your well-planned route gets shut down by the reality of the terrain on the ground. When you run into unexpected major obstacles like a swampy bog, you can try to go through them – which can take forever and make you wet and cold and slow down the rest of your movements (not recommended) – or you can try to "box" them, making a series of 90 degree turns that gets you around the obstacle and back on your original azimuth.

To box an obstacle, make a 90-degree turn to the left (or right) and walk far enough to bypass it while counting your steps. Turn 90 degrees to the right (back in the original direction), carefully measuring the distance to ensure you've passed the obstacle (calculated from the map). Then take another 90-degree turn to the right (back toward the original line of march) and walk the distance you recorded in step one. Finally, take a 90-degree turn to the left onto your original line of march and hope you're close to where you would have been if you hadn't needed to box it.

Boxing an obstacle takes a long time, and there's no guarantee that the ground along that route will be any better. You may have to stop your "box," head back to your start point, turn around, and head back a kilometer in the opposite direction and try the box again. It's incredibly discouraging to try boxing an obstacle twice and still not be able to get through easily because now you've lost so much time that your only option is to go straight through, which usually consumes more time than even the most challenging "box."

Because if you go straight through, you can easily find yourself trapped in the middle of a foul-smelling swamp, with water reaching up to your neck—a terrifying experience. Sometimes you get stuck and can't move backward or forward because your boots get sucked down into the mire. When that happens, you have to stop in the swamp, force yourself not to panic so you don't sink any further, inflate every waterproof bag in your rucksack, and use them as makeshift floats to get out.

Once out of the swamp, you're soaked—and at a minimum you're going to take off your boots to pour the water out and decide whether it's worth the time to put on dry socks. Running in wet boots and socks is a sure way to get a hell of a blister, but you worry that even those extra five minutes will ultimately cost you.

There's no way to know ahead of time if it's better to attempt to go around the obstacle or just bite the bullet and head straight through it. And every single "lane" of The Star Exam had at least one leg with a significantly challenging obstacle not depicted on the map. Most had two or more.

The very first time I did the Star Exam I'd boxed so many obstacles that I was running behind and made the choice to go through the swamp on my last leg to try and catch up. I got lucky and it worked out for me. But not for everyone. There are always a considerable number of students who fail The Star and have to repeat it. Fail it three times and you're kicked out of the Q-Course.

When I went through Phase 1 the second time as an officer, The Star was a disaster and I ended up failing it and having to retest. My hubris got the best of me because I expected to breeze through it. The looks the cadre shot me afterward made me just want to crawl into a hole and die.

My main shortcoming was that I was "just" competent, which would have sufficed in most scenarios. But being "not bad" doesn't cut it in the Q-Course. In my role as the "junior demo guy" on a team when I was enlisted, I'd only been given the "compass" position on a few training missions where it wasn't difficult. And even though I'd been a Scout Platoon leader after I was commissioned, we still operated in terrain that was always bounded by major roads or used a GPS - which meant you could never really get lost. I was good enough for the regular army, but not for Special Forces. "Regular" isn't "Special."

Brimming with misplaced self-confidence, I was sure I could "outsmart" the course and instead of exhausting myself, I'd plan better routes, move quickly, avoid all the nasty stuff, and cruise in hours ahead of time like the cool Green Beret that I was. While that might have worked in "normal" terrain, the area for The Star is anything but normal and I quickly found myself in one of those semi-flooded bogs that wasn't indicated on the map.

I didn't panic and calmly tried to box it. But my box was too small and I found the same bog halfway through my attempt. So, I tried to "box the box," which still didn't work, and before too long I had no idea where I was anymore and I was way behind time. But I was still overconfident in my ability to "work smart and not hard," so instead of just biting the bullet and going through all the nasty shit, I kept trying to maneuver around it.

Box #3 eventually proved successful and although I managed to stay out of the muck, it wasn't the only unexpected large obstacle I encountered that day. So despite an all-out sprint at the end while the sun was coming up, I was still a few minutes shy of making the time, which was one of the most humiliating and disheartening moments in my life. However, I learned a few valuable lessons that day. First," humble yourself or be humbled." When something is important, put your ego aside and just embrace the suck, no matter how nasty the muck is. Secondly, no matter how good your plan is or how smart you think you are, something is going to surprise you; so work as hard as you can as early as you can so you've got enough time to pick yourself up as often as you need. I immediately put that into practice for my second attempt and moved on. But I still carried a stain throughout the rest of the course.

Phase 2
Phase 2 was a blast when I was an enlisted soldier. Literally. I was in the Special Forces Engineering and Demolitions course, so we got to build things and then blow them up. There were a few pivotal moments during that course. For the first time in my life, I saw math as something that had real purpose and application. Algebra went from being a tedious requirement in high school to the secret language of battle mages because with the right equations we could figure out how to blow up or destroy just about anything using a small amount of explosives we carried on our back.

Phase 2 of the Officers Course had three parts. The first part consisted of classes on leadership tasks appropriate for our rank. This was done in each of the specialties to meet the requirements for the students' next leadership school requirements. The purpose was to understand the full capabilities of each specialty, including potential, strengths, and weaknesses, because that knowledge was essential to leading the entire team effectively. Because if we didn't know what each of the specialties could *really* do, we'd never be able to effectively employ them as a team.

Part 3 of Phase 2 focused on advanced leadership skills: detailed planning, enhanced decision-making, problem-solving, and risk management, as well as how to lead a team through those same activities. This included a lot about weapons, blowing things up (again), learning how to "cut" long-range antennas that could reach the other side of the world, and receiving the most comprehensive medical training of my career. But as much as we learned and as much fun as we had, we were primarily left with a profound respect for what each specialty brought to the table. There were many times in my life where I trusted my 18D's for medical advice more than the doctors on base.

It was a constant cycle of studying every nuance of a particular Special Forces mission (Unconventional Warfare, Strategic Recon, Direct Action, etc.), conducting practical exercises to reinforce the lessons, going to the field to plan and execute the mission, and then returning straight to the classroom to learn the next mission.

This wasn't like Phase 1 where we'd plan and execute simple recons, raids, and ambushes one after the other with limited planning time. The goal of these missions was to teach us how to *lead* a team through the 4-day mission planning process that SF teams use, a problem-solving and decision-making method that makes SF teams some of the best operational planners in the world.[19]

> So let's be clear. It's the leader's (your) job to ensure the team comes up with a fool-proof plan that achieves all the team's goals and that every member of the team knows the plan and all its details inside and out so that anyone could step up and take over to execute the plan. To make sure that happens, the leader should have some good processes and tools to ensure that everything gets covered, that root causes (not symptoms) are identified during problem solving, and that the best decisions are always made. It takes some time to do all of this correctly, so plan accordingly. Yes, you should plan for a successful planning process.

So even though it sometimes feels like you have to drag the team through the process, the complete mission planning process is essential to leading a Special Forces team. If a leader can't routinely organize an exceptional planning process where the team demonstrates exceptional proficiency, cognitive prowess, ingenuity, creativity, problem solving, and decision-making skills, their team will *never* get a "good mission," which ruins the morale of the team and causes everyone to lose respect for, or even hate, the leader. The leader's job is *not* to be the primary trigger puller, to

---

[19] This is the standard timeline for mission planning in isolation (no contact with the outside world). There are also plenty of missions that require months of planning.

calculate and emplace demo, give an emergency tracheotomy, or do that magic voodoo commo stuff. The leaders' job is to employ all those skills in the best possible manner and to bring out the magic that happens when all of those amazing abilities synergize to accomplish incredibly important – and sometimes seemingly impossible – missions.

There is a "capstone" exercise for each of the specialties. For my enlisted demolitions course, it was a mission to destroy a very large bridge (simulated). It's a difficult mission because it takes a lot of explosives to bring down a modern bridge; we only had as much C-4 as we could carry in our rucksacks, and we had additional demo missions to perform before the bridge. However, I don't remember that exercise being particularly tough. I did well in that course and would have been the Honor Graduate except that during the only "partner" assignment we'd been given during the course, my higher-ranked partner didn't put any effort into the work; so even though my personal grade was very high, our combined grade on that assignment knocked me out of the top spot by a single point.

I was bitter about losing the Honor Grad spot as it would have validated my skills and made me feel like I deserved to be in Special Forces. I argued that I shouldn't be punished for someone else's poor attitude and lack of effort. The cadre responded that while I was absolutely right, it didn't matter because we didn't accomplish the mission and if I'd been a better leader I'd have found a way to get him to do a better job.

Of course they were right. I wasn't a leader and I was afraid to have a difficult conversation with a superior – an experienced, older, senior sergeant. Yes, he *should* have known better; he *should* have cared about his own grades; he *should* have put more effort into the exercise – especially knowing that it would affect both our grades. He *should* have done a lot of things—but he didn't—and I had to come to grips with my own inadequacy and inability to anticipate and overcome mismatched expectations. Because it didn't matter what he should have done; all that mattered was what I did—or didn't do. We can never rely on "should."

> "Should" is the architect of destruction; remove it from your vocabulary immediately. "Should" creates mismatched expectations, the source of almost all conflict and misunderstanding. "Should" is the devil on your shoulder that whispers in your ear that it's okay to do something harmful or spiteful because "you should have that," or "they should treat you better" or "she should know how I feel," or "they shouldn't have done that." "Should" is the sword of the vindictive, it destroys friendships, ruins marriages, and sends countries to war with each other. There's no reason to ever say this word again because it's easily replaced. Change "I should be home by 10:00 pm" to "I plan to be home by 10:00."

"Should" leeches away your agency, your personal power, and says "I want to be home by ten but things outside of my control may interfere and I won't be able to overcome them. "Should" is what keeps you in a destructive loop where you keep thinking about how something "should" have happened differently. You may have goals, but they are focused on the other person or group that wronged you. You cannot move forward towards goals that benefit you until you break out of "should." If you ever find yourself saying "should" again, immediately stop what you're doing and figure out how you are setting yourself up for failure or creating conflict. Good communication and the ability to have difficult conversations are the key to clarifying expectations.

Losing the Honor Grad award was a good lesson for many reasons, the most important being that *personal success is intricately tied to the success of the team.* Leaders are ultimately responsible for results. *You can't be a leader and try to divorce yourself from bad results.*

Officer Stakes

While my Phase 2 capstone exercise for 18C wasn't particularly memorable, my second experience during "Officer Stakes" is another story, and I can still recall the sense of hopelessness I felt back then. The grueling 48 hour exercise tests proficiency in all the skills learned throughout Phase 2 at different stations. Because Phase 2 was so long, the number of things we could be tested on was daunting. But that wasn't the hard part. The hard part was that those "stations" were all 10 miles apart in the middle of the (often impenetrable) Uwharrie National Forest which is some of the toughest, most mountainous, and densest vegetation in the U.S. It was yet another Land Nav exercise, and it was the worst by far. 30% of my fellow classmates didn't pass Officer Stakes, a huge percentage considering that by the end of Phase 2, every officer that was still there was a stud. Officer Stakes is designed to surpass the difficulty of any tasks assigned to the sergeants and demonstrate the worthiness of the officers to eventually take charge of a team.

The Uwharrie National Forest and Mountains in North Carolina makes The Star Exam's terrain look like a farmer's field. The area where Officer Stakes is located is nothing but mountains covered by trees with no distinguishing characteristics except for the streams that run between the mountains. If you stand on top of one mountain and look around, you can't really determine the peak of the next mountain because the trees are so thick. Everything looks like a big green carpet with no way to distinguish landmarks.

And when I say the mountains are covered in trees and vegetation I mean thick vegetation and trees that grew so closely together that often it was impossible to walk between them. So wearing a bulky 80 pound rucksack while trying to pass between the trees was nearly impossible. Trying to move in a straight line and follow an azimuth just cannot be done. The only way to move at all in Uwharrie (in our training area) is to find *any* path through the trees and hope it takes you in the generally right direction. It was exactly like trying to walk a straight line in a maze – impossible.

Because it's a national forest there are lots of animals, and animals follow game trails, so we spent a lot of time walking straight up the mountains (90 degrees to our direction of travel) hoping to stumble across a trail that headed in the right direction. I managed to find one at some point but quickly realized it wasn't headed where I needed to go. That really sucked because it was just so wonderful to be able to move quickly that you wanted to stay on the trail for as long as you could, even if the only thing it was doing was taking you further from your goal.

There was one "high speed" route walking in the middle of the streams and rivers. There were no riverbanks because the mountains were so steep that the trees came straight down into the water. So the only option was to walk in the deep streams themselves. This had the advantage of unimpeded forward movement and the surety of knowing exactly where you were at all times. However, the stream beds are full of smooth rocks that you have to carefully walk on, so movement is slow and deliberate. We've all crossed rocky streams before so we know it can be tricky even when conditions are perfect.

But adding a heavy rucksack exponentially magnifies your imbalance. Even the slightest slip or misstep and you have to overcompensate for an additional 80 pounds to stop yourself from falling. And because you're walking up (or down) rather than across the stream, everything stays wet and inevitably you slide off a smooth rock and the added weight of the ruck takes you down. You try to minimize the damage but there is no way to avoid banging a knee or spraining an ankle. Even if you are able to windmill your arms and stay upright, the gyrations severely stress your knees and ankles.

Unfortunately, I was only able to stay in the stream for about two hours before I torqued my knee so badly that I was in pain with every step and was forced out of the water. My already slow progress became a crawl. Ideally, students are able to catch a few hours of sleep at night, but any possibility of rest was now out of the question for me, and it became a non-stop slog in constant pain. I consumed at least twenty 800-mg Motrins during those 48 hours, three or four at a time. I was *not* going to fail Officer Stakes like I'd failed The Star Exam.

Students aren't allowed to use roads, and if they're caught using one (or even walking parallel to it closer than 25 meters) they are immediately disqualified. One of my points was near an intersection and although I was able to approach the checkpoint through the woods, when I was given a new point to plot, I saw it was impossible to move in the direction I needed to go without walking on a road. There was only one "legal" route out of there and it was to climb a 200 meter high hill that went almost straight up and was covered with an impenetrable wall of thickets.

That was the closest I ever got to quitting. With my injured leg, I could not imagine climbing that hill and limping another eight miles through the mountains within the time I had left. After I'd plotted my course and saw that thicket-covered hill, I just sat there and contemplated my life for about 10 minutes, the evaluator silently watching. The smart thing would have been to let the instructor know I'd been injured and get myself recycled once it had healed. But there was no guarantee I wouldn't get hurt the next time (given that my knee probably wouldn't heal completely). And considering what had happened during The Star Exam, there was always the chance I'd mess up or get injured during a second attempt.

I finally screwed up my courage and used a stronger fear (shame) to overcome the pain and my other fears. I figured that I only had so many chances to make it through Officer Stakes and I needed to take advantage of every one; and quitting now wasn't going to increase my odds.

So I asked the evaluator to open his med kit, took off my BDU pants and wrapped my knee as tightly as I could, then covered it all with 100 mph tape to make it extra tight and ensure it didn't unravel. I couldn't bend my leg, but I put all my gear back on and hobbled off towards the hill.

My assessment hadn't been wrong. The only way to get up that hill was to crawl on my belly underneath the branches and pull my rucksack behind me with para cord attached to my leg. It probably took me two hours to get up that hill. I had to cut myself a tunnel with a small pair of pruning shears that we all carried with us for just such situations.

The instructor at each station calls in to HQ every time a student arrives and again when they begin movement to the next station, so the cadre is able to track the progress of each student, know roughly where they are in case of emergency, and pretty accurately determine if a student will make it in time. I was told afterwards that the cadre had given up on me and didn't think there was any way I'd make it, especially given my noticeable limp. But I was one of the lucky ones and managed to stumble into my last point with about 15 minutes to spare. Unfortunately, 30 percent of my classmates didn't make it, and we were a somber group of officers that met in the classroom afterwards and saw who was still left.

Phase 3

We began Phase 3 as a "reassembled" A-team with few of the original members from Phase 1 left. However, unlike our team in Phase 1, all the students from all of the different specialties were brimming with confidence and enthusiasm. While still far from being experts in our fields, we were now some of the most highly-trained specialists in the world. Phase 3 was the chance to put all that skill, knowledge, talent, and enthusiasm into a final exercise that would solidify everything we'd learned and to demonstrate that we could contribute something to an established A-Team – that we could be real Green Berets.

There was some classroom training at the beginning of Phase 3, but the vast majority of our time was spent conducting our capstone exercise named "Robin Sage". This began with five days of detailed Isolation planning followed by a long "infil" (infiltration – in this case a night parachute jump and a 10 mile night patrol to link up with our "partisans"), and about 18 days conducting the actual exercise.

"Robin Sage" is unique in terms of Army exercises in that it takes place in and around the homes and workplaces of real towns where almost every citizen plays a role. The scenario is that our SF Team has gone behind the lines to help partisans liberate themselves from a repressive regime that is oppressing the citizens. In order to simulate a complete environment, the exercise needs partisan fighters, an underground organization to support them, leaders and politicians (for both sides), police, enemy forces, citizens loyal to the new regime, and many normal people living their daily lives who are "tuned" in to the exercise and act in accordance with their roles should they see something or are asked to help in some way (like hide us in their barn if we show up in the middle of the night). Considering that multiple teams are conducting the exercise at the same time, a vast number of locals are needed. Because it's been conducted for over 50 years, entire generations of families have grown up being a part of the exercise, and roles and alliances are often inherited by sons and daughters when their parents are no longer able to participate. Many people have been a part of Robin Sage from the day they were born.

There are a few things that I still remember from my first Phase 3 Robin Sage (18C Sergeant course) because they were just so incredible that they're etched into my mind. After we'd

The Q-Course

linked up with our "guerrilla force" (G's) and moved to their base camp, they immediately asked for our medic. But instead of taking him to treat one of their injured, they grabbed him, tied him up, hung him from his ankles eight feet off the ground and placed a bowl beneath his head so that their "witch doctor" could drain all the knowledge out of him for his own use.

What's really crazy is that every scenario in Robin Sage is based on the actual experiences of SF teams. We knew that nothing bad would happen to our medic because it was an exercise, but it must have been terrifying for the team that experienced it in real life because when we tried to get our medic down, the entire guerilla force pulled their weapons and circled him. You can't start a firefight with the people that you've been sent to help, so we had to find a way to convince the Guerilla Chief (G-Chief) that a more effective way to give knowledge to their witch doctor was to let our medic down so he could pass the information laterally (head-to-head).

The second thing I remember vividly is when I was called to do "my" mission. Every member of the team gets an individual mission specific to their specialty in addition to all the team missions. The G-Chief took me to a small clearing in the woods where he normally trained his G's. He said that the addition of our team made it difficult for all his men to observe the details of our training and so he wanted me to build him a set of bleachers three rows high that could hold 30 of his men.

First of all, I'd never built a set of bleachers in my life. Building bleachers was *not* part of the 18C course. Secondly, all the bleachers I've ever seen are in stadiums or auditoriums, made out of aluminum and manufactured and assembled with bolts and screws by people using power tools. I hadn't thought to bring any power tools with me because, well, I was in the middle of the forest and there wasn't any power to plug into. Silly me. There also wasn't any metal or bolts or screws or anything that you would need to create a set of bleachers 3 rows high that could safely hold 30 people.

However, I did have a finger saw, a combat knife, and a forest full of trees. But even if I did figure out how to construct something out of wood, I had no way to attach all the elements together. We all carried 550 cord with us, but even if I collected every scrap our team carried, it wouldn't be near enough to securely lash all the seats, foot rests, and crossbeams. Then I remembered that we'd cached (buried) our parachutes close to our infil drop zone about 10 miles away. The suspension lines on a parachute are 550 cord (which is why it's also called "paracord"), so by cutting up a few parachutes I'd have all the cordage I needed. Once I explained to the G-Chief (who was also an OC - Observer Controller/Evaluator) that I was going to take a patrol to cut up a few U.S. Army issued parachutes, a large amount of rope magically became available (because parachutes are expensive). And after finding as many downed trees as we could, I managed to construct a set of bleachers with seats, footrests, and enough structural crossbars to make it safe. It wasn't comfortable, but the G-Chief didn't ask for comfort. It was only used a few times, but it was three rows high, seated 30 people, and it didn't collapse.

These two scenarios had a profound effect on me and taught me incredibly important lessons that shaped my life and career. The "witch doctor" scenario blew my mind and I had to somehow come to grips with the idea that someone could be absolutely, totally wrong and yet, I couldn't change their mind or ignore and criticize their ideas and deeply held beliefs simply because I knew "better." We didn't solve the "witch doctor" scenario through logic or argumentation. It wasn't until we acknowledged the G's belief about how knowledge is gained that we were able to use that to our advantage and suggest that removing a step (head-to-head rather than head-pot-head) was actually more effective and had less chance for "spillage".

The "bleachers" scenario helped drive home one of the more important lessons of SFAS – that the "impossible" is rarely that. But unlike Selection where we had an entire team come up with ideas, this was the very first time that I had to solve an "impossible" problem by myself. The insane amount of self-confidence that I gained from doing things that I'd never thought possible opened up the world to me. It no longer mattered what anyone else said I could or couldn't do, or what I could and couldn't be. It taught me that *what most people think is impossible is usually an opportunity.*

My first Phase 3 was truly a positive, life-changing experience.

But once again my "officer" Phase 3 was a completely different story. Our team's instructor/evaluator – we'll call him Sergeant First Class (SFC) Bone – loathed me and was determined to make my life a living hell. He started by pulling me aside on the first day to tell me that he didn't want me helping out the other members on my team too much. He said that it wouldn't be fair to grade them if I gave them all the answers. However, every time one of the team members didn't do well on something, he'd give me a hard time for not helping them more. So then I'd help my teammates and he'd give me bad marks for failing to follow instructions because I'd helped them. When I protested that he was giving me contradictory guidance, he just smiled and walked away.

I couldn't do anything right as far as SFC Bone was concerned. When I'd help "too much," he'd pull me aside and tell me in private. But when I didn't help out enough, he always criticized me in front of the entire team, causing a rift between me and the others by creating the impression that I didn't care about them. Knowing I couldn't win, I resolved that if I was going to get "dinged" for failure to follow instructions, I'd rather get the ding for helping than not helping and quickly resigned myself to the fact that I was probably going to fail Phase 3 and I'd hope for a different instructor after I'd been recycled. However, SFC Bone quickly caught on to that and threatened to fail my teammates if I helped them too much, which put me in the unenviable position of having to remain mute when SFC Bone was around. Thankfully there were times when he wasn't around.

He also tried to alienate me from the group by disparaging me when I wasn't around, saying things like "Oh, he already has his Special Forces tab, so he thinks he's too good for all of you," or "you should hear what he said about you during that last patrol." Painting me in a bad light was necessary because "peer evaluations" are an important part of the grading system, so my "peer evals" had to mirror the poor marks SFC Bone was giving me.

And while I generally managed to disprove his words through my actions, I wasn't always successful. After one particularly frustrating day, I attempted to give the team a pep talk and let them know that I was with them 100%. But I said it all wrong. What I wanted them to hear was "Guys, I really want to be here with you and to be a part of this team. You know I've already got the tab so I wouldn't be here now if I didn't really want to be here with you and for all of us to succeed."

What they heard, however, was arrogance. The message they received was "I've already got my stuff, so I don't need to be here with all of you."

While ultimately this screw-up would teach me one of the most important lessons of leadership, at the time the impact was terrible because no one told me how my words had come across. My intent was to help the team bond, to get us all together and to let them know that I truly cared for them and their welfare. But some of them heard the exact opposite and because no one responded to my feeble attempt at motivation, I thought they heard what I wanted to convey. And all the while some of them wondered if I'd just proven what SFC Bone had been saying all along.

Thankfully most of the guys knew me pretty well at this point and shrugged it off right away. Which was lucky because once we started Robin Sage, SFC Bone found the most ingenious ways to "challenge" me. For instance, I was once in a 2-person Observation Post (OP) for an 8 hour shift and he called me away to do something for him and report back to the main patrol base once I'd finished. After I'd reported to him, he very nicely told me to sit and wait for him and he'd come back soon to give me my next set of instructions. He let me sit there for hours, in full view of other team members and G's but not close enough to talk to anyone. When I tried to get in touch with him through one of the assistant instructors, I was told to sit and wait patiently.

This gave the impression that I was "hanging out in the rear" and had abandoned my buddy in the OP, meaning he couldn't go to the bathroom or eat or even blow his nose because you don't do those things in an OP. In wooded areas those activities are usually done by low crawling far to the rear of the OP so as not to reveal it.[20] But it's imperative to always have "eyes on target," meaning if my partner left to relieve himself, he'd fail his patrol. So he had to stay there all day, wondering where I was, getting angry that I hadn't returned, only to find out later that I'd spent all day hanging out in the rear "chilling." When I tried to explain the situation, SFC Bone told the others I misunderstood his instructions – probably on purpose – so I wouldn't have to go back to the OP.

I considered SFC Bone's behavior to be totally unprofessional, but I was a student and he was our senior instructor and could generally do what he wanted. We had two other instructors, but they worked for him, and he'd told them that he needed to ensure I really "have what it takes to be a team leader," so the extra attention was warranted and for my own good.

Robin Sage is essentially a series of graded exercises that all fit together, each one assigned to someone to evaluate them. However, as time went on, I began to get concerned because

---

20 This was dependent on the type of OP. On actual missions, we often dig a "hide site" and camouflage it perfectly - meaning there isn't any trail leading to the OP that someone could stumble across. Hide sites are usually occupied by a 3-man team and once in the hole, no one leaves until the mission is over. One person is always observing, a second sleeps, and the third is able to eat or take care of other business. Because you don't leave the hide site, physical elimination is accomplished by urinating into a deeper corner of the hide site and defecating into plastic bags which remain with you until exfil. This is all done in extremely close proximity and in full view of the other people in the hole. These missions usually last at least 3 days and the longest I ever occupied a hole was a full week.

I was never assigned a patrol. I later found out that SFC Bone intended for me to have the "big" mission at the very end of the exercise, the one that everyone had to pass in order to graduate. It was the only mission where everyone (the team and all the G's) participated together to destroy the enemy and put an "end to the war."

However, without a second patrol to be evaluated, if I failed the final patrol, my record would only show a "fail" and increase the likelihood that I'd fail Phase 3 and possibly the entire course.

Once the final mission was officially assigned to me and we started planning, I realized there was no way I was going to pass and I quickly resigned myself to the fact. However, I still needed to do as well as possible to ensure that the others on my team didn't get taken down with me.

Despite the fact that evaluators are supposed to remain silent and simply observe, mine openly told the group that my plan wouldn't work and that they were all going to fail, which set up the dynamic that everyone on the team was worried about their grade and saw me as the probable cause of their downfall.

And totally contrary to his role as an evaluator, he then told us *exactly* how to conduct the mission which was, of course, a completely different course of action (COA) that I had the team working on. We were all highly suspicious of his unorthodox behavior because he was essentially trying to give us the answers to the test. He should have never even given us suggestions, much less tell us exactly how to do it. Moreover, because he'd already openly opposed my COA and now told us exactly how to do it "correctly," some members of the team also began to argue against the plan saying that even if we didn't like it, we'd be stupid to not do what he told us. I told them that I knew I was going to fail so that we should stick with the plan because if it failed, then all the blame would fall on me for disregarding our new "guidance."

Since he'd guaranteed that my plan wouldn't work, SFC Bone "helped" it reach its natural outcome. The most egregious thing that he did was to wait until the recon teams had crossed a river and gotten into positions behind the enemy. We'd sent them 48 hours ahead of the attack so they would have plenty of time to sneak into position without getting seen and once there, they could constantly report on the situation, the number of soldiers on guard, and let us know if we needed to abort the mission.

In addition to being our evaluator, Sergeant Bone was also the Observer Controller (OC) for everything that went on in our area. Therefore, he had to know exactly where everyone was at all times for safety purposes. Once the recon teams were in position and well camouflaged, he walked over to one and literally stood in the middle of the OP between the two students. Then he called all of the enemy guards over to him (40 yards away) so he could "discuss things" with them. OCs are both the referees and the evaluators. They ensure no one gets hurt, no one cheats, and that the ultimate training objectives are achieved. As the OC, Sergeant Bone would have already briefed the enemy Opposing Force (OPFOR) on the training scenario, explained their mission, his expectations, and so on. He was their boss for the duration of the exercise.

The enemy guards were confused because OC's never called the OPFOR off of an objective to leave it unguarded. But they shrugged their shoulders and headed over to see him, taking all of their weapons with them (in the field no one is ever more than arms-length from their weapon).

The recon team went into shock. It took them a few moments to process what was happening because nothing like this had ever happened before. They tried to figure out what to do in hushed tones as the OPFOR approached. Once they realized they were being set up and there was no escape, they frantically tried to clear the radios so that once they were captured, the OPFOR wouldn't be able to monitor our frequencies and gain intel. But those initial moments of shock, inaction, and discussion meant that once they started to move in order to "zero out" the radios, the OPFOR saw their movement, ran over, leveled their weapons and took them prisoner. SFC Bone would later say that the recon team gave themselves away from their movements.

Once the OPFOR rolled up the first OP, SFC Bone went into "instructor mode" and asked the OPFOR if it was normal to only have one OP watching an objective. This encouraged them to search the woods on the other side of the road and they found our other OP as well. We were now blind, the OPFOR knew we were coming, and they had our radio frequency so they could anticipate everything we were going to do. And even though we used code words (you always assume that commo is compromised), it was still easy enough to figure out when we started our move towards the objective because the nature of the radio traffic changed and gave the OPFOR enough time to call for two truckloads of reinforcements and more machine guns.

Before the second OP was rolled up, they called back to let us know the mission was compromised and managed to zero out their own radios—so at least we knew something had happened. We wouldn't learn exactly how it had happened and what Sergeant Bone had done until after the exercise was over and the OPs told us what had transpired.

After we sent out the coded signal that our comms were compromised and to switch frequencies, the OPFOR began taunting us over our own radios. How did the OPFOR know we'd sent out the code word for compromised comms and to switch over to the new frequencies? Your guess is as good as mine. I remember the sinking feeling in the pit of my stomach when I realized how screwed we were. I didn't know the details then, but I knew instinctively that somehow or another, SFC Bone had found yet another way to "challenge" us.

In reality, a compromised mission is automatically aborted. To attempt the mission now would be suicide and a complete waste of all of our G's lives because we would face a reinforced enemy that knew we were coming. But it was training and regardless of the outcome, the exercise would be over and everyone would head back to garrison the next day. It's not like we could have faded into the woods, reestablished our guerilla base in a new safe area, and continued the war.

Before too long SFC Bone emerged from the woods with the evilest grin I'd ever seen. When I told him we should abort the mission because we'd been compromised, he told me to complete the mission because the others on my team needed to be evaluated.

So we did it. And of course it was a disaster. We never stopped trying to salvage the plan or find a way to overcome the new obstacles, but everything we tried was countered by some extrasensory ability the OPFOR had developed to know our every move.

The Q-Course

When it was over, with all of our team either killed or captured, SFC Bone came up to all of us and said "I told you it wouldn't work, but you just wouldn't listen." I apologized to my team for letting them down, we jumped on the trucks and headed back to the base. I felt more dejected than I'd ever been in my life.

Now that the entire Q-Course was over, we spent the next few days cleaning, turning in equipment, getting our evaluations, and conducting general recovery. I was incredibly relieved that the rest of the team had passed Robin Sage and I hadn't dragged them down with me. Unsurprisingly, I failed Robin Sage but still managed to pass Phase 3. We were finally released back to our "homeroom" cadres who were ultimately in charge of us. They gave us some general out-processing tasks, our follow-on assignments or schools, and gave us our final evaluations. These were the most important because they covered the entire course and took into account everything, including peer evaluations. I was sure that I'd be recycled because of my dismal Robin Sage performance, but astonishingly, I'd passed the course. And this time, I did celebrate.

The next day, however, my cadre unexpectedly told me to report to the commander's office—and my stomach dropped. Getting called to the commander's office on short notice is almost always a bad thing. As I walked to the headquarters building, my mind raced as I tried to think of anything I might have done that had just come to light. It wouldn't be the first time in my life I'd gotten in trouble for something I thought wasn't a big deal. I prayed that I was *only* going to get recycled and not kicked out of the course. My entire career was in jeopardy. I felt like I was going to vomit at any moment.

I became even more concerned when I walked in and saw not just the commander but also the sergeant major in charge of training and the rest of my permanent cadre. It was like a firing squad. I prepared myself for the worst.

So imagine my shock when they told me I wasn't being recycled, but instead they'd reversed my Robin Sage grade. Moreover, during our graduation ceremony, I'd be receiving the Honor Graduate Award for the officer's course and the overall course Leadership Award. This was unprecedented. Traditionally, the Leadership Award is presented to a single student from the entire class of officers and NCOs who is *not* an honor graduate but still deserves recognition for their overall performance.

Evidently, the two assistant evaluators who worked for Sergeant Bone had discussed all the "extra attention" I'd been given with the sergeant major and then the commander. In the end, the permanent course cadre gave me some extra credit for all of the extra training. Sergeant Bone did not show up for the graduation ceremony.

Lessons Learned

Like the last chapter, there are a few themes that run throughout the Q-Course:

- **You learn your lessons in the field** by "doing" and making mistakes. You learn the most important things while you are applying what you've been taught, not by reading.
- **The "suck" never ends.** While SFAS (Selection and Assessment) is hard, in many ways the Q-Course is

much harder both physically and mentally. Every day's challenge is harder than the day before. And there's no avoiding them.

- **If you can't figure out how to lead yourself you'll never lead a team**. That's the real lesson of Land Nav. If you can't show competence in the basics, a real SF team would eat you alive, so they'll never even let you get close to one.

- **Assessment never ends.** You will constantly be watched and judged by everyone.

- **You can still fail anywhere along the way** because there is no guarantee of success. In fact, you will probably fail quite a few times, but you can't let that stop you.

- **There is always a target on your back**. No matter what you do, someone will always be gunning for you. Accept it and plan accordingly.

- **No coasting.** Prior success doesn't guarantee future success. And while reputation will get you part of the way, being a Green Beret is a double-edged sword, and you must exceed the standard every day in every way.

- Like SFAS, the Q is also a **crucible experience**; you don't come out the same person as you went in.

- **You will never know everything**, so it's important to really know your required skill set and rely on others who have different ones if you want to create a great team.

- If you've committed to something, **Don't quit. Ever.** Even when you're absolutely sure that you're going to fail or that you won't make the time, tell yourself that it doesn't matter and do your best to finish strong. A strong failure is better than a weak surrender. Also, you just never know what will happen. Luck can't find you if you're not there to meet it.

It's pretty obvious how those same lessons also apply to you as you begin your journey and learn how to be the kind of leader that people will follow anywhere. Your process will include the following:

- **Leadership is a specialty skill** that requires its own training program. Just as there are different specialty skills for a team of Green Berets, your skills and tasks are different from the people you lead. While there are basic skills and knowledge that everyone needs to know in every job, your job is to lead and their job is to do. Learn how to do *your* job.

- **Lead yourself first.** None of us have any business leading others if we can't get ourselves sorted. The Land Nav metaphor is like a sledgehammer describing what we all need to do to be successful in life. Chapter Two was all about determining exactly where we are on the map and if we're up for a journey. The rest of this chapter is about defining your waypoints, identifying obstacles, and planning your route to get there. And if you can't lead yourself to where you want to go, think very hard about whether or not you should be entrusted to lead others.

- Just like in the Q, your path towards EPIC Leadership will **be difficult and hard** because it requires personal growth and character building; you will become a better and more confident leader. This is an advantage for you if you choose to take it because many people won't do the work required, leaving the field wide open for those who stick it out.

- The lessons aren't learned in a classroom. Rather, your training will be **with real people in real situations with real consequences**. It will be even harder to get to the elite level where you'll feel confident enough to lead lions.

- Your primary job will be to **build and maintain trust** so that even when your personal version of SFC Bone comes along and tries to screw it all up for your team, the team continues to follow you despite being unsure of a successful outcome.

- Building that trust is necessary because **you will make plenty of mistakes** along the way even after you've been trained. But your team will forgive you if your actions have consistently shown them that you are proficient in your job (leadership) and that you care for them and the success of the team.

- To successfully lead an elite team **the team's success must become more important** than your personal success. This is perhaps the hardest lesson of all, and why your personal growth is so necessary. Lions don't really need to be led, they need to be pointed in the right direction and unleashed. If you make sure they have everything they need and you take care of them, they will be incredibly successful. And as a result, you will be, too.

Your Personal Q-Course
Now that you've discovered your "Big Why" and completed your own Assessment, it's time to get some hardcore training of your own and upgrade your Leadership OS. So for the rest of this chapter we'll discuss using your assessment and developing your own personal training program. Your goal is to strengthen or improve any areas identified on the assessment so that you'll have the unshakeable inner core required to lead lions.

Rewriting Our Code
Changing our internal operating system is difficult and can take decades if we leave it to chance and experience. Fortunately, there are some ways we can speed up the process. The fastest and most effective is transformational learning through *paradigm shifts* in crucible environments. The phrase "paradigm shift" was originally a scientific term that describes a profound change in a fundamental model or perception of events. Paradigm shifts are *big* – like realizing the earth isn't flat, or the Law of Gravity, or Einstein's Theory of Relativity. A paradigm shift changes *everything* about our understanding of how things operate in a single moment.

We also experience paradigm shifts on a more personal level throughout our lives – like when new parents undergo a radical change in how they think and see themselves after the birth of their first child. Paradigm shifts are effective because we profoundly *feel* something about an experience and those strong emotional reactions imprint themselves on our brain and override our previous way of thinking; it's transformational learning. This is why SFAS, the Q-Course, BUDS, bootcamps, ropes courses, and other select training courses are such effective crucibles; they are controlled environments that place participants into scripted, highly tested, repeatable scenarios that create effective, predictable, and ideal paradigm shifts for the participants.[21]

To see why paradigm shifts are so powerful, let's revisit our "most people are basically lazy" paradigm from the last chapter. What exactly defines "laziness?" We usually characterize a lazy worker as being unmotivated, and their work is often late and/or substandard. They shun additional responsibility; can't wait to leave the office; cause resentment among other workers who have to pick up their "slack;" and still somehow seem to get less work than the others because they aren't dependable. If this is how you think of most people, then your primary tool is a whip.

---

[21] I used to "dip" smokeless tobacco because it felt like a little "pick-me-up" at 3:30 am on the 15th consecutive night of stressful combat patrols. But once started, it's a very difficult habit to break because the nicotine is absorbed straight into your system and it's highly addictive. When I wasn't outside where I could spit on the ground, I used a soda can to spit into. Nasty. Despite my numerous (6+) failed attempts to quit dipping using nicotine patches and drugs and anything else I could find, I instantaneously stopped dipping forever one afternoon while watching TV. I looked over the armrest of my chair to grab my spit can (which I placed on the floor next to me) just in time to see my 2 year old daughter about to take a drink from it. Horrified, I experienced a momentous paradigm shift when I realized that my bad habit was not just about me or my own health, but hers as well. I never dipped again and I will always vividly remember that exact moment; it still gives me chills 20+ years later. You also felt something simply by reading this story, giving you a taste of what it feels like to experience a paradigm shift for yourself.

But what happens if we experience a paradigm shift about lazy people? To do that we first examine whether or not our current paradigm is valid. Doing this is not easy because it opens us up to the idea that we may have been wrong all this time. Are people *really* lazy, or could there be something else going on that we hadn't thought about before?

Think about a teenager who never wants to do anything except play video games. His parents think he's lazy because he never helps around the house. But is he really lazy? How many hours a day does he play video games if someone doesn't drag him away from his game console? Six? Eight? Fourteen? Is that laziness? He'll skip meals, showers, school. He'll give up a huge portion of his life to play a game. That kid is *not* lazy; he is just not motivated to do *what his parents want him to do*. But if his job was to play video games (and that is a real job nowadays), he might never leave the office, and we'd all think of him as one of the hardest working people we know.

> Most people want something and if you give them the chance to earn it, you'll see them work incredibly hard for it. One of the "lazy" people I was asked to help had a teenage daughter who was a sports superstar - but all her games were on Wednesday afternoons so mom was never able to go and watch. "Gloria" fit the description of the typical lazy worker and wasn't well liked because no one felt she did her fair share of the work. When Gloria was given the opportunity to leave an hour early on Wednesdays to watch her kid's games as long as she completed all of her work to standard *and* take on an extra project, she jumped at it. Overnight our lazy worker

became a part of the team. And while she never became the most popular person on the team, her relationship with everyone else improved dramatically—as did everyone's overall performance.

So are "lazy" people really lazy, or do we just have to find the right way to motivate them? In most cases, if they're not performing well, they just aren't motivated. And once you realize that most people are willing to work hard to get something they want, you experience a paradigm shift and *everything* changes.

Instead of seeing lazy people everywhere, you now see opportunities for people to do better (and more) work than they would normally *if* you find the right lever.

Instead of a whip, your tool becomes a carrot, and the responsibility shifts from them (to do their job well regardless of circumstances) to *you* to find out what each person's carrot looks like, and then align everyone's carrots with what you want the team to accomplish.

There are second and third order effects as well. Everyone on your team becomes happier, more motivated, more efficient, and your team starts accomplishing more than it ever has. Because if you're spending the time necessary to understand what each person's carrot looks like, you have to *really* get to know them. And as your understanding of them deepens, so does the quality of your conversations and interactions with them – and your leadership style naturally and authentically changes. Don't worry about whether or not your reasons are "pure"; it doesn't matter. If your *only* reason to get to know them better is to make them more successful at work, you are still doing them a favor. You are still learning about them as people and it becomes the way the team operates. It becomes your team culture. And magic happens in good cultures. All from one little paradigm shift.

You might think that it's not fair that you should have to do all the work to figure out how to motivate them, and you'd be right. So what? Your purpose is to be a leader of elite teams, not to live in a fair world. However, keep in mind that the advantages that you'll get from leading an elite team aren't fair either. And – trust me on this – in the future you'll laugh at the irony that others will say it's not fair that you and your team are getting more (attention, accolades, budget, pay raises, "good" missions) than everyone else.

But elite performance must be earned; no one gets a Green Beret because it's "fair." If you want increased performance from your team, then you have to increase **your** performance and lead in a way that motivates everyone on your team and deftly aligns their goals and motivations with yours and the organization's. When you're leading lions, it's all about "aLionnment" of interests.

Can you imagine what amazing leaders we'd be if we examined *all* our paradigms and updated them to the most effective version? That's why paradigm shifts and crucibles are so powerful. They rewrite our code at the molecular level and it's permanent and instantaneous. You can't help but act accordingly.

So, the first method for changing your Leadership Operating System (LOS) is to enroll in a crucible – a highly reputable values-based program that utilizes guided discovery learning. It's why Outward Bound and at-risk youth programs have such an impact. Participants don't just learn something, they experience and "feel" something profound that stays with them and forever changes them in a positive way. I'm not talking about popular self-help gurus that want to motivate you. If there is hype or yelling or gimmicks, keep looking. You aren't looking for flashy, sexy, and exciting; you are looking for tough, professional, and introspective.

These programs have many advantages, including feedback from qualified mentors because crucible experiences often need interpreting in order for the greatest learning to occur. The downside to these courses is they don't necessarily target the areas you've identified for growth from your 360 Leadership Assessment. They can also be expensive and usually have a physical component, as well as a time commitment.

Very skilled and experienced leadership consultants and coaches can also help their clients experience powerful shifts that change paradigms and behaviors. Their method is similar to how the best mountain guides operate. They must know which paths or journeys will provide the best experience and the way to approach each vista for maximum impact. They have to understand what the client needs without telling them exactly what they're going to discover so the impact won't be diminished, help them find all the hidden paths, ensure the journey is arduous but achievable, and at the right moment put the client in the lead so they unexpectedly round a corner and experience an arresting revelation (or stunning vista) so it resonates deeply within their core and forever becomes a part of them.

Getting professional training and education from a well-respected program is another option. An established program has an advantage because it's already set the conditions for your success, will deliver enhanced learning, and provide constructive feedback. The best courses will also have a follow up program. Unfortunately, because they are more academic in nature, only the very best build paradigm shifts into their courses. Another disadvantage is the cost in terms of money and time. Any good course will cost you a few thousand dollars and at least 20 hours of instruction. But I caution you, what sounds like a great leadership course may not be so great. Any of them that are worthwhile will have a significant portion devoted to personal assessment and values clarification because good leadership always starts with being able to *lead yourself effectively.*

> Why all this emphasis on personal character for leadership? *Personality opens doors, but character keeps them open.* In the Army "**Be, Know, Do**" is drilled into your head as the leadership model starting on Day 2 of Basic Training. That's how important it is. And the order is critical. The most popular success models advertised today are "Do, Have, Be" (the more I Do, the more I'll Have, the happier I'll Be), or Know, Do, Have (so you Know what to Do to Have what you want). The worst (and unfortunately far too prevalent) version is Have, Do, Be (when I Have enough time/money/support, then I'll Do the things I need to do and *then* I'll Be happy). But Be, Know, Do is the correct order because studies

have shown that happiness and success come most often when we don't rely on other things to determine our happiness or who we'll Be. Studies have also shown that success follows happiness, not the other way around. So if we focus on Being the person we want to be, we'll Know the associated behaviors that we need to Do and success and happiness come naturally. Why wait until you're 65 or until you have 5 million dollars in the bank to Be the person you want to be? Start now.

Besides targeted paradigm shifts available through crucible programs and expert coaching, we also experience paradigm shifts unexpectedly and haphazardly throughout our lives, and we can put those lessons to good use if we recognize them for what they are. These include difficult periods where we've endured a bad job, a bad boss, no respect, no recognition, constant harassment, or other similar indignities.

We usually try to escape these situations as quickly as possible, but it's important to never waste a crisis. So if you find yourself in one of those situations, do the hard and painful work to think deeply about what happened and learn every possible lesson, even if it's what *not* to do. I've learned some of the most powerful leadership lessons from bad bosses. Unfortunately, there isn't a menu that allows us to order a specific crappy situation to affect a particular attitude change when it would be most beneficial to do so. Nonetheless, while random, they are still very powerful.

So, never waste a suckfest. The other thing you can do is to look back at some really unhappy periods of your life and find the lessons there, as well. Some of the greatest leadership lessons I learned weren't from a "crucible course" but from watching one truly great leader navigate through an incredibly toxic environment. The way they somehow quietly and confidently managed to take care of us, protect us, and motivate us while working for a tyrant sunk deep into my core and became the model of leadership that I committed myself to for the rest of my life.

Finally, you can attempt to trigger powerful learning experiences by putting yourself into difficult situations like intentionally joining a team with poor leadership or taking a stressful job for a company with a terrible culture for as long as you can stand it. However, these are simply crucibles that you enter willingly knowing the cost will be high but hoping it will be worth it in terms of what you'll learn and how you'll grow. The Paratrooper's Prayer reads in part:

"Lord give me that which all of us refuse – insecurity and restlessness, turmoil and struggle. And I ask you, Lord, that you give them to me forever so I will always have them, for I will not always have the courage to ask."

This course of action is not for the faint of heart.

If any of the options I've listed so far aren't available, acceptable, or you simply want to do it yourself and get started immediately, you can design your own training program so you can improve areas highlighted by your assessment and examine your paradigms to determine those that are effective and those that you need to rewrite yourself.

Creating Your Own Q-Course
If you go the self-development route, you'll still need to follow a proven process to be successful. Just like Land Navigation, your path will never be straightforward and you'll need to set waypoints along the way to ensure you're on track. If you want to use the same tools and worksheets that I use with my clients, you can get the *The Green Beret Way Workbook* and simply follow the instructions. But what I've outlined below is the same process that we use in the EPIC Leaders Course and the workbook. Doing the work is the hard part, the workbook just keeps it all in one place.

Phase 1: Identify strengths and developmental needs from the assessment; I recommend starting with everything relating to Trust because it is the basis for everything else. Pay particular attention to areas where others rated you very differently than you rated yourself. If you find major differences that you're unable to reconcile, go talk to a trusted friend or colleague and ask them for the brutal truth. This is why getting many people to do the 360 assessment for you is helpful; what is true will usually show up in more than one place and you won't go chasing outliers. But keep in mind that perception is more important than fact. It doesn't really matter if you're 100% honest if other people don't think you are. You are seeking the truth of how you appear to others, not what you want to hear.

Phase 2: *Part 1:* Dig a little deeper and conduct some situational analysis. Choose an area on your assessment where you scored very low or very high. Think of a time when you used/didn't use that particular trait or skill when doing something important like making a decision, dealing with an altercation, or some other stressful situation. Take 15 minutes and write everything you can about the situation:

- What is the background information on the event?
- What were you trying to accomplish?
- Did you meet your goal? Why or why not?
- Who was involved? What did they say and do?
- What did you feel?
- What did they feel?
- What did you do well?
- What could you have done better?
- What made the situation better (or worse)?
- What do you wish you knew/had then that you know/have now?
- Why did you do what you did?
- What were the reactions of others?
- Anything else you can think of. The more you write, the better.

Your goal is to discover insights from your experiences that you can work with. Do this exercise with at least two areas where you scored low and one where you scored high so you can figure out how to do it again in the future.

Additionally, if you had a particularly stressful situation at some point in your life and you're not sure exactly how to categorize it, simply write about it in the same manner and by the time you're done you'll have a pretty good idea of where it fits in. Follow those nagging feelings down the rabbit hole and stay there until you figure it out.

Part 2: Find a quiet spot and at least 30 minutes where you won't be disturbed and conduct some self-analysis by answering the following questions with as much specificity as possible:

- I am at my best when...
- The skill or ability at which I am best is...
- The personal quality that I rely on most for my success is...
- My natural talents and gifts are...
- What I really love to do at work is...
- What I really love to do in my personal time is...
- I am most knowledgeable about...
- I would love to learn more about...
- The accomplishment I am most proud of is...
- Others usually come to me for help with...
- Others think the best position for me would be...
- I want to be a person who...
- I am at my worst when...
- The skill or ability that is always difficult for me is...
- The value I struggle the most with is...
- I don't know as much as I should about...
- People close to me complain about...
- I usually go to others for help on...
- I wish I was better at...

- The situation that causes me the most frustration is...
- I am most hesitant when I try to...
- The reasons that some relationships didn't work out are...
- I am most concerned about my...
- Others think I am not skilled at...
- I'm afraid that others will find out that...
- I would become a more valued member of my organization if I...
- The things I really should be doing are...
- I am not being honest with myself about...

Part 3: Target identification and analysis. Go back through everything you've written and the comments others made on your 360 assessment and circle or highlight words, phrases, or patterns that emerge. If it's something you're good at – or something you need to work on – it will show up in multiple places.

When you're done with all the analysis, make the list of areas you're going to work on. For your strengths, you'll be focusing on how to expand upon them to "exploit success." In all SF missions, we plan numerous contingencies among multiple branches and sequels and one of the most important things to consider in the planning phase is "What do we do if everything goes better than expected? How do we exploit that success even more?" This is what you'll be doing with your strengths.

For your developmental needs and areas for improvement you'll be focusing on fixing the most important, especially any areas that pertain to character and integrity.

Phase 3: Capstone Exercises. Now it's time to put it all together. You'll start mission planning by conducting research and find out what activities, behaviors, or habits are associated with each of the areas you've chosen to work on. Trust, Integrity, and Communication are vitally important so I've included a list of activities and mindsets associated with them below as examples of how to do this step. If you choose to use *The Green Beret Way Workbook* or take the EPIC Leaders Course, then all of these activities, behaviors, traits, mindsets, and habits are already listed and formatted for you, as well as numerous others (Loyalty, Leadership Courage, etc)

Once we've planned the mission, it's time to do it under tough conditions in the field – real life. We do this by choosing an area we want to work on and for seven consecutive days really focus on the activities, habits, and mindsets associated with it. Using a notebook, draw an Enhanced Franklin Grid™ with days at the top and activities on the left. And every time you successfully do an activity give yourself a plus sign (+) in the box corresponding to that day. Each time you fail to do the right thing, you'll give yourself a minus (-). You don't need to "force it" by giving yourself a plus or minus every day. Just mark the days when something happens.

Communication

	M	T	W	Th	F	Sat	Sun
Active Listening							
Reflect words or feelings							
Set Clear Expectations							
Provide Real Feedback							
Share Plans or Vision							
Keep Others Informed							
Share X About Self							
Ask for Real Feedback							
Learn X New from Team							
(write your own)							
(write your own)							

Describe the situation: _____

_____

_____

_____

Leave plenty of room at the bottom of the grid and each time you give yourself a plus or minus for an activity, write the date and the specifics of the incident so that you have an opportunity to relive it and feel the emotions surrounding it. This is actually the most important step because it will reinforce good behaviors through a positive feedback loop and help you stop the bad ones; you'll enjoy reliving your triumphs and you'll cringe thinking about your missed opportunities. This feedback loop is the critical step that most "change engines" are missing.

Obviously the idea is to get more plusses than minuses, and you will over time. But don't worry if you don't do so well in the beginning. What's important is that you're now working in the realm of truth: recognizing and identifying your behaviors for what they really are. Pick a new area to work on each week and draw a similar grid. If you feel like you need to repeat a week, then do it. Do this every week until you've worked through every item on your list and you (and everyone around you) will notice how you've changed.

Most people don't think that it's possible to change character traits like integrity or humility, but they're wrong. Benjamin Franklin created the simplified version of this method when he was 20 years old to improve his character. And he believed that not only was he successful in changing his character for the better, but he attributed most of his success later in life to this exercise. I took Franklin's original grid and expanded each area to include the specific behaviors for each so we would know exactly what to work on. I also included a feedback loop at the bottom.

Moreover, this is nothing new—you've already done this. If you've ever rid yourself of a bad habit, then you instinctively conducted this very exercise. A common example many people can relate to is saying "um" all the time. I used to do this myself until someone was finally kind enough to point it out to me. Of course, I didn't believe them. However, once I was aware of it, I started to pay attention to how many times I was saying it, and guess what? I had a bad habit of saying "um." I didn't even have to think about how to fix it; it took care of itself because I was constantly on the lookout for it. When I'd find myself about to say it again, I'd pause and then continue without the "um." Before too long, the "um" mostly disappeared from my speech.

Paying attention to your behavior will bring big dividends. It's simple but hard to do.

Create Fierce Trust
As we discussed in Chapter 1, Fierce (Active) Trust is a necessary condition to build and lead elite teams that routinely accomplish the impossible. Active Trust is built from the 4 C's: Character, Communication, Consideration, and Coaching.

The 4 C's are incredibly important for leadership, but in truth, they are important for everything because business (and any relationship) moves at the speed of trust. Deloitte's "Ethics & Workplace Survey has consistently shown over the years that half of the people looking for a new job are primarily motivated by a lack of trust in their employers and 46% of those unhappy at work said the primary reason was a lack of transparent communication from their leadership.

You often hear "in business, it's all about who you know," and it's very true. However, *it doesn't matter who you know until they know who you are*. Read that again and consider that before anyone decides they are going to go out of their way to help you or give you something significant, they have to be able to trust you. *You must BE the person they want KNOW before they will give you the opportunity to DO great things.* It always comes back to Be, Know, Do. A similar saying is "they don't care how much you know until they know how much you care."

It's the same with leading lions. Until they have a sense of who you are they're not going to trust you with even simple things like discussing their personal lives.

Bob and Ted are now business partners with a close relationship, but it wasn't always that way. Both are former SF soldiers, so one would think that they'd be able to trust each other from the start. The two of them had served in the same unit but never at the same time and they'd never met while on active duty. They initially met when Bob's company was working on a proposal for a big client and they hoped Ted could help out as a subcontractor. So someone in Bob's company asked Ted to produce some data for his section. Ted produced a great report but in the end, the project didn't get approved by the client. Over the years Bob approached Ted a few more times, but Ted never seemed to be interested in working with him or his company. It wasn't until they both met at a convention and sat down to have a drink with each other that Bob finally realized what the problem was. Ted wasn't interested in working with Bob's company because to create the initial product for the proposal years before, Ted spent a lot of money conducting research and hiring people to get specific data for the proposal. Ted wasn't interested in working with someone who he didn't trust would bring a contract to fruition. Bob was floored when he heard this because he had no idea that Ted had spent so much time and money. He felt awful and immediately offered to compensate Ted for his effort. In fact, he offered to personally go work on an overseas project for Ted until he made up the cost, and it was obvious to Ted that Bob meant every word. That conversation showed Ted who Bob really was, and from then on they started working successfully together until they finally formed a joint company.

Because it's more difficult to identify behaviors associated with Fierce Trust, I've included lists that I use in my practice, on the Leadership Assessment, and in the workbook so you can use them as part of your Enhanced Franklin Grids™ as part of your personal plan to upgrade your LOS. It's as simple as copying the items from the areas below into the 1st column of your grids.

1. Integrity is by far the most important thing you need to build trust. How do we authentically demonstrate integrity? It's all the little things we do every day that show people who we *really* are. It means always:

- Saying what you mean and meaning what you say.

- Living your values. Emerson wrote, "Who you are speaks so loudly I can't hear what you're saying." Or, "Actions speak louder than words." You must "walk the walk" and not just "talk the talk." So if you publicly espouse "politeness to others," then you can't berate and threaten others. If you say something is important, then you'd better mean it, support it, and enforce it.

- Leading by example. There can be no double standards for you and the rest of the team. If you require everyone to be in the office from 9-5 every day, then you must always be there, too, if you're not traveling or meeting on official company business. If you're late one day because of traffic, you must apologize to the team because you are accountable to them for your behavior just as they are accountable to you. If there is a cap on how much money you can spend on food and hotel rooms for company travel, then you must follow those guidelines, too. A big way to build credibility in this area is to embrace the idea that leaders eat last, meaning you make sure that all your people get the good stuff before you do.

- <u>Always keeping promises</u>. If you are unable to keep a promise, then you must ask to be released from it and explain the circumstances. If something happens where you are unable to keep your promise (a hurricane prevents traveling to an event), then you must honor your word and do everything that you can to make it right. *You must always honor your word.* You will not always be able to keep your word because of external factors, but you can always find a way to honor your word. This also means you can be trusted to keep others' secrets.

- <u>Being honest in both word and deed</u>. Don't steal anything from the company, don't take liberties with company policies, never lie about anything, and never imply that something is true (or untrue) when it's not. Pay close attention to the last one. We do this far more than we realize and don't notice because "technically" we're not lying. But we're not being truthful.

- <u>Following through.</u> In addition to meeting expectations and commitments, it also means that you follow through with consequences. If you threaten a consequence for poor performance, then you must not wimp out when it comes time to deliver that consequence. Even your kids will trust you more if you follow through on punishments for things they know they shouldn't do.

- <u>Never saying anything about someone that you wouldn't say to their face</u>. If you talk badly about someone else behind *their* back – and if that person is even remotely competent – then people will always wonder what you are saying about them behind their backs. You may get away with this once or twice, but eventually, this behavior will say more about you than about the people you're talking about.

2. Secure - Self-Confidence. Being secure in who you are builds trust because it allows you to lead with humility and without fear. If you're not concerned with your ego or "looking good," you can listen to others, get their advice and counsel, and accept feedback gracefully. It means that you're okay with saying "I don't know," but still doing your best to handle issues at your level and not pass them off because you're afraid of making a mistake. It means owning every decision, even the ones from higher up with which you don't agree. It allows you to acknowledge when you're wrong and give true apologies. It means not using defeatist language like "well, we just have to do it because they told us to," or "it just can't be done." When you are truly secure with yourself, you exude a quiet self-confidence that calms and strengthens everyone around you. And most importantly, someone who is truly self-confident and secure is able to share the credit with others (or even give them all of it) and is not afraid to share information and knowledge. Both are critically important if you want to build and lead elite teams.

3. Sound Judgment. People need to know they can trust your judgment if you're going to build an elite team. This includes putting your focus and energy on the "right" things, not making rash decisions, ensuring you listen to everyone and get all the facts, being able to articulate the reasons for doing things a particular way, the ability to weigh pros and cons from multiple perspectives, as well as ensuring that you don't do anything that will cause others to lose respect for you.

4. Fairness and Consistency. Elite teams are always pushing boundaries, trying new things, or even challenging sacred cows. They do this because they are very creative and are always trying to find a better way, a disruptive method, or the next "must-have" product. They cannot push boundaries if you aren't consistent and *greatness is rarely achieved without pushing or crossing boundaries*. Steven Covey writes that, "All significant breakthroughs are actually break-withs old knowledge and traditions." Fairness and Consistency is about setting boundaries, disciplining everyone appropriately and the same, and not choosing favorites. Without it, your team will stop striving for excellence because they'll be fearful of consequences if they get something wrong.

Your team needs to have confidence in you and know that you will always treat everyone the same. They need to know that you won't "shoot from the hip" and you'll get input from the team before making big decisions. And one of the best ways to gain trust is by establishing clear, equitable expectations and metrics for success because then there aren't any surprises or mismatched expectations that lead to conflict and resentment.

5. Loyalty. If you're going to expect the impossible from your team, they need to know you have their backs and that you'll keep everyone "on mission." The concept of loyalty is often problematic because poor managers think that loyalty means personal loyalty to them above the company, team, or mission (they give, I receive). But a true leader never demands loyalty from those who work for them. Rather, a real leader knows that *true* personal loyalty is never given; it's only earned through their own actions over time. So great leaders don't waste even a moment trying to secure the loyalty of their team. Instead, they see loyalty as one of their responsibilities to their team and its mission (I give, they receive).

It's an interesting dynamic. The next time you want to gauge someone's leadership level or potential, ask them what loyalty means to them and see if the flow is inwards or outwards. The kind of loyalty you want to embody means fighting for your team and the resources they need to accomplish the mission. However, it doesn't mean coddling your people at the expense of the mission. We were always taught in Special Forces (and in most of the Armed Forces) that it's: Mission, Men, then Me. Loyalty means shielding them from others (your boss, other departments, meaningless taskers) to prevent them from being taken "off mission." Loyalty is taking 100% of the blame when things go wrong even if it is 100% their fault (because ultimately it is your fault because you failed to supervise them properly). And when you do talk to them about what they did wrong, you don't do it in front of the rest of the team. Conversely, when things go well, you give your team all the praise; you'll never try to take credit for their work or ideas. This is very hard for younger and first-time managers who are still primarily operating from fear which is why Self-Confidence (above) is so critical to EPIC leadership. Recognizing the efforts of others, even if small, will earn you good will and build trust and teamwork.

6. Competence. If they're going to follow you, they need to know that *you* know where you're going and how to get there. However, leaders/managers are often moved to new departments or get promoted and they might not have the technical knowledge that everyone else does in their new position. That's okay – as long as you don't try and pretend that you know more than you do (integrity, authenticity). Your team will give you a grace period to learn the specifics of the new job and they'll respect that you embrace learning and growing. It's okay to ask questions and lean on them for their input. It shows them you have self-confidence. But you must immediately demonstrate competency in your leadership ability because that's what they really need and that's what they expect. They will happily train you to become a superstar in your new role and make you look good if you demonstrate that you are a competent leader because they'll want to keep you around; everyone likes working for a good leader. You also demonstrate competency when you have a plan for the team to successfully reach their goals.

7. Consideration is one of the 4 C's and therefore a critical component of Trust. There is a lot of talk these days about "Empathetic Leadership," and that is certainly a part of Consideration. But it's not the entire story. Empathy is about listening, understanding, connecting, and being able to identify with others. An Empathetic Leader is aware of their team's thoughts and feelings and brings that perspective into decisions and actions. A 2019 study by Texas A&M showed that employee innovation and productivity are significantly increased by Empathetic Leadership. [22]

The essence of empathy is Caring and Consideration. If you don't care about the people you're working with, then you won't bother to learn any of the necessary listening skills or use them when appropriate. And you'll never become a great - much less an EPIC (Empathetic, Purposeful, Inspirational, Character) leader. From a completely mercenary standpoint, good leaders must care about their people simply so they can learn what motivates them, the areas in which they excel or have difficulties with, and how to use them most effectively. But EPIC leaders *genuinely* care about their team and in addition to really learning who they are, they constantly demonstrate consideration through active/empathetic listening (listening to understand rather than to reply) **in addition to**:

- **Forgiveness.** You can't hold a grudge against a team member if they've "worked it off" and haven't repeated the transgression. This doesn't apply for major integrity violations or incidents involving the safety and security of other team members where immediate termination is required.

- **Their Success.** You must genuinely be concerned about their success and well-being. Sometimes this

---

[22] http://cits.tamiu.edu/kock/pubs/journals/2019/Kock_etal_2019_JLOS_EmpathMngtJobPerf.pdf

means giving them away by actively helping them get promoted or moving to other divisions where they have better opportunities.

- **The Platinum Rule.** The Golden Rule says, "Do unto others as you would have them do unto you." But not everyone thinks like you, so you must understand your team well enough to know what motivates them and use the Platinum Rule instead: "Do unto others as *they* would have done unto them." You might love big parties, but throwing a surprise birthday party for one of your highly introverted team members would not be appreciated at all. The Platinum Rule requires you to get below the surface and *really* know and understand your team.

- **Kindness, Courtesy, and Respect.** In the "Be" section we previously discussed the need for leaders to have self-discipline and self-control. So even when we are angry and are not at our best, we need self-control to ensure we never take it out on our team and that we always demonstrate the highest courtesy and respect, with a significant helping of kindness when appropriate.

Conclusion

By now you are starting to understand why I keep referring to this as hard and difficult work. And if you thought facing the truth of your 360 Assessment sucked, then you've come to realize that the actual training and practice is far more difficult. Some things we've discussed so far:

- **What got you here won't get you there.** While the assessment was hard, the only thing it did was to allow you to get your foot in the door for the real training - which is even harder.

- **Assessment never ends.** People will always be evaluating you and it's never too late to fail.

- **Reputation and previous success doesn't guarantee success later on**. There're no free passes and you can never depend on what you did before to make it easier for you now. If anything, early successes mean that people will expect even more from you in the future.

- **The team always comes first.** Focus on the success of the team even when it seems like you will personally crash and burn. While counterintuitive, when you make the team's success paramount, it will also usually turn out much better for you; the leader cannot be considered successful unless the team succeeds.

- **Your job is *not* to do their job.** Your job is to make sure they have what they need to get things done which is why leaders eat last. You should know enough about their jobs to ensure you can step in, but you have a completely different skill set and it's your job to master it for the good of the team.

- **It *is* possible to change your character** and become whoever you want to be. It's Be, Know, and Do, in that order. Character is king because *it doesn't matter who (or what) you know until they know who you are*. Just practice the behaviors associated with those traits and you'll be able to fake it till you make it. It *will* get easier and it *will* change you.

And finally, **it's all about creating Fierce Trust** and if the only thing you do after reading this book is to focus on the items that build Active Trust, you'll be well on your way to becoming a truly great leader.

CHAPTER FOUR

Language School

Communicate Effectively
Learning to communicate effectively is essential for Green Berets to accomplish their missions, and it will dramatically improve your life and success as well. As with everything before, there is a high price to pay to learn a new language. While not physically demanding, effective communication with angry loved ones will easily be one of the hardest things you'll ever do.

Why Learn a Foreign Language?
We are often asked "why do Green Berets go to language school? Don't you do commando stuff? Why do you need to know another language to do that?" It's a fair question - and a very important one - because language is what sets the Green Berets apart from all other Special Operations in the world (except for intelligence agencies). The reason language is so fundamental to SF is found in our mission set. Special Forces teams conduct five primary missions: Unconventional Warfare; Foreign Internal Defense; Direct Action; Strategic Reconnaissance; and Counterterrorism.[23]

23 Secondary missions include: Security Force Assistance (SFA); Information Operations (IO); Psychological Operations (PYSOPs); and Counter-Proliferation (CP). Language skills are also extremely important for SFA, IO, and PYSOPs.

The first mission – Unconventional Warfare (UW) – is the raison d'etre of the U.S. Army Special Forces, the reason we were brought into existence. Our motto "De Oppresso Liber" means "to free the oppressed" and that's what UW (aka insurgency or guerrilla warfare) is all about. It means working by, with, and through indigenous forces to help them achieve their independence or overthrow a government that is illegitimate and repressive. An excellent example of this was the overthrow of the Taliban in Afghanistan after 9-11, a classic SF UW mission in every sense.

The second – Foreign Internal Defense (FID) – is literally the other side of (the) COIN (counterinsurgency). Whereas UW is an insurgency, FID is counterinsurgency warfare, helping legitimate democratically-elected governments stop terrorist organizations from seizing power. A good example of FID is the decades-long SF support of the Columbian counterinsurgency campaign against the FARC (Fuerzas Armadas Revolucionarias de Colombia), especially since the 1980s, which has seen Columbia become a stable and much safer country.

Both of these missions, our two most important, require Green Berets to live, train, and work closely with foreign troops and civilians. Yes, there are usually some interpreters around, but good interpreters are few and far between and there are never enough interpreters for the entire team. Moreover, how does anyone really know if the interpreter is any good unless you know the language yourself? For longer and more established deployments a vetting process is established that assigns a proficiency and security level to interpreters, but that is never in place at the start of a conflict and Green Berets are always the first on the ground.

A few native volunteer interpreters always show up, but normally it's somebody's cousin who took some English classes in school. Will you trust soldiers' lives to a tactical plan that has been "translated" by someone who may not even know the word for "ambush?" Absolutely not. Therefore the responsibility of communication falls on the SF team because even if you do have an interpreter, you must know the language well enough to know if the interpreter is translating correctly or getting the correct nuance.

Speaking for hours at a time in another language is exhausting, so it's nice to have an interpreter around to handle some of the load or help you with a word that you can't think of at that very moment. But I have personally worked with interpreters who were really working for "the other side" and purposely tried to mislead allied forces and then leak information to the bad guys to compromise our plans. One of them even tattooed the enemy's symbol on her back thinking we'd never find out about it. Successful SF teams do not rely on interpreters for critical communication. Green Berets must have at least a rudimentary knowledge of the language of the country in which they are working.

This is vitally important for our study of leadership because what Green Berets do in UW and FID is an advanced form of leadership because an SF captain is advising a foreign Colonel (at a minimum), but most probably a general or warlord. And the SF sergeants are advising officers (or their equivalent). You can't *make* an Afghan warlord or a Russian Airborne colonel do what you want. They are lions! But you can exert leadership through your role as an advisor, you can influence their actions by the resources you provide them and the Trust you establish with them. As an advisor, your job is to align the interests of the indigenous forces with those of the U.S. by using the "art" of leadership to *get them to do what you want them to do because they want to do it.* Green Berets work "by, with, and through" local forces; this is **exactly** what you must do as a leader of an elite team.

After all, what is "advising"? Isn't that pretty much the same as Coaching? And how do you build rapport? Through Trust that is built by your Character, the belief that you have their best interests at heart (Consideration), and your ability to Communicate all of that to them in a way they understand. Once again we come back to the Circle of Trust that surrounds our Leadership Model.

The understanding of the nuances of language is so important that when Special Forces were first founded, Senator Henry Cabot Lodge created legislation known as the "Lodge Act" (Alien Enlistee Program of 1950) that allowed refugees from countries behind the Iron Curtain to enlist in the U.S. Army and become members of the 10th Special Forces Group (the original SF organization). The Lodge Act was specifically aimed at creating an Unconventional Warfare unit filled with soldiers that were native language speakers with in-depth knowledge of the country, people, and culture of communist nations that the 10th Special Forces Group was prepared to engage with in the event of a war.

This was not a new concept even in the 1950's as it was the basis for the OSS (Office of Strategic Service, the parent organization of both the Green Berets and the CIA) Jedburgh Teams that operated behind the lines in WWII. Language and culture were, and always will be, one of the most important skills of Green Berets, which is why graduating language school is now a prerequisite for matriculating into the last phase of the Q-Course in its current configuration.

It's What to Say AND How to Say It

But unlike the 1950's "Lodge Act" Green Berets, most of today's prospective SF soldiers have never studied a foreign language before. Everyone must score well enough on the DLAB (Defense Language Aptitude Battery) to qualify for Special Forces. But that test is based on Esperanto and is essentially a logic test and anyone who has ever studied a foreign language will tell you that you can't master a foreign language through logic alone. The older a language is, the more exceptions have drifted into everyday speech, the more foreign words have slipped into the lexicon, and the more contractions and permutations have contorted the language.

So while basic logic and a lot of vocabulary memorization will get just about anyone to a rudimentary level of speaking, if you want to be fluent in a language, you will eventually spend a significant portion of your time learning all the crazy exceptions.

Of course, native speakers grow up with the anomalies and so it doesn't seem strange to them. English speakers have no problem understanding, "The camel herder decided to desert his dessert in the desert," or, "Evan had to write to the right people to exert his rights during his rites." There's no "pine" or "apple" in a pineapple, nor does it come from a pine tree.

When you learn to communicate effectively, you'll need to do the same thing – understand that each person has a list of (sometimes crazy) exceptions and your "logic" often doesn't work.

But even before you get to experience the joy of exceptions, there is the shock that comes from studying a language in the first place, especially as an adult. It's a well- established fact that children learn languages much more easily than adults. One of my early Russian teachers grew up trilingual and it was simple for her. As she told us: "It just seemed natural. I spoke to all the people in my life in their own language. My mother spoke Russian, I spoke to my father in German and to my nanny in French. I thought everyone did that." And that really is the heart of how we want to communicate as well. By learning *each person's* unique language.

For most of the SF students going through language school, it's their first time learning a language. So even something as simple as the realization that other languages have identifiable cases, declinations, and conjugations is mind-blowing because even though English has them, most people don't know about them because we rarely identify them.[24] And once you throw

---

24 English has three cases: Nominative; Possessive; and Objective. While the Nominative and Objective cases are usually the same (greatly contributing to the practical obsolescence of English cases) there are some instances where they are different (he, his, him; I, mine, me). HE is angry because HIS brother won't give HIM HIS ball.

in noun genders it becomes more difficult (the word "tablet" is masculine in Russian but feminine in German). And if it wasn't already confusing enough, both the spelling of the word and the article preceding the word can change depending on whether it is in the nominative, accusative, genitive, or dative case.

It's enough to make you want to stick pencils in your eyeballs.

So while not physically taxing, for the majority of Green Berets, language school is mentally draining and, as is the case with everything Green Berets have to do in training, there is a high standard to meet in order to pass and move on to the next phase of training.

And it's more than language school. It's also a "culture school" because all of the instructors are native speakers and part of their job is to also teach students about the country and customs of the language they're learning.

Green Berets aren't successful just because they have the skills to speak a different language. They also must know what to say and when and how to say it. Herein lies the difference between simply knowing a language and how to effectively communicate. Even though learning a new language is difficult, it's a skill, and the skill is the easy part. The second element is best expressed as "consideration." The word "consideration" has two meanings.

The first is careful thought and deliberation in forming a decision or taking action. The second is having or showing regard for others. But basically both definitions mean to think carefully about something or someone. "What to say" is a combination of (considered) awareness, knowledge and experience, along with good intent (consideration for the people you're working with), which is all influenced heavily by culture. Small things can be critically important to your success. Whether it's how and when to bow your head, shake someone's hand, or drink a shot of vodka with them.

That's why "Cultural Awareness" is one of the seven core values of Special Forces.

People from some cultures won't do business or work with you until you've spent a sufficient amount of time getting to know them. It doesn't matter how good your idea is or how advantageous a course of action is. What matters first is building a relationship. *Because it doesn't matter who you know until they know who you are.*

It's also about what culturally "not" to do, like refusing a cup of tea or coffee, showing the soles of your shoes or feet, eating food with your left hand, insisting on timeliness, or not freaking out when soldiers from another country come up behind you, grab your hand, and begin to walk with you hand-in-hand.

Everyday effective communication has the same requirements because every person has their own set of cultural considerations – things to do or not to do – if you want to be able to get past the surface and really connect with them.

Pronunciation is another important part of culture and consideration because if you don't pay attention to the way a language is supposed to sound (at least a little), it's very probable that the people you are trying to talk to will just tune you out completely or find a way to leave the conversation prematurely. Russians have a term for this called "cutting the ears." It is used when a foreigner is speaking the language with such a bad accent that it's painful to listen to. I didn't understand the concept until I once heard an American speaking Russian so badly that it even made me cringe. Even though the speaker was grammatically correct and had a huge vocabulary, hearing him speak Russian with a heavy US southern accent was just so jarring that he had a difficult time working with the Russians. No one wanted to talk to him.

So it's not just knowing what to say and the right words to use; it's also about *how* to say it, delivering your message in a way that doesn't push the listener away. It's making the extra effort to get the accent and pronunciation right so that the other person will pay attention to the words and the ideas you're trying to impart.

Culture and language (consideration + skill) go hand-in-hand in terms of mission success. It's so important that I've devoted the last chapter of Part 2 just to "culture."

When I was enlisted, they hadn't yet established the language school at Ft. Bragg, so we learned languages at the Defense Language Institute (DLI) in Monterey, California. The Spanish course is four months long, German is six months, but Chinese, Arabic, and Russian are one-year long — and I needed every single day.

Foreign languages don't come easily to me and despite my best efforts, after a few months I was teetering on the edge of failing. My teacher suggested I join the DLI Russian Choir to help me understand the language a bit more naturally. I didn't want to because it would take time away from my homework every day, but mostly because the Russian Choir was not a particularly popular choice for most of the male soldiers.[25] It

---

25 It didn't help that the proper pronunciation of "Russian choir" is "rooski xor (whore)." You can let your imagination run wild with all the potential jokes associated with that.

was kind of like joining the cheerleading squad in high school, looked down upon by a lot of guys. But my teacher promised it would help me, so I joined.

She was right, it did help because to sing a song in another language you have to get the pronunciation right and you memorize and constantly use (sing) complex sentences. We dressed up in traditional costumes and went around and performed at area store openings, holiday events, culture days, and any place the choir director could find to show us off. It was really embarrassing at times, but it helped me with word order and cases and I learned a lot of traditional Russian folk songs by heart, a treasure trove of Russian culture that I vastly underestimated at the time.

> Many years later during a mission with Russian Airborne Forces (politically sensitive because it was one of the first times that US and Russian troops had conducted joint patrols since WWII and the fall of the Soviet Union), it was critical to quickly build rapport and start working cooperatively with the Russians so that we could stop the war in our region.
>
> Understandably there wasn't much trust between the two sides and the Russians had been standoffish, restricted access to their headquarters, and wouldn't allow us to participate in operational planning. But at one point they had a party, and they invited us to attend. After lots of vodka the Russian officers began singing traditional songs. First of all, I was shocked because I didn't really think that people did that, and secondly because all the (what I'd thought were silly and worthless) songs

I'd learned by heart back in DLI were the same ones the Russians were singing!

So I began singing along with them, and it was their turn to be surprised! The ones closest to me stopped singing and looked at me like I was a little green man from outer space. Because I'd had to memorize so many songs for the Russian DLI choir, I'd learned a lot of songs that they'd forgotten the words to, but that their grandmothers used to sing to them.

I obviously wasn't a spy because I didn't speak the language well enough, so they were convinced that my family's lineage was Russian because, in their words, I had a Roo'sskaya Doo-sha' (a Russian soul) and deep down inside, I was really one of them. And the very next day we were finally invited into their HQ to conduct joint planning – which was instrumental for the success of that mission.

It was only the deep trust we built over time, much of it through language and cultural knowledge, that made it possible for us to go to the Russian commander one night at 9:00 pm and say, "Sir, we can't tell you why, but tomorrow morning at 06:00 we need 12 of your trucks and 130 of your soldiers," and he gave them to us. The joint operation we carried out the next day was a massive success and we (Russians and Americans together) seized almost all of the weapons and ammo needed to keep the conflict going, pretty much shutting down any large-scale violence or attacks in that region.

That "silly" choir was easily one of the most important things I did to be successful in my Special Forces career.

> The impact and importance of language skills and cultural knowledge simply cannot be overestimated.

Fluency Requires A Lifetime

After I'd completed the rest of my requirements to become a Green Beret the first time and finally made it to a team, I tried to maintain my language skills in a variety of ways, including college courses. It takes constant effort to improve and maintain language skills.

Once I became an officer and graduated the Q-Course a second time, I went to language school again – this time the Special Forces Language school at Ft. Bragg, the one that every Green Beret goes through now. The SF language school is different from DLI or traditional language programs. Although it teaches grammar rules and cases, it primarily focuses on practical application, learning the vocabulary and phrases needed for our specialties: assembling and disassembling weapons; setting explosives; providing battlefield first aid; planning operations; etc. We didn't spend a lot of time trying to master declensions and conjugations. Rather, the idea was that through enough practice we'd get a feel for what sounded right and what didn't. And it wouldn't matter if we made some mistakes as long as we got our point across.

In addition to our language training, we spent a lot of time learning and understanding the culture because while language lets you communicate, people from another country don't believe you fully *understand* them until you can demonstrate that you know and respect their culture. So we'd go to restaurants that served Russian (or Georgian) food and learned how to cook some of it ourselves on our instructor's backyard grill. We took field trips to cities that had large Russian populations and poked our heads into grocery stores that specialized in imported Russian household products and food. We even went to universities to sit in with grad students who were learning the language.

And while I knew quite a bit about Russian history, geography, and politics (all the "culture" stuff they taught in university), this was the first time that I felt like I was learning about real culture. But again, we were just scratching the surface and what we learned only prepared us enough to get "in country". Language and culture training never stops and regional differences abound, just as in the U.S.

If an SF student can't learn their language, they usually have one chance to try an easier one. However, because the current configuration of the Q-Course has language school before Phase 3, it's very possible that students who don't get the required scores in language don't move on and don't graduate because you can't be a Green Beret if you can't speak a foreign language.

This is especially true because language skills are held in much higher esteem than when I graduated from DLI and today all SF soldiers are required to pass an annual Defense Language Proficiency Test (DLPT) for their language. Professional fluency is encouraged by a bonus that increases as proficiency does, up to an extra $1,000 per month for reading, writing, and speaking 2 languages at just below the level of native speakers.

It took me about 18 years of effort (on and off) before I was able to "max" my Russian language pay because learning and being proficient in another language is hard for most of us and it requires a lifetime to become truly fluent.

However, despite the years of studying and classes and constant brain freeze, the effort was worth it, and I used my Russian language and culture skills up to and beyond my very last day of active duty when I was working in Sochi, Russia for NBC Sports during the 2014 Winter Olympics, an amazing experience that I would have never gotten if I hadn't spent all that time learning to properly communicate and operate in someone else's world.

Lessons Learned

- **It can take a lifetime of effort** to be able to communicate effectively in someone else's language. It's difficult (for most people) and requires a high price. Are you seeing a pattern yet?

- Green Berets **cannot perform their most important missions without learning the languages** of the countries they work in. Effective communication in the host nation's language is essential for Special Forces to exercise leadership while Advising, Training, and Equipping their allies because Green Berets work By, With, and Through them to accomplish strategic goals and impossible missions.

- Exceptions abound and often what you're trying to learn or understand **makes absolutely no sense at all**. A language cannot be mastered through logic; it will always require memorization and repetition before a non-native speaker is able to get it right.

- **Green Berets are 100% responsible for communication**; there is never any expectation that the people that we are working with will learn English or provide translators.
- Moreover, you must take on the added responsibility to **communicate in the way that they want to hear it** – otherwise it "cuts their ears" and they turn you off.
- **No coasting.** Prior success doesn't guarantee future success; yet another lesson repeated from the last chapter. Sadly, any communication skills you manage to acquire will quickly fade away if they aren't used and practiced regularly.
- Effective communication is more than just learning another person's language. To truly connect with someone you **must learn both their language and culture** and learn how to live in their world.
- Fluency takes time. Until you become a master and use it often, **you will still need to stop and think** about what to say before you say it.
- **The effort is worth it.** Knowing another language opens you up to a world of opportunities you wouldn't have had otherwise. The advantages you can accrue far outweigh the price and will significantly change your life for the better.

Now it's time to apply those lessons to *your* communication and language program.

- **To truly communicate and lead effectively you must learn a different "language."** This new way of speaking also has different "rules." There is a proper word order, and you will have to plan what you say ahead of time. It is difficult and requires a high price.

- Just because you get it right once, doesn't mean you won't **have to get it right every time.** However, just as with a foreign language, if you've shown that you know how to communicate with someone, they will usually give you a chance to get it right once they see you struggling to find the right words or phrases.

- **You will not be able to perform at the highest levels** and build/lead elite teams without learning this new language because you will not be able to work By, With, and Through the lions on your team. Long-established research from multiple sources has shown that the majority of highly successful people and organizations have learned how to communicate in this way. Yes, there are exceptions, but even Steve Jobs got fired from his own company (Apple) because he didn't do this well.

- **You are 100% responsible for effective communication**; you must do *all the work all the time, every time*. Sometimes this will seem unbearably unfair. It is. But suck it up. If you want to be a master communicator then it's 100% on you to get your message across in a way it can be understood by the other person. It is 100% your responsibility to make sure you're communicating the way they want; you cannot expect them to adapt to you. If you're extremely lucky, the other person is also striving to be a master communicator and they will feel 100% of the responsibility on their shoulders, as well. When this happens you will have a very rewarding conversation and probably solve all problems and issues in record time. And you will probably become friends.

- **This will take a lifetime to master**, but it will get easier the more you practice and use it. It will seem weird and stilted at times as you think of the right "vocab" and "structure."

- When using your new form of communication, you will hear and try to make sense of things that **make no sense at all.** You will hear things as ridiculous as a man's mustache being "feminine." And yes, there will be lots of exceptions.

- Without a doubt this skill **will change your life for the better.** I have personally seen people fix relationships that they believed irretrievably lost, fix marriages, and create much better leaders *and* human beings. In my opinion this is the **single most important skill you will *ever* learn in your entire life.**

Your Personal Q-Course

The good news is that the training required to speak this new language is pretty straightforward because it's a skill that anyone can learn. But before we start our training, we first need to understand why we need this new language/way to communicate in the first place. Why does effective communication get its very own chapter?

If you remember from Chapter One, EPIC leaders provide Purpose, Direction, Motivation, and Resources (PDMR) in an atmosphere of **Fierce / Active Trust** gained through Character, Communication, Coaching, and Consideration (the 4 C's).

Here's the Leadership Model again. Communication is the first element in the Circle of Trust which encompasses all our leadership tasks. "Good" communication builds Active Trust which, in turn, facilitates effective execution of almost every leadership task in one way or another.

But more to the point, effective communication is probably the most important skill for a leader to have because without people to lead, you're not a leader. And the only way to get them to do what you want them to do is to communicate effectively with them.

What does "Good Communication" mean?
But now the tricky part. Everyone talks about the importance of good communication, but what does that really mean? Is it keeping your boss informed of every little thing? Is it CC'ing

every detail of a project to everyone who's working on the project? Is it having four meetings a day to ensure everyone is "up to speed" on everything? When your boss gets up in front of everyone and says, "We all need to communicate better" for the 20th time, is she only talking about keeping people informed of "the important stuff"? Is there something more than simply learning to become proficient in Active/Empathetic Listening?

Despite frequently talking about how important it is, people have a hard time defining good communication.

That's because true communication is more than just an action. It's not just a skill. **Real communication is about your values: it is an authentic expression of your Generosity of Spirit – of your Consideration and your Character.**

Knowledge is power. When somebody doesn't share information that would be useful for others, it's usually because that person is afraid of something or they just can't be bothered to pass it on because it would be more work. Either way, it's an issue with their Character or Consideration; it's a telling sign that the person isn't generous. Oh, sure, that person might be very generous when it comes to buying lunch or doing other things that demonstrate their wealth. But if it's only about buying things or giving you things, then it's usually more about that person's insecurities, their need for status, and their need to be liked. It is inauthentic generosity.

Even if that person is very skilled in empathetic listening, they are still not really communicating. *Intent matters.* And ironically, it's often the people who are calling for "better communication" who are the worst communicators. What many of them really mean is "give **me** more information" because of the knowledge and power it gives them.

The idea that knowledge sharing is a requirement for true generosity is an ancient concept found in all major religions and philosophical texts but rarely discussed today. Examples include:

- Christianity: "Having all the knowledge in the world is useless without the desire to share."[26]
- Judaism: Actively obstructing the flow of knowledge is suggested to be the destruction of mankind.[27]
- Islam: The Muslim Hadith on knowledge sharing states that the messenger of Allah said, "Whoever is asked about knowledge and he conceals it, Allah will clothe him with a bridle of fire on the Day of Resurrection."[28]
- Dharmic: The Vidya Daan (विद्या दान), translated as knowledge charity, is the value of sharing knowledge and is a tenet of Buddhism, Hinduism, Sikhism, and all other Dharmic ("Eastern") religions.

Notre Dame University's "Generosity Project" studies the science of generosity and in tracing the word's etymology found that in the middle ages the word came to be associated with a "nobility of thought" and "an achieved mark of admirable personal quality and action." And even today there are historical associations that inform our meaning of the word, including the idea that generosity has not been viewed as a normal trait of ordinary (or all) people, but rather one "to be practiced by those of higher quality or greater goodness." [29]

---

26 "And though I have the gift of prophecy, and understand all mysteries, and all knowledge; and though I have all faith, so that I could remove mountains, and have not charity, I am nothing."—KJV: 1 Corinthians 13:2
27 and "my people are destroyed from lack of knowledge." —Hosea 4:6
28 Sunan al-Tirmidhī 2649
29 Notre Dame University: https://generosityresearch.nd.edu/more-about-the-initiative/what-is-generosity/

This relates directly to leadership. By definition alone, if you want to lead *elite* teams, you're not shooting for ordinary. Generosity of spirit builds the trust and cohesion elite teams need to face immense challenges. In this sense, communication as an act of selfless knowledge sharing ties directly to the notions of nobility the Generosity Project identifies. For elite teams, nothing less than "uncommon" generosity will do.

The virtue of "Knowledge Sharing" is further articulated in the 4th "C", Coaching. True generosity of spirit means that you want your team members to succeed. Coaching is what happens when the other C's are in place, when you have enough Consideration/Caring for the other person to be willing to share your knowledge, and Communicate it to them in a spirit of humility and fearlessness (Character).

So what is *real* Communication? Think in terms of Be, Know, Do.

> Real Communication is genuine Generosity of Spirit that makes knowledge sharing an integral part of leadership. It's knowing when empathetic communication is needed and having the skill to do it well. It's the discipline to do all of that regularly—even when you don't want to, and especially when the other person doesn't want to hear it. And finally, it's a commitment to coach the rest of the team to ensure they do it, too.

This task of improving communication skills is a perfect example of why we need to address values and integrity (Be), before training specific skills (Know). Why? It's hard to communicate well. Sometimes overwhelmingly so. The skills required aren't especially difficult, but actually executing the task is *hard*. We won't become expert communicators until we address our character because we won't have enough courage and self-confidence to be "generous in spirit" or be considerate enough for real knowledge sharing. In other words, we must build our own foundation and ensure it's rock solid before we can begin to be strong enough to support others. That's ultimately what good communication is: carrying the full weight and responsibility of every exchange if needed.

While we occasionally get lucky, we cannot consistently achieve excellence in any aspect of our lives without a strong foundation upon which to build our skills, natural talent, affections, and ambitions. Artists must study their craft, athletes must master the basics, lifelong relationships must have trust. You get the point. The greatest sword ever made is useless if you don't have the strength to wield it.

But even when you've clarified your values and have the right attitude, you still won't want to share everything all the time. And you're busy, so sometimes you won't want to take the extra steps and time needed to ensure that important information gets to everyone who needs it. And as you'll see in the section on empathetic communication, sometimes it takes everything you have to commit to the process and see it through. It takes real generosity and strength to give constructive feedback to someone who needs it—but doesn't want it. Most people can't do it.

Here are some examples of real communication that lead to an atmosphere of Fierce Trust:

- Sharing the complete vision and plan (not just the parts that will motivate people).

- Setting unambiguous, achievable, agreed-upon metrics and expectations for everything important and anything that directly impacts your team members' evaluations, promotions, company standing, or training.

- As soon as you fully understand them yourself, tell your team all the issues that your section/department/company is facing and any information that may be potentially harmful to them like possible layoffs or company changes. Do not, however, spread rumors or conjecture until you can confirm something. You don't want to needlessly worry people, so find the truth and understand its impact and *then* let your team know. If someone asks about an issue (because they heard a rumor elsewhere), acknowledge the information that you know, but also tell them that you are still determining its truth and impact before sharing with the group.

- Providing clarity for everything. I've heard company officers purposely obscure things they tell their employees. Technically, they didn't lie, but the way in which they presented information gave employees the idea that they would be eligible for certain benefits when they weren't. Even technically truthful statements can be deceptive when used to confuse rather than inform, and will destroy your integrity.

- Giving real and effective feedback. As a leader you *must* understand and truly believe that it is a great kindness to let a team member know they aren't performing, and give them a chance to improve before they lose their job or their fellow team members' respect. Many leaders shy away from this task, especially with people who are resistant to any sort of feedback, so I've developed tools that can help you do this effectively.

- Asking for and being open to constructive feedback yourself. Listening well is 2/3rds of effective communication, so being open to hearing feedback and improving yourself may seem one-sided, but the actions you take afterwards will speak volumes about what you learned and if you listened. Your team (and your boss) will be watching. Learn to love feedback and to use it to constantly improve yourself.

- Active/Empathetic Communication skills. If I was King for a Day, my first decree would be that everyone in the world would spend at least eight hours learning this incredibly valuable skill, and overnight the world would be a much better place. This is not hyperbole; it is by far the single most important thing that any human being could ever learn. Mastering this skill will *profoundly* change your life.

- Learning about your team members. While the purpose of "small talk" may be to ease into a conversation, showing genuine interest in the lives of your team members is a form of deep communication that will inform and advise your thoughts and actions in many ways. Knowing that Janelle's daughter has her volleyball games on Thursday gives you a lot of "actionable" information that you can use to keep Janelle motivated and happy. But your connection with Janelle (and the trust she will have in you) is deepened simply by showing authentic concern about her and what's important to her.

- The flip side of that is <u>sharing more of yourself</u> than you might normally be comfortable with - just as you are going to care enough to really learn about your team and what makes them tick, they will benefit by learning the same about you. The more you share, the more trust you gain and ultimately the deeper the commitment you develop between all the members of the team.

So should you CC everyone on every email? Absolutely not. Should you CC every member of the team on an initial email to inform everyone of what's going on and announce that future emails on the thread would be for a specific subset of people (unless someone requests to stay on)? That's probably a good idea.

Should you use a Slack channel for specific team members to allow immediate access to information they might need? Sounds like a good idea if you establish hard rules about what's allowed and what's not.

Should you have a daily meeting with all 150 of the company's employees? Maybe. If you ensure that *all* the information that everyone needs is front-loaded and then people are released after the first 15 - 20 minutes (unless they choose to stay).

There are hundreds more scenarios, but the easy way to answer all of them is to ask yourself these questions:

- For whom is the information useful?
- What is the proper method of dissemination (email, in-person meeting, virtual meeting, Slack, shotgun blast, empathetic listening, etc.)?
- Does the method of dissemination ensure *everyone* who needs it gets *all* the information?
- Am I wasting other peoples' time by disseminating information that they don't need or want? Have I provided a means for people to opt-out early and often?

But in truth, you only have to ask yourself: *"Am I being generous with my knowledge and considerate enough to ensure it is shared properly and completely?"*

Some companies have adopted cultures that don't just encourage openness, they demand "radical truth and transparency" or "radical candor, " meaning that everything gets shared or is available unless it's protected by law (SSN, HIPAA, etc.) or the company's general counsel indicates it puts the company at risk. These companies record all important meetings and make the videos available to everyone. They make salary and bonus information available to everyone, and one of the companies I work with even requires every employee to give at least three pieces of constructive feedback per week to another employee, and they enforce it.

How Communication Breaks Down

Poor communication in the form of "mismatched expectations" accounts for **99%** of interpersonal problems. So, in addition to knowledge sharing and "expectation leveling" a great communicator must be proficient in Empathetic Communications. This is a relatively simple skill that can prove extremely difficult to do well until we can get past our own ego. We use this special language because it allows us to get past the normal obstacles that prevent us from communicating effectively with one another.

The Shannon-Weaver Model of Communication

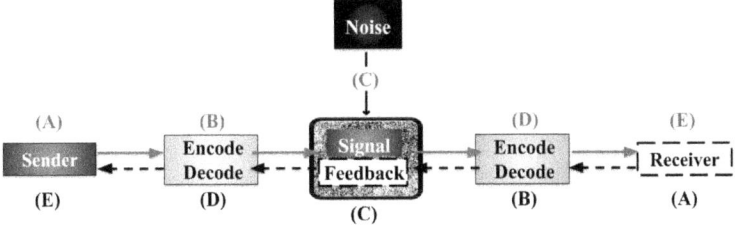

Normal communication has some inherent problems that we don't usually see or appreciate. The Shannon-Weaver model of communication graphically represents how basic communication flows and the areas for problems to occur. The sender (A) wants to convey a very specific thought and chooses a method(s) for sending it. This step is more complex than simply choosing to speak or send an email or write a letter, etc. There are all kinds of unconscious inputs that become part of "encoding" (B) including tone of voice, inflection, body language, etc. In fact, studies indicate that 93% of communication is non-verbal and *only 7% is from the words themselves.*

Here's a quick example to show you what I mean. Compare these seven identical phrases with completely different meanings:

I didn't say you had a problem.
I ***didn't*** say you had a problem.
I didn't ***say*** you had a problem.
I didn't say ***you*** had a problem.
I didn't say you ***had*** a problem.
I didn't say you had ***a*** problem.
I didn't say you had a ***problem***.

Yet inflection is only 38% of communication. Body language and facial expressions are the greatest contributors to communication at 55%. So while we initially don't assign much importance to the "encode" box, it's easy to see that it is the cause of many of our communication missteps.

Once you put your message out there (with all the associated encoding), it must pass through an environment that always has some "noise" or "static" (C). This includes all the external factors that neither the sender nor receiver can control. It could be something as simple as actual noise (a truck backing up and beeping as you're trying to say something) or psychological noise (the other person is stressed because they're very busy or had a bad day). Your message must pass through that noise before the other person even starts to decode it.

Your intention does not equal their interpretation! You might have meant to say something encouraging to the receiver, but after it's passed through the noise and any distortion, they still have to decode (D) what's coming at them. And regardless of your intentions, they may decode the message in an entirely different way. This could be for any number of reasons.

> Remember in the last chapter when I tried to give some inspiring words to my team during Phase 3 - and they heard "arrogance" instead of "camaraderie"? It was only after the course was over and one member of our team came up to me and said "man, I'm sorry, I was wrong about you" that I finally learned how badly I'd screwed up. When I asked him what he meant, he told me about how he'd felt after I'd given my little speech. While the team still trusted me, some of them thought I was just an arrogant jerk. I was dumbfounded; I literally stood there with my jaw open and couldn't speak for a few moments as I tried to clarify that he was talking about my "team building" speech. Once I realized that we really were talking about the same thing, I was crushed. To this day I am still ashamed that I communicated so poorly, that I'd somehow managed to say the exact opposite of what I wanted to convey. Unfortunately, this was only one example of the many times in my life where I tried to say one thing and it came out as another.

At some point we have all said something to someone else that was taken completely the wrong way, and it takes a while to figure out why, doesn't it? Sometimes it's just that we don't have the same relationship with certain words that others do. We all know of words that elicit strong emotions for some people, but others can use them and it's not considered insulting. There are plenty of language landmines out there that we can unknowingly step on without meaning to, but that still doesn't prevent another person from feeling anger or pain, and that means they immediately stop listening to your original message.

If, for whatever reason, the message doesn't get to the receiver (E) in the way it's intended, then it's highly likely that the situation will deteriorate because the receiver now becomes the sender and they are responding to an incorrectly understood initial message — meaning they are responding to a "different" message and their response must therefore be inherently flawed. Look again at the examples listed above and you'll notice that each of the "problem" statements takes the argument in a completely different direction. What are the chances the response is addressing the originally intended message? To compound the issue, the receiver's "flawed" response goes through its own path of encode-noise-decode. So it's easy to see how a conversation can quickly devolve into a shouting match where each side is arguing about something different as it continuously spirals downwards.

Empathetic communication short-circuits the encode-noise-decode pattern of communication by adding another step to ensure the receiver gets the message as intended. It's as simple as saying, "So you didn't say I had a problem, but someone else did, right?" When both the sender and the receiver agree that the receiver understands the message properly, then the receiver responds, confident in the fact that both parties are in harmony with the originally intended message. It's important to note that the sender and receiver **do not have to agree on the validity of the message,** simply that they agree the original message has been understood as intended.

Language School

Empathetic Communication

```
                        Noise
                         |
                        (C)
                         |
  (A)        (B)         ▼         (D)        (E)
 ┌──────┐  ┌────────┐ ┌────────┐ ┌────────┐ ┌──────────┐
 │Sender│→ │ Encode │→│ Signal │→│ Encode │→│ Receiver │
 │      │← │ Decode │←│Feedback│←│ Decode │←│          │
 └──────┘  └────────┘ └────────┘ └────────┘ └──────────┘
  (F)        (E)        (D)        (C)        (B)
    ↑                                            ↑
     ╲              (A)                        ╱
      ╲         ┌─Check──────┐              ╱
       ╲───────│ Understanding │───────────╱
               └───────────────┘
```

If for some reason the sender doesn't agree with the receiver's understanding of the message, they correct it. "No, that's not right, there's a problem, but it's with Dan."

Then the receiver tries again. "Okay, so this project that Dan and I are working on is tough and Dan did something we need to fix; is that right?"

Sender: "Yes, section two of the report, Dan's part, makes it seem like our division didn't do our job, and that's not right! This is wrong and you need to fix it!"

Even though the sender is still argumentative, both parties are now sure that the original message is completely understood so that any subsequent dialogue is at least addressing the real issue.

Then it's the receiver's turn. Even if the original sender doesn't know how to communicate empathetically, the situation will still be far less explosive because the receiver validates what the speaker thinks and feels, and once someone feels understood, it takes the heat out of any argument.

The "witch doctor" scenario from the last chapter opened my mind up to the idea that someone could be absolutely, totally wrong and yet, their ideas can't be ignored or criticized; someone's deeply held beliefs cannot be changed simply because "I know better." We didn't solve the witch doctor scenario through logic or argumentation. It was only after we validated their "crazy" ideas and feelings that they were ready to listen. We never agreed with them, but we acknowledged the G's belief about how knowledge is gained and then used that to our advantage to craft a solution that fit their worldview — removing a step (head-to-head rather than head-pot-head) was actually more effective and had less chance for "spillage".

This idea of valuing someone else's ideas or culture is critical for Green Berets to establish rapport and achieve mission success because no one will work with you (much less listen to your suggestions) if you haven't first validated their beliefs and ideas. We don't have to agree with them; all that matters is that we listen and convey to our counterpart that we totally and completely understand what they're saying.

Additionally, this lesson has helped me be a far more empathetic person and to realize that, no matter how smart I think I am, I am not always right and I should listen more and talk less.

Empathetic+ Communication™

So what's this new language that you must know to be successful in building and leading elite teams? It's called Empathetic Communication and as you'll see, it is a different language with its own lexicon, rules, exceptions, idiosyncrasies, and "crazy ideas" to work through as you struggle to understand someone else's worldview.

There are different methodologies for Empathetic Communication, but they all share a few essential elements: the listener reflects the thoughts (and feelings) of the speaker; the listener completely focuses on what the speaker is saying and not what their response is going to be; the conversation doesn't progress until both sides are sure that they completely understand the situation (original message); and the focus is on what happened and not on the other person's character ("when you said those clothes didn't look good on me I got angry", rather than "you're a jerk!").

I developed Empathetic+ Communication (EMP+ - pronounced "EmPlus") for very tense conflict resolution scenarios – like when a company is literally falling apart because their C-Suite can't get along. It's often difficult to just get both parties into the same room, much less speaking to each other. In those cases, I must be the "honest broker" and be trusted by both parties to lead the process. Using EMP+ I've never had a case where we have not successfully resolved the conflict and repaired relationships. I've had people who refused to be in the same building with each other leave our EMP+ session with their arms around each other in tears saying how much they love each other.

But you don't need a third party. You can do EMP+ on your own if you learn the process and take full responsibility for the *entire* conversation. The skills are quite simple, but they can be overwhelmingly hard to do when your own emotions are also running high.

Here's the entire process: identify the need for EMP+; reflect thoughts and feelings; ask if you got it right; and see if there's anything else to discuss. Just four simple steps. Sounds easy, right? Keep reading.

Normally, I explain the concept first and then show you the graphic. But this time, I'm showing you the tool up front, and again at the end, because as you read the next section, it might feel like there's a lot to remember. Don't worry. Everything is captured in the tool, so just focus on understanding the concepts.

Steps for Empathetic+ Communication (EMP+ "EmPlus")

GUIDANCE:	SPEAKER	LISTENER	GUIDANCE:
* "Because" is critical. * Avoid YOU statements whenever possible. State facts and don't assign motivations - "you did this because you were ...." or "you were mean" - instead, stick to the protocol. * Keep items short enough that the other person can remember / restate - one item at a time. You'll get through all of them. * ALWAYS let the other person go first (unless you are the one bringing up a subject in the first place). Letting them go first and successfully reflecting will build a significant amount of goodwill and make it far more likely that they will listen to you.	1. When ____ happened (when you said ____) 2. I felt ____ 3. Because ____	1. **Reflect:** When I said/did ____ you felt ____ because ____ 2. **Confirm:** Is that right? 3. **Ask:** Is there More? ... after "no" ... (optional) • Mention anything you've learned • List any points of agreement • Apologize (if appropriate)	* Listen ONLY with the intent to understand. You may take notes so you don't worry about forgetting something. Your job is to LISTEN so you can reflect, build trust, and give them "air." * If caught off guard, you can always start with "You're upset" to give you a few moments to listen. * **Reflect:** Statements, *not* questions. Attempt to reflect so clearly, vividly, and fairly that the other person says, "wow, thanks! I wish I'd thought of saying it that way." * Your INTENT is most important. It's OK to get it wrong, they'll correct you and then reflect again. * **Confirm:** If "NO", ask speaker to say it again; reflect until you get a "yes." * **Ask:** If yes, allow them to state the next point and reflect. If no, ask if you may state your point of view. It is YOUR responsibility to get your point across respectfully, and in the way that they best understand.

YOU are 100% responsible for EMP+ Communication.

© 2023 Robert W. Schaefer | All rights reserved | Use only with permission

Step Zero is the activation "pre-step." It's understanding when you need to switch to **EMP+**. Most of our daily conversations do not require this advanced form of communication and our interactions would sound stilted if we always used it. Think of it as walking sideways. It's very useful when we need to get around an obstacle, but it would be weird if we walked sideways all day long. There is a time and a place for it.

You know it's time to use EMP+ when someone is angry or emotions are running high. It's essential during arguments, but often the need for EMP+ is more subtle—like when your sister breaks up with her boyfriend or your friend loses their job. Our instinct is to help by trying to "fix" it, saying things like, "You're better off without him," or, "They never appreciated you anyway." But when you choose to use EMP+, the first rule is always the same: **let them speak first. Don't interrupt**. Let them get it all out. This is critical.

Step One - Reflect their words and/or feelings. What the speaker needs most is for you to listen—without inserting yourself into their story. That means no questions, advice, opinions, or judgments. An empathetic response simply reflects what they're feeling. For example: "You seem really upset about the breakup," or, "Wow, that must be a shock—losing your job so suddenly." In both cases, you stay out of their story. By reflecting, you give them the psychological space to say what they really need to say. You become a true sounding board—just reflecting what you hear.

Step Two - Confirm you understand the message. This step is essential for conflicts, as it ensures both people agree that the message being sent is the message being received. It's the extra step (the new "A") in the model on page 177. After reflecting what you believe they're saying, simply ask, "Is that right?" Don't worry if it's not. They'll correct you—and they'll still appreciate the effort. Reflect and confirm again until they indicate that you got it.

Step Three is to ensure we've gotten everything. This step helps uncover any other issues that might be part of the problem and confirms you've gotten to the heart of it. Just ask, "What else about this is bothering you?" Most of us have had conversations that went on for hours, only to realize the real issue was something completely different from what the person started with. You've probably done the same—talked with someone close about one thing, only to realize later that something else was really driving how you felt.

There's a concept called *symbolic value*—when something of low value takes on deep meaning because it represents something else, usually of much greater importance. It's like saying "1 = 57" with a straight face and absolutely believing it. When something carries symbolic value for someone, it can be confusing—because nothing they say will make sense until you figure out what the symbol actually represents. When a normally reasonable person insists the sky is green and gets angry when you say, "No, it's blue," it feels like you're arguing with a crazy person. But in that moment, the symbol and what it represents are the same thing for them.

> I used to occasionally leave empty sweetener packets on the counter because I'd be in a rush to get out in the mornings. I always planned to pick them up later, but after grabbing my coffee and juggling a backpack and keys, I usually didn't have the hands for it. And to me, it was no big deal.
>
> But every once in a while, my wife would get really angry about the packets. I'd say, "Why are you so upset? It's just a few wrappers—I'll clean them up later." That only made her angrier, which confused me even more. Because it wasn't really about the sweetener packets.

The packets had symbolic value. To my wife, they represented something much bigger: that I was taking her for granted. That I expected her to clean up after me. That I didn't respect her.

But the argument never started there. It started with frustration over some bits of paper. And we'd go back and forth for a long time because I thought we were talking about sweetener packets—when what she was really trying to express was that she felt unappreciated.

Once I understood what the packets meant to her, I stopped leaving them out. Not because the paper mattered, but because she did.

It often takes time, when practicing EMP+, to get to the heart of the matter which is why Step 3 is so important. It's as simple as asking, "What else is bothering you?" or, "Is there more?" If there is, you go back to Step One and work through the new issue. Then you ask again. And you keep repeating the process until they finally say, "No."

This repetition matters. Going through all three steps more than once almost always brings up something new. Sometimes it's connected to the first issue. Other times, after a few rounds, it reveals something much deeper that wasn't visible at the start. Most people don't even realize there's an underlying issue when they begin talking. They won't find it unless you walk patiently through each layer of the conversation.

They have to feel completely understood at each layer before they'll even consider peeling back the next one. If you rush the process or try to force it, they'll shut down, and whatever deeper issue was there will stay buried. But if you stay with them—if you take the time to genuinely listen and show that you care—they'll often get there on their own. And when they do, they usually start solving the real problem without you having to do anything except keep repeating Steps 1–3 and staying fully present.

It sounds simple enough: recognize the need for EMP+, reflect their thoughts and feelings, ask if you got it right, and check if there's anything else they want to talk about. An easy way to remember it is "RCA"—Reflect, Confirm, Ask. Some of you might remember the old RCA (Radio Corporation of America) logo—the dog sitting in front of the gramophone. It's the perfect metaphor. That image is all about listening. And that's exactly what we're doing: listening. Then RCA—Reflect, Confirm, Ask. How hard could that be?

It's often unbelievably hard—especially when you're upset with someone you care about, and what you really want is for them to listen to you, too. But if they're not trained, or even if they are but just don't want to at that moment, it can feel impossible. You'll be working hard to stay calm, trying to understand their point of view, while they won't even consider yours. That's enough to make even the most experienced EMP+ communicators want to walk away. This takes practice. Be patient with yourself if you don't get it right the first few times. In my communications course, I give students half a day just to practice the basics of EMP+, because even at the most basic level, it's a real challenge.

Even if you're a neutral third party helping two other people work through this process, it can still be hard. It's easy to unconsciously take sides without meaning to—and the moment you do, the entire process starts to fall apart.

Here are some additional tips for using EMP+ effectively:

- When you're listening to someone, listen *only* with the intent to reflect your understanding — not to reply with your own thoughts or arguments. The moment you start thinking about what you're going to say next, you're no longer really listening. You'll miss the heart of what they're saying, and when you try to check in with "Is that right?", it will land flat — or even make things worse.

- If the other person says something you want to respond to, don't address it right away. Just write it down so you don't forget. Ask them to pause for a moment and let them know what they're saying is important—and that you want to write it down so you can come back to it later. I've never had anyone refuse. If anything, it shows you're taking them seriously.

- Even though you're writing it down for your own benefit, it still sends a powerful message of goodwill. Focus *only* on reflecting what you hear, and you really can't get this step wrong. You'll be concentrating so closely on remembering their words and feelings that it naturally pushes out the urge to plan your next move.

- Attempt to reflect so succinctly, perfectly, and thoughtfully that the other person says, "Wow! I couldn't have said it better myself" or, "I wish I'd thought to say it that way." Use statements and not questions to make this easier.

- After they respond with a "No" in Step Three (is there anything else?) you should do three more things as appropriate:
  - Mention anything you've learned
  - List any points of agreement
  - Apologize for anything that you are genuinely sorry for. You aren't giving in, but if you raised your voice and it upset the other person and you really didn't want to do that, then it's appropriate to apologize for just that part.

Now would be a good time to go back and review the "lessons learned" section of this chapter—because it will make a lot more sense now. This form of communication is like learning a new language. It has its own rules. It's incredibly hard to do. A lot of times, what the other person says won't make any sense to you. You have to get it right every time. You'll need to stop and think carefully about what you're going to say—and how you're going to say it. You are 100% responsible for every part of the process. And it will take a lifetime to master.

Just like Green Beret missions, nothing moves forward until the other side feels that you genuinely understand what their world looks like.

Your Turn
And now, finally, it's your turn to talk. But just like listening, there are some rules for this part, too. Why? Because if you want the other person to actually *hear* you — not just endure

you — you have to speak in a way that keeps them open. If you "cut their ears" by yelling, accusing, or calling them names, they'll shut down fast. You won't change their mind — you'll just harden it.

The moment you push too hard, you lose them. And no matter how right you are, you'll just be wasting your breath and getting more frustrated because they're no longer listening. If the goal is to be heard — and it is — then how you speak matters just as much as what you say.

But, that's not their fault. You are also *completely responsible* for this part of the conversation as well, which is why I say you must take 100% responsibility for empathetic communication.

Is this incredibly unfair? Absolutely. It's completely one-sided and this is why we have to work on our foundation before we learn this skill because otherwise we will not have the strength, courage, or consideration to do it at all, much less do it well. Just remember the ultimate benefits of communicating this way far outweigh the temporary pain.

There are three simple steps to speaking as well: discuss actions, avoid "you" statements, and give them a "because". Again, sounds easy right?

Step One: Describe actions, not people! If you want them to listen, don't talk about *them,* talk about what happened and *separate the person from the action.* No one (except someone who loves you immensely and is trained in EMP+) is going to stand there and continue to listen to you if the only thing you say is how terrible they are. If you are calling them "stupid," and their ideas "ridiculous," you are just making the problem worse.

No name calling. Ever. Words have power and you can never take it back after you call your loved one "a piece of garbage." Those insults stay with them forever even if you did not mean them. And if you call them names every time you have a disagreement, over time those constant insults will erode your relationship with them. You can apologize later, but an idea will remain in the back of their mind that what you really think of them only comes out when you're angry.

Instead of attacking their character, describe the action that upset you. Use phrasing like: "When you said I looked fat in those jeans," or "When you didn't put the sweetener packets in the garbage," or "When [specific action] happened." People can change their actions much more easily than they can change their character. And often, they didn't even realize their actions might upset you. They're not an asshole because they didn't put the lid on the garbage can correctly—they just didn't do it the way you prefer. The "action" sentence is immediately followed by...

Step Two: use "I" statements. Specifically the words "I felt" (angry, sad, unloved, frustrated, livid, confused, hurt, etc.). This step is merely adding those words to the end of your first sentence. Examples:

- "When you said I looked fat in those jeans, **I felt** sad and angry."
- "When the boss came over and accused us of not working hard and you didn't tell her that I had actually done my part, **I felt** deflated and betrayed."
- "When you yelled at the other driver for cutting in front of us, **it startled me** and **I felt** frustrated and scared.

Don't use words like "it made me feel." Instead use "I felt." While subtle, you are always 100% in charge of your own feelings and emotions and you might think that when someone else yells at you it *makes* you angry, but it doesn't make you do anything unless you let it. Never give up your power or agency to someone else.

This is graduate-level EMP+ thinking, but it's never too early to start practicing this. We will never be able to control what another person does, thinks, or feels. The only thing we have complete control over is our own thoughts, feelings, and actions. So own it. No one can "make" you do anything unless you're weak enough to let them.

Step Three: explain why. Specifically, use the word "because." This is the most powerful part of your statement—it gives the other person a chance to understand why something upset you. While it might seem obvious, this is the step most people skip. People often don't realize the effect their actions have on others. They probably didn't mean to upset you—they just didn't know how you were going to perceive what they said or did, so they had no way to anticipate your reaction.

What we're really dealing with here is a cognitive bias known as false consensus or egocentricity—the assumption that everyone thinks the same way we do. If something makes sense to me, and I consider myself intelligent, educated, lucid, and reasonable, then *of course* others will think exactly the same—unless, of course, they're not intelligent, educated, lucid, or reasonable. It's easy to spot this bias when we watch heated political debates between people with opposing views. That's often why those arguments devolve into name-calling. What we're not as good at is recognizing this bias in ourselves.

Unfortunately, our egocentricity shows up most often with the people we care about. You may have heard of the idea of love languages - words or actions that make us feel loved. In many relationships, at least one of those love languages doesn't make sense to the other person.

For example, Person A might feel that acts of service, like loading the dishwasher, are a clear expression of love. To them, it says, "I love you." But to someone else, that might sound completely absurd. How could putting dishes away mean "I love you"?

Half of you reading this are probably thinking, "Well, duh—of course it does." The other half is thinking, "What? That's ridiculous. No one actually believes that."

When Person A (John) assumes his partner thinks and feels the same way he does, he might start to feel angry or frustrated with Person B (Robin) because she never does the dishes, even if it's not her chore. For John, it doesn't matter who's responsible for loading the dishwasher. To him, love means that every once in a while, Robin will do one of his chores just to show she cares.

But if acts of service doesn't mean love to Robin, she's probably not going to do the dishes, and at some point, an argument may break out that leaves her wondering what the hell is going on. The argument makes no sense to her. And now Robin starts getting upset too, because from her perspective, John is angry at her for no reason.

The third step of EMP+ (using the word "because") clarifies what's going on and the two people can actually start to understand each other. If John was trained in EMP+, putting all three steps together would look something like this:

When I work late and I come home and you haven't done the dishes (step one), I feel sad and unloved (step two) because (step three) if you really loved me, you'd take care of those for me every once in a while so when I come home I can just relax and not have to do more work.

If Robin were trained in EMP+, she'd probably still look at John like he had a third eye in the middle of his forehead—because what he's saying doesn't make any sense to her. But she'd keep her cool and walk through Steps One and Two. "You think doing the dishes means I love you? And if I don't do them occasionally, it means I don't love you? Is that right?"

Being 100% responsible for every part of communication is hard. Even when you're using EMP+, it's likely the untrained person will get more upset—and the trained partner will have to stay calm and keep using the process, even as emotions escalate.

Egocentrism plays a role here, too. John loves Robin and thinks she's reasonable, so *of course* Robin must think the same way he does. That means she must know that "acts of service" equals love—so if she's not doing the dishes, it's on purpose!

And to make things worse, it seems like Robin is *pretending* not to understand the argument—which only escalates things. *She's doing that on purpose, too!* And if your partner is intentionally doing something to hurt you, then of course they must be a jerk, so it's totally appropriate to call them a jerk!

It's at this point John (or anyone) will often start name-calling or assigning motivations to the other person ("You don't love me! You're a jerk because you don't do the dishes!").

Can you see how something like this could easily spiral into a major argument, with each person convinced the other is being completely unreasonable? And how a couple might keep having the same fight over and over—simply because neither one understands what the other is actually thinking?

Any solid form of empathetic communication short-circuits this kind of miscommunication. It helps people focus on the real issue instead of getting pulled into the black hole. Because if Robin isn't trained in EMP+, she could easily, and justifiably, from her perspective, get angry at John for giving her a hard time about something that isn't even her chore. How dare he? What a jerk!

Now both people are calling each other names, and the argument just keeps spiraling out of control.

Steps for Empathetic+ Communication (EMP+ "EmPlus")

GUIDANCE:	SPEAKER	LISTENER	GUIDANCE:
* "Because" is critical. * Avoid YOU statements whenever possible. State facts and don't assign motivations - 'you did this because you were ...' or "you were mean" - instead, stick to the protocol. * Keep items short enough that the other person can remember / restate - one item at a time. You'll get through all of them. * ALWAYS let the other person go first (unless you are the one bringing up a subject in the first place). Letting them go first and successfully reflecting will build a significant amount of goodwill and make it far more likely that they will listen to you.	1. When ____ happened (when you said ____) 2. I felt ____ 3. Because ____	1. **Reflect:** When I said/did ___, you felt ___ because ___ 2. **Confirm:** Is that right? 3. **Ask:** Is there More? ... after "no" ... (optional) • Mention anything you've learned • List any points of agreement • Apologize (if appropriate)	* Listen ONLY with the intent to understand. You may take notes so you don't worry about forgetting something. Your job is to LISTEN so you can reflect, build trust, and give them "air." * If caught off guard, you can always start with "You're upset" to give you a few moments to listen. * Reflect: Statements, not questions. Attempt to reflect so clearly, vividly, and fairly that the other person says, "wow, thanks! I wish I'd thought of saying it that way." * Your INTENT is most important. It's OK to get it wrong, they'll correct you and then reflect again. * Confirm: If "NO", ask speaker to say it again; reflect until you get a 'yes." * Ask: If yes, allow them to state the next point and reflect. If no, ask if you may state your point of view. It is YOUR responsibility to get your point across respectfully, and in the way that they best understand.

YOU are 100% responsible for EMP+ Communication.

© 2023 Robert W. Schaefer | All rights reserved | Use only with permission

Here's the protocol again. Now that it makes sense, you can actually use it as a tool. It's designed for both people to follow, but you can use it solo. When I'm running a conflict resolution session, I give these rules to both sides and make it clear that we're all going to use them—I coach everyone through the process to keep it on track.[30]

That said, it's probably not going to work if you suddenly whip this out in the middle of an argument with your spouse or kids and demand they follow it. I don't recommend that. What does work is talking about how you'd like to handle conflict before the next argument happens—and introducing these steps as part of that conversation.

Putting It All Together
Even if the other person doesn't want to try EMP+, you can still use the protocol effectively on your own. You'll especially see how powerful it is during arguments with your kids. If you think your partner or coworkers have some wild ideas, remember—teenagers' brains are still developing. They will genuinely believe things that feel inconceivable to the rest of us.

It's not just about pushing boundaries or seeking independence. Research shows that the brain continues developing into the mid-20s. So not only do your kids think differently than you—they think differently than their future selves will. EMP+ helps you work through those tough moments with empathy and structure. And if you can use EMP+ effectively with kids, using it with your team—or even your boss—will feel like a piece of cake.

When an argument starts (or you've recognized the need to use EMP+), let them go first so that they will feel understood. Once they feel *completely* understood they are far more willing to listen to what you have to say.

---

[30] There is additional guidance for third-party conflict resolution facilitators, but that's beyond the scope of this book.

If you are the one initiating a conversation about a sensitive topic, you'll start as the speaker and *expect* the other person to get defensive and begin justifying their actions. Immediately switch to "listener" mode and RCA – Reflect, Confirm, and Ask for more – as they talk about how they feel about your original statement. Once they're done, you switch back over to the speaker using the "action, feelings, because" protocol.

Following the protocol is extremely important because one little slip can cause a conversation to go sideways in a heartbeat. We must separate the individual from their actions! So we don't talk about them, we don't accuse them, we don't call them names or assign motivations to their actions. Instead we use "I" statements and talk about ourselves.

"When you promise to come home by 10 p.m. and don't make it back until after 2" (Step One), "I get so worried" (Step Two), "because I know you're a good kid, so in my mind, all I can think is that you've been in an accident or someone's hurt you" (Step Three). They can come up with a thousand reasons why they should be allowed to stay out later, but they can't argue with the fact that you worry because you love them.

They'll respond with, "But Jennifer gets to stay out later!" And you'll reflect: "So because Jennifer gets to stay out later, you think you should be able to as well. Is that right?" (Wait for confirmation.) "Is there more?"

Then they might say, "The only reason you don't let me stay out later is because you don't trust me!" And you'll reflect again: "You feel like the reason we don't let you stay out later is because we don't trust you. Is that right?" (Wait for confirmation.) "What else?"

Eventually, they'll run out of reasons—or start to realize their argument doesn't hold up. But more importantly, you'll notice something shift: the conversation stays calmer. Kids often struggle to feel heard by their parents. But when they see that we're really listening—even if we don't agree—it takes the fight out of the argument.

By using EMP+, and sticking with it even when it's hard, you'll eventually reach a moment when your kid looks at you and says something like, "So what do we do?" And because they really listened to you (because you listened to them first), they'll offer good suggestions. And if they don't, you simply stay in the process and respond with: "But if you do that" (Step One), "I'll still feel worried" (Step Two), "because..." (Step Three).

One of the hardest parts of using EMP+ is that you have to think before you speak. Just like with a foreign language, you have to find the right words - and the right way to say them. It also forces you to actually consider *why* you're upset or worried, instead of just reacting in anger. *You're going to respond, not react.*

And that pause, while you gather your thoughts, is a good thing. It shows the other person that you're working hard, that you're taking them seriously, that you respect them. It also gives everyone a little space to cool down, which keeps the conversation productive.

With practice, you'll be able to communicate effectively with anyone, even about the hardest topics, even if they have no training or are resistant to hearing your point of view. That's why I'm so confident this will change your life. When you take 100% responsibility for every part of the conversation, you'll be able to work real magic. You'll improve your relationships dramatically, even if the other person has no idea what you're doing.

Becoming a Lion Whisperer

You will rarely face anything at work as difficult as what you experience in your personal life. So if you can use EMP+ effectively at home, you can use it anywhere. As the leader of an elite team, you must be proficient in empathetic communication to motivate your lions. They're incredibly smart and talented—and if you don't truly listen to them, they will mentally dismiss your intelligence and lose all respect for you.

So, how and when will you use EMP+ at work? The answer is: **everywhere, and all the time.** First, you'll establish a culture of respect, teamwork, and trust—especially when you teach your team how to use EMP+ and insist they use it with each other when issues arise. Making sure everyone is heard and understood is the best way to ensure diversity of thought—and that's how you and your team will always make the best decisions. You'll also see immediate results when interacting with:

Clients and customers. The most obvious time to use EMP+ is when a client or customer is upset: *"So you're saying the last shipment of widgets wasn't the quality we agreed on, correct? Okay, what else?"* But EMP+ goes beyond solving problems. You should use it at the beginning of every client relationship and with each new project or order. Don't assume you know what they want, use EMP+ to make sure there are no mismatched expectations: *"So the most important part of this project is completing it on time, am I right? Okay, what else matters?"* Continue using EMP+ at each project check-in to keep things on track. In fact, there's at least one very popular, well-respected, and expensive "selling system" that's built entirely around this process.

Your boss and your peers. When your boss, or anyone else in the organization, gets angry, EMP+ is the fastest way to deescalate the situation, whether that anger is directed at you or not. Don't argue. Shift immediately into listener mode and use RCA: Reflect, Confirm, and Ask for more, just like you would with your kids. Eventually, they'll run out of steam. At that point, you'll have the space to either share your point of view (if the anger was directed at you) or offer new information they didn't have (if it was about someone else).

Evaluations. The art of leadership is getting people to do what you want them to do because they want to do it. As discussed earlier, this comes down to aligning goals and expectations. You use EMP+ at the beginning of a rating period to make sure everyone is 100% clear on what success looks like—metrics, resources provided, the parameters they'll need to follow, the methods for accountability, and the consequences, both good and bad, for meeting or missing goals. Using this approach with lions gives them the autonomy they need to excel and allows them to manage themselves.

At the end of the rating period, there shouldn't be any question about whether the metrics were achieved. That means there won't be any uncomfortable conversations. However, until you're fully proficient with the evaluation process, you'll still run into the occasional issue. In those cases, you'll use EMP+ at the end of the cycle to talk everything through. Your team members will appreciate this way of doing business, and your boss will, too—especially when you structure the same type of agreement for yourself.

Conflict within your team. If you need to facilitate conflict resolution between team members (or family) you become the impartial facilitator, and EMP+ is both your tool and your rule book. Your role is not to be "the boss" who eventually picks a winner, unless the disagreement is about a specific course of action. Rather, you serve as a neutral referee. Your job is to help both sides work it out by guiding the conversation and making sure everyone sticks to the process.

In these cases, give both parties a copy of the protocol, keep one for yourself, and have a notepad ready to take notes. As their supervisor, you have the authority to enforce the rules. Expect the session to last at least an hour. But plan for at least twice that time in preparation—because if you want it to succeed, you'll begin by meeting with each person individually, giving them space to vent while you practice being the Listener: Reflect, Confirm, and Ask (RCA) for more.

This accomplishes two very important things. First, it gives you a clearer picture of the real problem. And often, while you're listening, something will click—you'll have an "aha" moment and see exactly where things went off track between them. But when that happens, *do not* simply explain what the real issue is to the other person during their individual session. *It doesn't matter if you know what the problem is*, what matters is both parties come to that realization on their own from working through the process and *being heard by the other person*. Each person must have their own "aha" moment and your job is to lead them there. Knowing what the issue is ahead of time will help you guide the conversation in that direction. But don't rush it. It's critical that both sides fully air everything they're upset about.

The second reason you meet with both parties individually before bringing them together is to "pre-exhaust" them. Both sides are angry. Both are frustrated that the other person isn't listening. But venting to their boss, someone who holds authority, is hugely cathartic. Whether or not that other "jerk" ever figures it out, at least the boss knows the "truth."

This is different from venting to a spouse or a friend. You're the boss. That makes it feel official. And once they've said everything to you, they'll be more willing to sit down with the other person—because now, in their mind, the truth is on the record. They're sure the other person will finally have to hear it. And they believe you'll back them up.

Of course, you're not going to say that to either side when you're meeting with them ahead of time because you won't have to. They'll naturally assume that because you've listened to them and ensured they felt understood, that you'll see things their way and so, in their mind, the "conflict resolution session" will really be all about making the other side "see sense."

Do not shortchange the preparation period. This is the most important part of the process. The rule of thumb is to spend twice as much time in prep (talking to both sides) as the actual session will take. If this is a long-entrenched problem, there may be a lot to work through, and the session itself might take a long time. But by listening carefully and understanding the issues from both sides, you can guide the conversation so the most important and contentious issues get addressed first. And usually, once two or three of those are resolved, the rest tend to fall away—because they're no longer worth holding onto for either person.

Being able to handle conflicts between your lions will boost your reputation across the organization. It's one of the most visible signs of real leadership. Not only will you have shown that you know how to listen to individuals and align their goals with the team's goals to drive success, you'll have proven that you can calm angry lions and get the team back on track, working together again. There isn't a person in the world who doesn't respect that ability.

Negotiating. The art of negotiating is a specialty, and there are plenty of books and seminars on the subject. Most negotiating techniques are built around helping you win, or at least not lose. Little thought is usually given to what the other side gets, as long as your side comes out ahead. In the short term, that approach can work—if you don't care about maintaining the relationship. But if you've ever been on the losing end of a deal, you know how resentment builds. When you feel like you got "screwed," you're always looking for a way to get back at the other side. And if circumstances shift and you find yourself in a stronger position, you won't hesitate to make up for what you lost, and then some, in any renegotiation.

However that method isn't effective in maintaining long-term relationships - whether they be family members, clients, vendors, suppliers, or any other valued relationship. What happens in a marriage if one person always insists on winning and never listens to the other person? *All strong, lasting relationships are mutually beneficial.*

Moreover, you can never know if an organization (or someone else) may be important in your future. Especially in business, circumstances change, and a current competitor may be a valued supplier in the future. For long-term growth and sustainability, always keep in mind during any negotiation that today's adversary might be tomorrow's most important partner, customer, or supplier.

EMP+ Negotiating™ is based on the Special Forces Decision-Making Process (discussed in Chapter Seven) and is designed to always discover the best solutions to any issue. And what is a negotiation, if not a set of issues that need to be resolved?

Whereas standard negotiation strategy positions the two parties as adversaries, EMP+ Negotiating™ makes the well-being of important relationships a requirement for arriving at the best solution. This method always assumes that every relationship is worth maintaining and works to ensure that both sides get what they need, (though not necessarily everything they want), in order to be successful.

EMP+ Negotiating training is beyond the scope of this book, but its engine is the protocol we've already discussed—using EMP+ to discover the needs and wants of both parties. The "because" is especially important in negotiation, because one side may believe a need can only be met in a specific way, while the other side might know of a different solution that fulfills the need and benefits both parties.

While the process generally takes longer and requires greater dedication to finding the best solutions, EMP+ Negotiating™ is successful because, when done effectively, it allows both parties to arrive at outcomes that are far better than either side could have conceived on their own. By making the health of the long-term relationship a requirement, it also allows for the option of a friendly no-deal—where both sides agree that they can't meet each other's needs and part amicably, without a deal this time. But because of the mutual respect built during the negotiation, it's usually only a matter of time before those same parties are able to work out a deal on something else.

Performance Issues. In my experience, what new or inexperienced leaders hate the most is dealing with a team member's poor performance or bad behavior. Most of us don't like conflict, and we tend to assume that any conversation about performance will turn contentious. On top of that, newer team members may not value constructive feedback, which creates a real fear that saying something could actually make the situation worse.

Most managers are never trained to handle confrontation. They don't have any tools, they haven't done anything to mitigate their fear, and the people they ask for advice usually don't have any training either. So they avoid confrontation, or they half-address it until things get bad—then they lash out in anger and resentment. Additionally, the team members who are performing well will start to lose respect for a manager who doesn't deal with conflict and allows different standards for different people.

Difficult conversations are an example of "good communication." Letting someone know about an issue they need to improve on is actually a gift and it shows that you care about them. This is coaching and it requires discipline, courage, and consideration to get effective results.

EMP+ is the tool that allows you to do this well. First, it provides a clear protocol for addressing issues. But more importantly, it helps people solve their own performance or behavior problems. Why? Because we flip the usual script.

Instead of opening a counseling session by telling someone what they're doing wrong—that's confrontational—we listen. We make sure the time and place are right, and instead of confronting them, we ask what's going on. Then we reflect.

Manager: "Thanks for coming in, Jim. How are things? How's your family? Tell me how things are going with your project. Are there any issues you need help with?" Note: Jim probably knows why he's been called in. This gives him a chance to bring up his recent tardiness on his own terms. If he does, reflect and help him work through it. If he doesn't, and after he's had a chance to talk (and you've listened), you can bring it up.
Manager: "I've noticed lately that you've been coming in late. You've never done that before. Is something going on? Is there a problem somewhere that I can help you with?"
Jim: "Well, you know, traffic has gotten worse, and so sometimes I just don't make it on time."
Manager: "So you're saying the reason you've been late is because traffic has gotten worse. Is that right? Is there more?"
Jim: "Uh, yeah, that's right. And no, nothing else."
Manager: "Could this be affecting others in the office?" *Notice there's no "you" or accusations.*
Jim: "No, not really. We all work on our own stuff, so it's not a big deal."
Manager: "But what about Jill? She has to turn in her financial reports every morning by 10 a.m., and she needs your data—with time to analyze it—before she can turn it in. So when she gets the data from you later than usual (step 1 -describe actions), she feels upset and frantic (step 2 - describe

feelings) because she's afraid she won't get her work done on time (step 3 - because)."

Jim: "Oh, yeah, I guess I forgot about that. Did she get in trouble because some of her reports were late?"

Manager: "Yeah. She's been late a few times in the past month, and people get angry and blame *her* when that happens. She just hasn't felt comfortable talking to you about it because she's new and you've been here for a while."

Jim: "Oh. sorry. I didn't realize that. I need to go and apologize to her. She's nice and I don't want to put her in that situation. I guess I need to start leaving a few minutes earlier. They're doing construction around my house and it's taking forever. But I've still been leaving the house at the same time figuring the construction would be over any day."

Can you see the difference? There's no confrontation. Instead of getting defensive, Jim is being led through the conversation, realizes his behavior is affecting other people, and comes up with the solution himself. The manager is still using the EMP+ speaker protocol, even though he's talking about Jill. There's nothing in that conversation that would make Jim feel attacked. If anything, he'll be thankful you brought it up—because he doesn't want Jill to resent him.

Remember the idea of paradigm shifts? That's what you're helping Jim do—see the impact of his behavior from someone else's point of view. And if this is all there is to it, Jim will decide on his own to start showing up on time.

More often than not, when a good employee starts having performance issues, there's something else going on. In the case above, after using EMP+ and making Jim feel safe, any underlying issues will eventually surface—even things Jim hadn't realized himself. It's the process that brings those deeper issues to light.

And while it might feel like the meeting is taking far more time than it should (this talk could last well over an hour, compared to the quick "Jim, you've been late—don't let it happen again"), *it's actually much faster* than the usual methods. Why? Because you only have the difficult conversation once—and Jim solves the issue himself, quickly and permanently.

In this case, after using EMP+ for 20 minutes and discussing his tardiness, Jim says something like, "It's just so hard to get up in the mornings lately. I'm not sleeping well at night." Aha! Now we're getting somewhere. Now you're addressing the root cause—not just the symptom. At this point, you know exactly what to do: Reflect, Confirm, Ask for more.

Maybe Jim is having problems with his spouse, his kids, PTSD, financial stress—who knows. By staying with the process, you've done more than just manage. You've shown that you actually care about Jim and what's going on. You might be the first person he's ever opened up to about this. And this might be the first time he really feels understood.

That's the moment you stop being "just the manager." That's the moment you become a leader in Jim's eyes.

And maybe at the end, you let him know the company has resources that could help. But even if all you've done is listen and reflect, you'll have helped Jim—and he'll be far more likely to come up with his own solution to both the tardiness and the deeper issue.

Having difficult conversations is a deep topic that deserves its own book. The key to success is using empathetic communication through EMP+. If you approach any difficult situation with the right attitude, if you genuinely want to understand the problem and solve it, and you use EMP+, sticking with the process even when it gets hard, you'll achieve significantly better results.

Conclusion

Empathetic communication may appear simple, but it's often harder than even the most difficult foreign language. But you can't be a leader without being able to communicate—and if you're going to lead lions, you'll need to become a "lion whisperer." That means ensuring they feel understood, aligning their goals with the organization's, and helping them work through thorny issues. The definition I offered earlier should make more sense now.

> Real Communication is genuine Generosity of Spirit that makes knowledge sharing an integral part of leadership. It's knowing when empathetic communication is needed and having the skill to do it well. It's the discipline to do all of that regularly—even when you don't want to, and especially when the other person doesn't want to hear it. And finally, it's a commitment to coach the rest of the team to ensure they do it, too.

It should now be obvious why "language school" comes after assessment and the Q-Course. It takes a lot of Character to communicate this way. There's a lot to learn—on top of the unfair burden of taking full responsibility for doing all the work all the time. Even when others are yelling at you,

you have to keep your cool, follow the rules, get it right every time, think carefully about what to say and how to say it, and stick with the process even when every part of you wants to walk away.

And yet, it's all worth it—because you'll have the life you want. A life full of deep, meaningful, lasting relationships, both at work and at home. And you and your team will do what others think is impossible. *Routinely.*

CHAPTER FIVE

Airborne and SERE

MASTER YOUR FEAR

The greatest obstacle to becoming a great leader isn't incompetence or inexperience — it's fear. When we manage through fear, we constantly sabotage our team's potential for success — often without even knowing it. Fear rarely shows up as panic; it hides in hesitation, control, defensiveness, avoidance, micromanagement, or blame. In this chapter, we'll confront that head-on. You'll learn a scientifically proven, repeatable process that shows you how to lead from opportunity, not fear. No one is born courageous — not even Green Berets. Courage is learned. And once you learn it for yourself, you can teach it to others. That's where great teams begin.

The vast majority of managers I see are fearful. There's the fear of being wrong; of being blamed; of failing; of your people not liking you; of your team not respecting you; of admitting you don't know how to do something; of losing a big client; of missing an opportunity; of taking a chance; of not knowing what to do; of what others think of you; of not getting a raise; of not getting promoted; of others discovering that you don't really know what you're *doing; of being in the background; of not getting the credit; of having your teammates and peers be more successful than you. And those are just the basics. These fears erode the confidence and trust the team has in you, and without that, you will not have the foundation you need to build truly great teams.*

SERE School

There's one final experience Green Berets go through before they're sent to their teams and begin their SF careers. It's technically referred to as a training course, but anyone who's been through the Survival, Evasion, Resistance, and Escape (SERE) Level C Course will tell you that, while there's some outstanding training, SERE is primarily about building resiliency and conquering fear.

What makes it effective isn't just what you go through, it's how it's structured. SERE works because it deliberately exposes you to escalating levels of physical and psychological stress in a controlled way, giving your mind and body the tools to adapt. In doing so, it mirrors what scientists refer to as "stress inoculation." The process builds a kind of internal resistance—an ability to recognize fear, stay grounded inside it, and still make decisions. That ability isn't theoretical. It's trained. And it lasts.[31]

---

31 The concept of *stress inoculation* was developed by psychologist Donald Meichenbaum in the 1970s. It's a form of resilience training that uses gradual, controlled exposure to stressors to help individuals develop cognitive and emotional tools for managing fear, anxiety, and high-pressure environments. See: Meichenbaum, D. (2007). *Stress Inoculation Training: A preventative and treatment approach*. In Lehrer, Woolfolk & Sime (Eds.), *Principles and Practice of Stress Management*. Guilford Press.

Some details of the SERE Level C course are restricted (and some are classified) primarily because much of the effectiveness of SERE would be lost if students knew exactly what to expect ahead of time. But there's still much about the course we can discuss, especially as it relates to its methodology.

The original SERE school was started by the US Army Air Forces during WWII to teach pilots how to survive if they were shot down or had to make emergency landings behind enemy lines or in inhospitable areas. During WWII, the U.S. Navy discovered that 75% of pilots who were shot down or forced into emergency landings made it down alive, yet ultimately, only 5% survived until they could be recovered because they didn't know how to find food, fresh water, create shelters to protect themselves from the elements, or even swim.

Because of the efficacy of the first course, multiple survival courses soon popped up around the country in areas that reflected their regional aspects (ocean, jungle, arctic, etc.) and focused primarily on physical survival. However, during the Korean War, enemy forces did not abide by the articles of the Geneva Convention regarding the treatment of prisoners of war and the schools began to address darker aspects of survival like how to endure torture and prisoner-of-war camps so U.S. service personnel could return to the U.S. with their honor intact (by not assisting the enemy, especially by not revealing information that would harm other U.S. forces).

In the early 1980s, Green Beret Colonel Nick Rowe helped design and implement a new SERE training program based on his five years in a North Vietnamese POW camp. In addition to survival training, the new course also exposed soldiers to the harsh reality of becoming a POW and taught them how to resist interrogation and maintain their morale and discipline while in captivity.

His experience showed that fear isn't eliminated by willpower—it's reshaped through repetition, reflection, and recovery. SERE became a way to systematize that transformation so others didn't have to suffer the way he did to learn it.

When I went through the Q-Course as an enlisted soldier, SERE school wasn't a requirement because there was still a week of survival training built into Phase 1. That was a great week of instruction on all aspects of survival in a wooded environment (where it was assumed most Green Berets would find themselves) and was capped off by a three-day individual survival exercise with a list of things that had to be accomplished. You were only able to take a few items with you: a knife, a small amount of 550 cord, a box of matches, a rain poncho, your canteen and canteen cup, and a signal mirror – items that a Green Beret was expected to carry on their person at all times.

We made fish hooks out of bones and used the guts of 550 cord for fishing lines and gill nets, started and kept a fire going at all times, made traps for game (and hopefully caught something so we'd have something to eat). We could survive three days without food if we didn't catch fish or game, but it was tough if you didn't. One of my buddies got so hungry on the third day that he dug up the bones of some small thing he'd killed and cooked and sucked the maggots right off the bones.

Different Levels Based on Mission

When I went back through the Q-Course as an officer, the week of survival training in Phase 1 had been replaced by an additional week of small unit tactics because the SERE Level C course had become a requirement for graduation. (Note: The following information about SERE training is publicly available and unclassified.)

There are three levels of SERE training that are progressively more demanding. Overall, the SERE program is designed to prepare military personnel for the worst-case scenario and to give them the skills and knowledge they need to survive in hostile environments and evade capture if necessary.

But more than that, it teaches you how to operate inside fear without being consumed by it. And the way it does that is systematic. SERE doesn't just throw you into chaos—it walks you through it step by step: education, tools, exposure, experience, and then repetition. That's what inoculation really is. You're exposed to fear in controlled doses, long enough to adapt, but not long enough to break. Over time, that changes how you respond.[32]

Level A is the basic level of SERE training. It covers the fundamentals of survival in the wilderness, including how to find and purify water, build a shelter, start a fire, and find food. It also covers basic navigation skills, such as how to use a map and compass. Additionally, it teaches evasion techniques to avoid being captured and how to use basic communication devices such as radios. Anyone in the military is eligible for Level A.

---

32 Controlled exposure to fear activates the brain's threat detection systems, but repeated exposure under safe conditions reduces reactivity in the amygdala and strengthens regulatory pathways in the prefrontal cortex. This allows individuals to recognize fear signals without becoming overwhelmed by them. See: Schiller, D., Levy, I., et al. (2009). "Preventing the return of fear in humans using reconsolidation update mechanisms." Nature, 463(7277), 49–53.

SERE Level B is more selective and designed for anyone deployed to a combat zone. It builds on the skills learned in SERE Level A and includes more advanced survival skills, such as how to find and prepare wild edibles, how to navigate without a compass or map, and how to build more advanced shelters. It also includes training on how to resist interrogation and torture techniques.

SERE Level C is the most advanced. It's primarily for special operations forces, pilots, military attaches and others who are at a high risk of being abducted, captured, held hostage, and tortured. Level C has three phases: Survival, Evasion, and Resistance. The Survival Phase is the first part of Level C and it was pretty much the same as the survival phase from the Q-Course.

During the evasion phase, students learn how to navigate through hostile territory without being detected. They learn how to create improvised tools and weapons, how to use camouflage and concealment to blend in with their surroundings, and how to navigate without a compass or map. The field exercise during this phase is a hands-on test where students are hunted for days by "enemy forces" with tracking dogs and have to evade capture and survive while on the move using whatever is available. Ultimately though, this phase ends with being captured no matter how well you evade during the exercise.

During the Resistance phase students are placed in a mock prison camp where the cadre treats them like POWs and subjects them to individual and collective tests of their training and ability to resist interrogation, exploitation, and torture techniques that may be used against them. There's little food, less sleep, and exposure to great discomfort throughout the phase which, when combined with the previous phase, creates exhausted and frazzled students which allow the cadre to test them at their limits.

There are many stories and legends about what students endure during the prison camp portion of the Level C course. What I can say is that the Prison Camp phase was definitely one of the worst suckfests of my life, but it was also probably the best training I've ever had. It didn't just change what I thought I could endure — it redefined it.

While the stated purpose of the course is to prepare Green Berets for worst-case scenarios and give them the skills and knowledge they need to survive in the worst environments, the most important goal of the course is to instill resilience, which is intertwined with fear in a complex relationship. Developing resilience can help individuals manage fear, while facing and overcoming fear can also build resilience.

Not only do operators gain the knowledge and skills to survive in conditions that would kill most people, facing and overcoming their fears helps them develop a sense of mastery and confidence which can increase their resilience in future challenges. Moreover, building resilience is a form of inoculation against stress and adversity, not just against those circumstances they've been exposed to, but all types of fear and adversity in general. Just as a vaccine can prepare the immune system to fight off a virus, developing resilience prepares Green Berets to cope with significant challenges and fear itself.

We can use that same methodology when it comes to overcoming our own fears. It is a gradual 5-Step process that starts with **education** (explaining and fully understanding the types of dangers to expect in different environments), providing strategies for dealing with those dangers (**training and tools**), and placing students in controlled scenarios where they can practice those strategies (**exposure and experience**), which ultimately results in **inoculation**.

That's a BIG deal. The most validated and widely used methods in clinical psychology offer powerful tools for *reactive* treatment of fear - after the damage is done. But none of them provide a unified, *preventative*, stepwise process that makes the mechanisms explicit, repeatable, and teachable the way this one does. That's why we'll be using this process to inoculate our own fears, doubts, and self-protection reflexes.

There is one more required school for Green Berets. It's also designed to teach you to conquer fear. And while we can't talk about all the aspects of SERE, we can freely discuss Airborne School.

U.S. Army Airborne School
For Green Berets, special operations, and other airborne forces, using a parachute is just a way to get to work. Whereas most people drive cars or take the metro to the office or job site, special operations forces often rely on parachutes to get into their area of operations because almost all SF missions are conducted behind enemy lines. As such, prospective Green Berets must graduate U.S. Army Airborne School *before* showing up to the Q-Course because "air ops" are a basic method of infiltration and most Q-Course training missions incorporate them into the scenarios.

Winged Badge of Courage

However, the vast majority of soldiers going through Airborne School are not prospective Green Berets and most Airborne School grads *never* jump out of a plane again after they've completed their required five jumps. That's because Jump Wings are by far the most widely earned "volunteer" badge in the Army and you'll find members from every service branch in every Airborne School class. Why? Because airborne training is one of the best ways in the world to *confront and overcome fear* and those jump wings, worn proudly above your heart, is a conspicuous "winged badge of courage."

Old airborne school training posters are festooned with slogans like "it's the last step to becoming a man," "it's a real man's life," "if you've got the guts," and "Airborne - the Finest." Airborne jokes are full of off-color humor like "Why did I become a paratrooper? Because baseball, football, and basketball only require one ball." "Airborne - balls so big we need a bag around our waist just to carry them" (refers to the fact that when jumping with your rucksack you wear it attached to the front of your legs). And "Nads, you either have them or you don't" (with a large Airborne symbol at the bottom of the poster.

While this may seem sexist, don't say that to female paratroopers. They are just as proud (if not prouder) of the fact that they have more guts than most of the male soldiers in the Army.

While we'll see that Airborne School uses the same formula for fear inoculation that I've outlined already, the in-your-face bravado described above is incredibly important, as it is key to a secondary (supplementary) means of conquering fear: shame. Functionally, it is pitting one fear against another.

It's well documented that soldiers don't fight for their country as much as they do for their buddies to their left and right. All the posters, jokes, and mocking nicknames for "non-airborne" personnel are designed to make airborne soldiers feel superior, the kind of soldier that doesn't run from fear or battle. Because even though they have the training and should be ready to face the enemy bravely, what really drives them forward into danger is the fear of letting their team down. The fear of losing friends or being seen as someone that the team can't depend on when things get tough (someone too afraid to be airborne) is stronger than their fear of battle or jumping out of a plane. In this case, it's a stronger fear that triggers the "fight" response, rather than "flight" or "freeze".

All that pride and esprit de corps points to one simple fact: airborne operations are inherently dangerous, and they're scary as hell the first 20 or so times you do them. No matter how many jumps you've made, there should always be an edge of concern. It's commonly accepted that the scariest jump most airborne soldiers ever make is their second. You don't really know what to expect on your first; everything's moving fast, people are yelling, and you just go with the flow and jump. But on your second jump, you know exactly what's coming. Volunteering to do it again after living through the terror of the first is a true mark of courage. Knowing you'll be terrified, knowing the risks, and doing it anyway — that's what it means to overcome fear.

So Many Things To Fear

The introduction to this chapter has a laundry list of common fears that leaders, managers, executives, and supervisors face daily. However, when you ask them what their fears are, they can only think of a few, if any. But show them the list and the honest ones nod their heads and say, "Oh yeah, definitely all of those things." There are so many things that can go wrong that we can't even think of them all at once. It's overwhelming.

It's the same with airborne operations. They're far more dangerous than sport parachuting, which is a solo activity with highly maneuverable parachutes and gentle, walk-off landings. Most airborne operations involve hundreds of people — and just like leadership, you have to execute as an individual while also taking care of your team.

I'm going to describe basic air operations so you can understand all the things that can go wrong during a single parachute drop. Then I'll explain how Airborne School is designed to address each of those risks and explain the methods they use because you'll be using them to inoculate yourself against your own fears.

Airborne School lasts three weeks: Ground Week, Tower Week, and Jump Week. Jumping out of a plane safely involves much more than the "jumping out" part — and in fact, that part isn't even the most dangerous. There are plenty of things that can kill you or the rest of your stick (the group of jumpers exiting with you on the same pass), which is why the first two weeks are designed to educate, train, expose, and give students experience in everything they'll do on a real jump — and all the ways it can go wrong. These include:

- **Actions inside the aircraft** make up the longest — and ironically, most dangerous — phase of any airborne operation. A single mistake here can kill a lot of soldiers. Once you've jumped and are actually airborne, even the worst accident typically affects only two or three others. That's why the ability to use hand-and-arm signals alongside shouted instructions — especially when the aircraft doors are open and no one can hear — has to be drilled until it's second nature. On a C-141, that means 150 jumpers responding quickly and precisely. If someone screws up and lets their parachute deploy inside the aircraft while others are already hooked to the static line, the chute will be sucked out the door, dragging 30 or more soldiers into the rear of the aircraft at 130 miles per hour. And even without an emergency, delays inside the aircraft can cause the plane to overfly the drop zone — meaning jumpers could end up in trees, on buildings, or tangled in power lines, where the chances of serious injury or death go way up.

- **Aircraft exit and body control.** A lot can go wrong if a jumper exits the aircraft improperly or fails to maintain correct body position until the parachute opens. This is where most accidents happen and include such dangers as getting caught in the door or being towed in the air bouncing against the outside of the airplane until they can land and drag your body along the tarmac. Poor body positioning accounts for nearly all parachute malfunctions.

- **Controlled descent.** The goal is to avoid colliding with other jumpers and steer your parachute — which offers limited maneuverability — toward a clear landing area rather than a road, power line, or building. But in case you do collide with someone or end up in trees, water, or wires, you're taught emergency procedures to minimize the damage. The last few hundred feet are critical: that's when you release any gear you're carrying (like your rucksack or weapon) and position your body to execute a proper Parachute Landing Fall (PLF).
- **Landing.** Most injuries don't come from jumping. It's the landing that hurts. Malfunctions in the air make for rough landings, but even when everything goes right, you still have to execute a proper PLF. This isn't the smooth "walk-off" landing you see in sport parachuting. With static-line jumps, you don't land — you hit the ground in a controlled fall. Good PLFs come from repetition and muscle memory. Even then, bad PLFs account for most airborne injuries: broken legs, sprained ankles, blown knees, concussions, and more.
- **Parachute Control.** It's not over after the PLF. Even a slight breeze on the drop zone can cause your parachute to re-inflate and drag you — sometimes violently — across the field, risking injury to you and anyone in your path. That's why you have to get up immediately, take control of your chute, and secure it before it does any more damage.

In Airborne School, each of the areas above is taught through a progression. First comes classroom instruction to explain the concept and the "why." Then instructors demonstrate what "right" looks like. After that, students perform the actions on the ground. Finally, most lessons include a training apparatus elevated off the ground to add realism without exposing students to any real injury.

Weeks one and two of Airborne School focus on breaking down every dangerous part of an airborne operation, giving students tools (drills) to execute each task successfully, and then practicing those drills in increasingly realistic scenarios using mock-ups (more tools). After repeated ground practice, exit procedures are rehearsed in a parachute harness attached to a mock aircraft door suspended 34 feet above the ground.

Your body harness is attached to a cable running alongside the mock tower, so when you jump, it closely replicates what you'll experience exiting an actual aircraft. The freefall from the 34-foot tower isn't as long, but it's still real — and when you're standing in the door, 34 feet feels scary as hell. It's just high enough to trigger the same fear response you'll feel in a real jump, but low enough that even if the equipment failed (which it doesn't), there'd be no serious injury. It's a brilliant training tool: it lets you face real fear in a safe environment and repeat the drills until they're second nature. When it's time for the real thing, jumping from the plane is actually easier than the tower.

Tower Week gets its name from the 250-foot towers used to practice turning in the air. Originally built as an attraction for the 1939 New York World's Fair, the 250-foot Jump Towers are another tool to inoculate soldiers against fear and ensure they can perform the key tasks required to control their parachute and land safely. When it's your turn, you're strapped into a parachute harness connected to a fully deployed chute, which is attached to a large metal ring. A cable hauls you 250 feet into the air. Once you give the "okay" to the black hats (Airborne instructors), they release the parachute from the metal ring and you drop. Most students get time for two short turns under canopy before it's time to prepare for their PLF.

But you don't start on the 250-foot tower. First, you do hundreds of PLFs off a shoulder-high platform. It's just high enough to run through all the preparatory steps, generate enough speed to mimic a real landing, and trigger just enough fear to make it matter. In Airborne School, you land in sawdust pits to reduce the risk of injury. But PLF practice doesn't end there. It's part of every pre-jump training for every airborne operation, even after jump school. And *those* platforms? They face cold, hard ground — the same kind jumpers usually land on.

Jump Week is the real thing. Students must complete five parachute jumps from 1,200 feet from a C-130 aircraft. The first jump is a "Hollywood" jump — named because, in the movies, paratroopers never carry their combat gear. In reality, soldiers always jump with their weapons and rucksacks because the jump is just how you get to work. After landing, the mission begins and you need all your gear. But for the first and second jumps, everything is kept as simple as possible. The third jump is usually a combat equipment jump, though the rucksacks are still kept light. At that point, it's more about learning the added complexity than carrying a real load.

Combat equipment jumps require soldiers to rig their rucksacks to their parachute harnesses underneath their reserve chutes, attaching them at the waist. During normal operations this setup makes walking nearly impossible because the rucksacks are heavy and completely block the front of their legs. Because a clean exit is critical, leg straps are routed around the jumper's legs and pulled tight to prevent the ruck from flipping up, slamming you in the face, or catching the jet stream and twisting your body midair. The tighter the straps, the safer the exit — but the harder it is to move inside the aircraft and launch yourself cleanly out the door. Bottom line: there are no perfect exits when you're jumping a ruck.

In addition to the rucksack, a soldier's rifle (or machine gun, shoulder-fired missile, etc.) is packed in a padded case and strapped to their side, further limiting mobility. A true combat equipment jump with a fully loaded ruck is brutally hard. Special Forces mission rucks start at 120 pounds, and having that much weight strapped to your waist makes standing upright a struggle. You don't walk when you're jumping with combat gear — you lean back and waddle like a penguin.

The rucksack and weapon are both attached to a 15-foot lowering line. At around 150 feet above the ground, the jumper pulls a release strap that disconnects the leg straps securing the ruck to the body and lets it hang 15 feet below. This creates enough clearance to execute a proper PLF without slamming into your own gear on landing. The weapons case is also secured to the lowering line, and once the ruck is lowered, the jumper pulls a second release to let the weapon drop as well. The lowering line is critical — you can't perform a safe PLF with 120+ pounds strapped to the front of your legs. Ask any paratrooper who's had to "burn in" with a ruck and a weapon, and they'll have quite the story to tell.

The fourth jump is a night combat equipment jump, adding another layer of complexity to everything students have trained for. The challenge with night jumps is that you can't see the ground. Depending on the moonlight, you may not be able to steer your parachute at all — you just drift with the wind until you hit the ground. If the pilots and jumpmasters have correctly calculated the release point using wind speed, direction, and altitude, you'll drift to the drop zone without needing to steer. But wind conditions shift. What was a good release point 30 minutes ago might not be good enough by the time you jump.

The second challenge with night jumps is that you might not see the ground until it's too late to lower your equipment and prepare for a good PLF. Night combat equipment jumps are no joke, and I don't know anyone who enjoys them.

The fifth jump is another Hollywood jump, sort of a celebratory "easy" jump to finish off your airborne training.

Think about that last sentence for a moment. By the time you get to the fifth jump you've completed so much training, rehearsed all the actions so many times, and conquered your fear so completely, that doing something that terrified you on Day 1 is now something that is "easy," almost like a parting gift from the Airborne cadre. You've become inoculated to the fear and gained a huge measure of self-confidence and resiliency, which will in turn allow you to face other types of fear more easily.[33] It's no wonder that earning your "wings" is such a big deal.

---

33 Studies show that fear learning and desensitization can generalize across different contexts — meaning a recalibrated response in one domain (like physical risk) can reduce fear sensitivity in others (like social or performance-based threats). See: Dunsmoor, J. E., & Paz, R. (2015). "Fear Generalization and Anxiety: Behavioral and Neural Mechanisms." Biological Psychiatry, 78(5), 336–343

Lessons Learned

During this portion of Green Beret training there are a couple of strong themes that should be crystal clear:

- Courage is not the lack of fear; courage is not letting fear control your actions.

- No one is born fearless and just like everyone else, Green Berets go through a process in order to do very dangerous things.

- Airborne school is about confronting physical fear while SERE school is primarily psychological. But the method for overcoming the fear associated with each is the same.

- No matter how good you are, no matter how much you practice, there will be a little pain involved. But the more preparation and training, the less chance there is for anything more than some discomfort and a few bruises.

- Stress and fear are closely related and, just like stress, we can inoculate ourselves to specific fears through a process: **education** - explaining the types of dangers and providing strategies and **tools** for dealing with those dangers (**training**), and being placed in controlled scenarios in order to practice, practice, practice those strategies (**exposure, experience**, and ultimately - **inoculation**).

These lessons are vitally important for you as you confront the hardest part of your leadership journey thus far, as you move from a fear-based manager to an opportunity-based leader.

- This will hurt. And it won't be easy. But, as Ray Dalio says. "Pain + Reflection = Progress." The last easy day was yesterday. But great leaders do the work necessary to ensure they never let their fear control their actions.

- Just as Green Berets aren't born fearless, neither are you. And just as all SPECOPS personnel go through processes and are able to master their fears, you can, too.

- You were initially afraid to ride a bike, but you overcame your fear. The same processes you used to conquer your physical fears will be the way you inoculate yourself against psychological fears.

- Just like jumping out of a plane, some people will think you're crazy and that your actions are foolish. They'll tell you there are easier ways to get where you want to go, and they'll be right. You will still have to "volunteer" every time you exert EPIC leadership.

- Confronting your fears will build a huge well of self-confidence and resiliency and make it easier for you to confront even more fearsome activities. And by internalizing these principles and dedicating yourself to personal growth, you will be equipped to lead an exceptional team that achieves remarkable success.

Before we dive into the major fear-based patterns that hold people back from becoming great leaders, we need to first understand why fearlessness matters in the first place.

Then we'll look at how fear shows up in leadership — and why it's something you can dismantle, not just manage. After that, we'll cover the specific techniques you'll use to do it. With that foundation in place, we'll turn to the deeper issues that must be addressed to build the kind of Fierce Trust required to lead an extraordinary team.

Manage from Fear or Lead to Opportunity.
Great leaders are focused on achieving the mission and motivated by opportunity. They see potential rather than pitfalls and operate from purpose and opportunity. They are constantly looking at the goal far ahead and don't fear the potential pitfalls along the way because they have a vision and confidence in themselves and their team. Their Leadership OS is purpose-based because they are focused on the team and its success.

Unfortunately many leaders (especially new managers) are motivated by, and operate out of, fear. They aren't focused on the end goal. All they see are the dangers along the way and everything they do is designed to keep themselves from falling in. They are focused on what's right in front of them because they're worried about themselves. They aren't going to take a chance at a potentially big win if there's even a small chance they could lose. They aren't really trying to make something good happen as much as they are trying to prevent something bad from impacting them personally.

If we're dealing with lions and our Leadership OS is fear-based, we're like a lion tamer and our tools are whips, leashes and cages. We're trying to control them while keeping ourselves safe. But if you are operating from opportunity and purpose, then you are the leader of the pack. You let the lions run free to hunt on their own. They come back and follow you and recognize you as the Alpha Lion because you've "aLioned" their goals with yours. Lions have choices; they choose to stay in your pride because you give them what they need to be successful on their own hunts. But standing in front of lions trying to convince them to do what you want without cages or whips is scary, which is why many don't try. It's easier to stay fearful and protect ourselves.

The Science Is Clear

This isn't just my opinion. Research supports what my own empirical evidence has made clear: most leadership failure can be traced back to fear. Not fear of danger or harm—but fear of exposure, fear of failure, fear of loss. Fear is among the most studied emotional responses in modern psychology. Its impact on cognition, behavior, and decision-making has been well documented across domains from trauma recovery to executive performance.

Leaders operating under fear of losing control, losing status, or being revealed as inadequate, frequently create fear-based environments. This kind of leadership behavior isn't just ineffective; it actively sabotages trust, limits innovation, and accelerates team breakdown. A 2023 study in Administrative Sciences showed that fear-based cultures dramatically reduce psychological safety, eroding employee commitment and organizational health.[34] Another report published through

---

34 Çakar, K., & Sürücü, L. (2023). The impact of fear-based leadership on psychological safety and organizational outcomes. Administrative Sciences, 13(2), 56.

ResearchGate concluded that when leaders act out of fear, the ripple effects often include dysfunctional communication, reduced morale, and disengaged employees.[35]

Fear also distorts decision-making. Seminal studies from leadership psychology and behavioral economics both show that fear of failure leads to hesitation, overcontrol, and defensive behaviors, the very things that prevent adaptive leadership.[36] And in business environments driven by speed and innovation, fear quickly becomes a hidden drag on performance. It causes managers to avoid hard conversations, reject feedback, hoard control, and mistake perception for progress.

When the original ground-breaking research on fear was published by Kahneman and Tversky in 1979, the implications for business were so profound that Kahneman was awarded the Nobel Prize in Economic Sciences — a rare honor for a psychologist. Their work helped launch the entire field of behavioral economics and transformed how companies think about risk, incentives, and decision-making.

And yet, the most important insight from their research — that fear silently shapes behavior, often more than logic or strategy — has been almost entirely overlooked in leadership development. Over the past 45 years we've redesigned marketing, pricing, and consumer behavior models based on their findings. But when it comes to leadership and team performance, we're still operating as if fear isn't part of the equation.

---

35 Hubbart, J. A. (2024). Understanding and Mitigating Leadership Fear-Based Behaviors on Employee and Organizational Success. ResearchGate.
36 Kahneman, D., & Tversky, A. (1979). Prospect Theory: An Analysis of Decision under Risk. Econometrica, 47(2), 263–291. Kahneman received the Noble Prize in Economic Sciences in 2002 for this groundbreaking and foundational work. Sadly Tversky had passed away by then.

That's why fear has to be addressed directly. Not as a feeling to be dismissed or pushed down, but as a recurring obstacle that demands a specific, trained response. Because fear doesn't just erode performance, it shapes cultures. And if left unaddressed, it remains the default operating system that causes most leadership breakdowns.

> Considering that fear is the most corrosive force in leadership, how is it that almost no leadership programs address it directly? And of the microscopic fraction that even touch it through adjacent frames like vulnerability, resilience or safety, very few offer a systematic, repeatable, scientifically grounded method for overcoming it. We've built an entire industry around developing leaders and somehow overlooked the single force most likely to undermine it.

Fear is The Default LOS

Fear isn't just the default in our Leadership Operating System, it's the default state of the human nervous system. This isn't dysfunction; it's design. The system evolved to detect and respond to threats long before we had language, strategy, or logic. What we now call "fear" was once the mechanism that kept us alive — whether by avoiding predators, surviving tribal rejection, or navigating physical violence.

And evolution hasn't updated the hardware. The human brain still processes psychological threats, like social rejection, status loss, or professional failure, using the same neural pathways it uses to respond to physical danger. *Our brains don't distinguish between a threat to our safety and a threat to our status.*[37] And because most of us were never taught how to update the software, the default response remains the same: protect, defend, survive. But those instincts, while once useful, are now mismatched to the environments in which we work and lead.

The result is a cascade of predictable physiological changes: elevated cortisol and adrenaline; muscle tension and blood redirection; and narrowed focus and cognitive rigidity. In neuroscience, this is called an **amygdala hijack** — when the brain's threat-detection system overrides the prefrontal cortex and defaults to reflexive survival behaviors: fight, flight, or freeze. In other words, System 1 automatically takes over from System 2. And while these responses are biologically rational, they're organizationally maladaptive.

There are no good or effective biologically-wired responses to fear in today's work environment. But unless we retrain them, they're all we've got and when triggered in the wrong context, they cause real damage.[38]

---

[37] Social-evaluative threats—like fear of embarrassment, judgment, or exposure—activate the same physiological stress systems as physical danger, including the hypothalamic-pituitary-adrenal (HPA) axis and cortisol release. See: Dickerson, S. S., & Kemeny, M. E. (2004). "Acute Stressors and Cortisol Response: A Theoretical Integration and Synthesis of Laboratory Research." Psychological Bulletin, 130(3), 355–391

[38] This table represents a small illustrative sample. Full mappings are explored in the EPIC Leaders Course and supporting FIT™ training materials.

Reflex	Fear Manifestation	Default Response and Impact
Fight	Fear of not getting credit	Hoarding recognition, undermining team wins > eroded trust
Flight	Fear of failure	Risk aversion, hiding in low-stakes work > stagnation
Freeze	Fear of being blamed if I make the wrong call	Decision paralysis > progress halts, missed opportunities

That's why we simply cannot afford to neglect addressing fear in leadership and management training anymore. Retraining is necessary. The 5-Step process we're going to use doesn't remove fear. It reconditions your nervous system to respond more effectively. It turns unconscious reaction into conscious leadership. Over time, fear loses its grip and courage becomes a trained, embodied response.

Fear is like the Matrix. Once you are able to see it woven into our everyday interactions, you can never "unsee" it again. It is everywhere among managers and once it clicks, you'll wonder how you never noticed it before.

I mentioned this before but it bears repeating because even if *you* are past most of your fears, your subordinate leaders probably aren't. Managers say they aren't afraid of anything - until you present the list. Review the partial list at the beginning of the chapter. Now it will all make sense.

Not surprisingly, these fears also induce a significant amount of stress and the two often feed off of each other to the point that some managers would much rather do nothing (freeze) than make a wrong decision. It's easier (and safer) to say "no" than to take a chance.

And while we have to face those fears head-on, that's not the destination, it's the starting line. What we're really after is something much higher because we're trying to build a highly successful team, a team of lions that routinely achieves the impossible. *But you cannot tame or herd lions to excellence.* You can imagine how scary it is standing in a pen of lions with nothing to protect you. Now imagine you want them all to go from one pen to another without whips or leashes or prods. I don't care how much experience you have with other animals, step #1 in dealing with lions will be mastering your fear. Only after you've done that will you be able to exercise the art of leadership and get the lions to go where you want them to go because *they* want to go.

A common example is stepping into a new leadership role. Walking onto an established team is intimidating — even more so when it's a high-performing one. Plenty of managers try to mask that fear by blustering, showing off how busy they are, and trying to prove they deserve the title. But in doing so, they often sow the seeds of their own downfall. Experienced leaders take a different approach. They enter with respect and a healthy dose of caution. They're not worried about being questioned, so they don't feel the need to prove anything, especially in the first few months. Unless they've been brought in to turn around a sinking ship, they focus on listening, learning, and understanding the team and its mission before trying to "fix" anything.

I learned this the hard way as a young sergeant. I joined an established A-Team that was already deployed on a dangerous deployment, and I was afraid I'd be seen as an untrained burden — the guy who'd get left behind to guard the camp every time the team went out on a mission. So I tried to put them at ease by letting them know I'd learn fast, that I already had some experience. What they heard was arrogance. Blustering. Boasting. It turned most of the team against me right out of the gate. One of the guys was kind enough to pull me aside later and explain how my message had actually landed. It took months of hard work, keeping my mouth shut, guarding the camp, and running mail runs to earn some trust back. I eventually got most of the team to accept me. But not all. And because we weren't fully cohesive, I became a liability. Six months later, I transferred to a new team so we could all get a reset and be successful again.

Much later, when I joined my first A-Team as a commander, I was *very* nervous — even though I'd already served on multiple teams and even been in combat with one, which was rare at the time. I was determined not to repeat my earlier mistake. Just like before, the team was already deployed on a dangerous mission — bullets flying, bombings every night. So my experience *should have* made it easier because I really did know a lot more than most captains taking over a team. But in reality I was probably far more scared than any of them. I knew I couldn't afford to screw up those first few weeks or I'd become a burden to a team that was already neck deep in "the shit."

Think about that for a moment ... I wasn't scared of bullets, ambushes, bombings, IEDs, or enemy artillery, I was scared about taking over a really good team and screwing it up.

And yet, I'd argue that what I faced wasn't nearly as scary as what first-time managers go through when they're promoted from within — suddenly put in charge of the same group they just spent the last few years working alongside as peers and friends.

Whether or not we choose to admit it, the mantle of leader forces us into a great number of fearful and stressful situations. And they start the very moment you join a team.

Courage Is A Learned Skill
The opposite of fear is *not* courage, it's recklessness. Fear tells you to be careful and shows all the things you need to take into account to avoid the danger, plan contingencies, and accomplish your mission. Being courageous means being afraid but not letting the fear dictate your actions.

I'm not talking about bravery or physical courage — the kind that lets soldiers run toward gunfire and perform legendary deeds. I'm talking about moral courage, which can be just as hard to summon. In fact, I'd argue that showing moral courage day in and day out is just as praiseworthy, because everyday people, those who aren't trained for bravery, can still rise to the occasion in extreme moments. A mild-mannered stay-at-home parent turns ferocious when their child is threatened. Total strangers dive into rivers or run into burning houses to save someone else. That kind of courage is instinctive. Moral courage is chosen.

Opportunities to show moral courage usually come in small, everyday interactions, moments where the second- and third-order effects aren't obvious, and doing the easier thing will feel tempting. The work, stress, discomfort, and pain required to do the right thing often won't seem worth it in the moment.

It takes courage to admit to your subordinates that you don't know how to do something as well as they do. It takes courage to give your team all the credit for something that's gone well and to take full blame when things go bad even when it wasn't your fault. Moral courage means having lots of difficult conversations, and most of us hate confrontation. This is especially hard for new managers and fledgling entrepreneurs because they got here by doing things — but now they're being asked to "do" leadership, which is a completely different skill set they've likely never studied, let alone trained for.

But that is the nature of leadership. We must always be willing to have difficult conversations and make difficult decisions because that is how we achieve objectives.

Everyone talks about the need to have courage, but their exhortations and platitudes often ring hollow because they rarely (if ever) tell you *how* to develop it. As if you should wake up the next morning and immediately begin living your life more courageously because someone told you to. The truth is that all courage must be learned. Jumping into the deep end before you know how to swim, just to say you are being courageous, could be fatal. That's the fear that holds most of us back: not fear of action itself, but fear that doing the "right thing" won't work, especially when the payoff isn't guaranteed and feels a long way off.

Here is an actual (and typical) example of how a large organization tries to cultivate moral courage. They simply posted some nice sounding words on their intranet and sent an email to all employees directing them to read it. The "training" reads in part:

> *"In order to display moral courage, you must have the ethical awareness and sensitivity to analyze and respond to a moral problem. You must commit to act in an ethical manner as well as follow the code of ethics. (You) need to learn to identify, strengthen, and develop your self-efficacy. Courage to be moral requires: Obligations to honor: What is the right thing to do? Danger to manage: What do I need to handle my fear and uncertainty? Expression and action: What action is needed to meet my obligations and to maintain my integrity?"*

I swear I didn't just make that up. That is from a real company. And while it sounds great, you can't magically wake up one morning and *have* courage; you must *learn* courage.

You don't take a brand new military recruit and throw them into combat on their first day and expect them to demonstrate physical courage. So why is there an expectation that the rest of us can display *moral* courage without any training?

Perhaps it's because most people don't believe you can learn courage. But you can ride a bike, can't you? The deep end of the pool isn't very scary once you've learned to swim, right?

> *While fear inoculation isn't a new concept, its application has almost completely been confined to clinical therapy or elite professional training—military, firefighting, law enforcement. And even in those worlds, the five-step process is often used instinctively, not explicitly. What we're doing here is laying bare the method, naming the structure, and saying that learning to overcome fear doesn't belong in just the psychologist's office or training*

volunteers to conduct exceptionally dangerous activities. This belongs in everyday leadership development. Because - as should be crystal clear by now, **fear is the greatest inhibitor of good leadership, yet no one is teaching us how to overcome it!**

You can – and you already have – learned courage. The path to developing moral courage lies in understanding how we learn physical courage. In the Green Beret training pipeline, fear isn't treated as a psychological obstacle, it's addressed as a practical one. Courage isn't taught as a character trait, it's trained as a behavior. *However,* with repeated and progressively more challenging exposure, that behavior becomes more stable and more transferable, until it manifests in other areas and *starts to become a character trait.*

Very few, if any, Green Berets start off their careers brimming with physical courage. Most begin as scared privates or cadets, jumping off buses while red-faced drill sergeants scream in their faces. They cower in their foxholes for a few seconds the first time blanks are fired over their head in basic training, overwhelmed by the noise and confusion. For most, the first real test of courage comes when they willingly throw themselves out of an airplane 1,200 feet above the ground and trust their lives to a flimsy piece of fabric with holes in it.[39] Only much later are they capable of the kind of bravery that Hollywood makes movies about.

That bravery comes from a repeatable formula that I call FIT™ — Fear Inoculation Training. It's the same five-step cycle

---

39   Basic round parachutes have holes, called vents, and cut panels designed to allow limited steering. Even though you know they're supposed to be there, they still make you nervous when you're new.

we've been exploring throughout this chapter to explain how elite environments build courage under pressure:

1. **Education.** Identify, examine, and understand the fear (real issue) and how to beat it.
2. **Training**, Get guidance and feedback from experienced mentors.
3. **Tools.** Making plans and acquiring strategies, drills, or equipment that reduce uncertainty — including internal compasses like PDMR to guide action under stress.
4. **Exposure.** Facing the fear in a controlled setting. Immediately afterwards reflect and analyze the lessons learned.
5. **Experience.** Repeating it enough times to build confidence and normalize stress.[40]

Then back to Step 1 for increased proficiency and mastery. Each cycle builds more stability, more confidence, and more control. The more often you move through it, the less power fear has. Eventually, the cycle doesn't just help you survive hard things, it can even make you seek them out: sport parachuting, rock climbing, SCUBA, bike riding, etc.

This cycle gives people a sense of control in dangerous situations, and that's the key. Research shows that the feeling of control, not the situation itself, is what reduces fear and stress. The level of stress hormones doesn't match the

---

[40] Although FIT is drawn as a cycle, we spell out Step 5 – Experience to prevent a common failure mode: after one controlled exposure and debrief, leaders assume the loop is complete and stop. Explicitly naming the repetition phase forces deliberate, progressively harder reps—the element scientifically proven (Meichenbaum, SIT; Kolb, Experiential Learning) to convert insight into automatic, stress-proof behavior.

objective difficulty of the task, it matches the *perception* of the difficulty. The body follows the mind. And that's why we can beat fear.

But the last and most important thing required for physical bravery is a mission and purpose, a compelling reason to listen to our hearts instead of our heads. Firemen do not run into burning buildings just for a paycheck. There are easier ways to make money.

That's how people develop physical courage and it is *exactly* the way that we develop moral courage, too.

> It's worth pointing out that this model doesn't come from academic theory. It was derived through empirical analysis of real-world practices used in elite environments where people are trained to master fear under pressure. We know we can trust it because FIT™ not only aligns with established core psychological models—it integrates them. The five steps reflect the same core mechanisms used in cognitive behavioral therapy, exposure therapy, stress inoculation, Self-Determination Theory, and Bandura's mastery modeling.[41] This isn't an aspirational framework;

---

41 The FIT™ cycle operationalizes five foundational psychological frameworks: (1) Stress Inoculation Training (SIT), which emphasizes staged exposure to stressors with applied coping strategies; (2) Graduated Exposure Therapy (GET), which builds tolerance through structured encounters with feared stimuli; (3) Cognitive Reframing, a central technique in Cognitive Behavioral Therapy (CBT), which rewires fear-based thought patterns; and (4) Mastery Modeling, based on Bandura's self-efficacy theory, which builds confidence through graduated success and observational learning; and Self Determination Theory (SDT) which drives motivation through autonomy, competence, and connection. Each of these models has decades of independent validation. FIT™ explicitly sequences all five into a single, teachable cycle. A full academic treatment of the model, including clinical applications and case studies, is available upon request.

it's been validated scientifically through multiple models and proven operationally through more than 80 years of refinement, battlefield training, and performance at the highest levels.

What makes this five-step methodology so effective is that it operates on two levels. At the surface, it's practical and teachable — a repeatable cycle for helping anyone overcome fear. But underneath, it mirrors and unifies the four core psychological mechanisms that make behavioral change stick: Scaffolding, Agency, Reframing, and Reinforcement. These aren't steps. They're the why behind the how. The five step cycle is what you do. The mechanisms are what make it work. Together, they bridge the best of high-stakes training and modern cognitive science and translate it into a leadership enhancement process that works under real-world pressure[42]

Most leadership programs never get close to this because nearly all of them rely on sublimation: suppress the fear, push through it, act like it's not there. FIT™ takes the opposite approach. It demands integration. Name the fear. Understand the pattern. Retrain the response. Even the best programs still focus on tactics and visible behaviors like communication skills, delegation techniques, and performance metrics. They treat fear as incidental (if at all). But fear isn't incidental. It's

---

42   Unlike traditional clinical protocols, FIT™ makes the implicit explicit. It draws on the core mechanisms that clinicians already rely on - Agency, Scaffolding, Reframing, and Reinforcement - but sequences them into a repeatable structure. This model doesn't compete with existing therapies; it enhances them. For psychologists and clinicians working with fear, trauma, or performance under pressure, FIT™ offers what many have sensed but lacked: a practical, integrative framework that names what works and shows how to teach it. It's not a replacement — it's an upgrade.

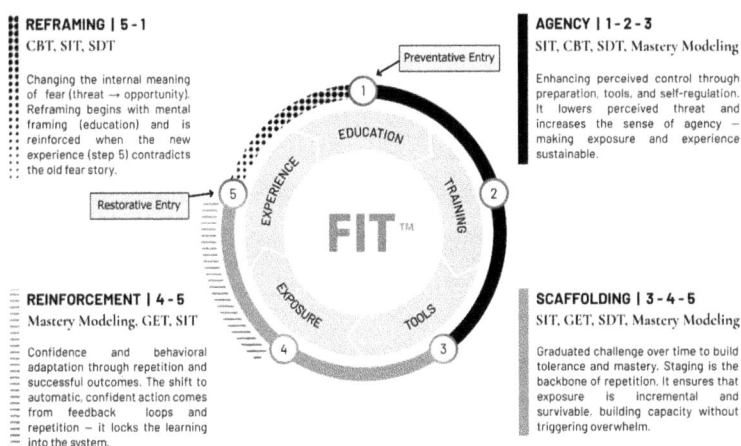

central. The real issue is what happens to a leader when their stress spikes because the problem isn't tactical. It's internal.

As discussed back in Chapter One, Kahneman showed that under stress, the brain switches from System 2 (slow, logical, deliberate), to System 1 (fast, reactive, automatic). In that moment, it's not your best intentions that guide you. It's the current version of your Leadership Operating System (LOS), the default code that's been with you from birth and reinforced over years of experience.

And that's why most leadership programs, motivational techniques, and academic theories break down under pressure. They were taught to System 2 — but fear activates System 1. FIT™ doesn't just teach better strategies. It rewires the default. It updates your Leadership Operating System so that when fear takes over, you don't fall back on avoidance or control. You default to courage.

Shame is Stronger Than Fear
A supplemental accelerant for building moral courage – using a greater fear to trigger our "fight" response – is also based on physical courage. The Fight or Flight (or Freeze) sympathetic nervous system response releases hormones into our body and helped our ancestors survive encounters with dangerous animals, warring tribes, and a host of prehistoric dangers.

And while we usually only associate fight, flight, or freeze with physical danger, we respond similarly when reacting to angry accusations or when someone yells at us. And while it might not be as strong, the "fight" response often kicks in when someone calls us names or insults us. Our "fight" response (to the fear of being thought weak) motivates us to do things that we wouldn't normally do, and people can manipulate us through it.

So just as fear can cause us to freeze and then run like crazy when our "flight" instinct kicks in, it can also trigger our "fight" instinct.

Shame is stronger than fear (normal fear) and shame is very good at triggering our "fight" instinct. Shame is a deep-rooted fear that someone will find out about a character flaw or a dark secret that we aren't proud of. Many, many soldiers throughout history have died rather than be thought of as cowardly, so *do not* underestimate the power of shame. Napoleon wrote, "It's amazing what a man will do for a colored ribbon." I am not immune to this either, having schemed to get on an SF team that was getting ready to deploy into a war zone because I wanted to go to war (and get my combat patch and Combat Infantryman's Badge). I'm no different than millions of other veterans from every country and era. What do we fear? We're afraid of being "less than" those who have been in combat. We fear that others won't respect us or trust us to do our job properly because we don't have "real experience."

This type of fear can, and does, get us killed. But we can also use the power of shame (or a greater fear) to our advantage if we reframe our situation. If it's your responsibility to ensure your team surpasses the sales quota so everyone gets a big bonus, then your fear of "losing out" can supersede your fear of admitting you don't know something so that someone else's idea can take the team over the top. The shame of being last in a competition will almost always encourage us to work harder. [43] [44]

You might not have thought about it this way before, but if you look back, it's clear that whatever courage you've developed came through one or both of these same methods. Parents, mentors, teachers, coaches, bosses — someone helped you work through the fears you've already overcome. Maybe it wasn't a formal process like the 5 Steps I've described, but the structure was still there. Think about learning to ride a bike: someone explained what to do and how to do it. They showed you. They gave you training

---

[43] Shame functions within FIT™ as a powerful subtype — one that can catalyze action through reframing. In these moments, we instinctively choose the lesser of two fears: the fear of letting someone down, for example, outweighs the fear of personal harm or exposure. That mental equation becomes the new meaning, and the action that follows is a live example of reframing in motion. It's not a detour from the model — it's a direct expression of it.

[44] Zhao, Q., Li, X., & Wang, Y. (2023). The Neural Signatures of Shame, Embarrassment, and Guilt: A Voxel-Based Meta-Analysis. Brain Sciences, 13(4), 559. Additionally, leading psychologists like Paul Gilbert and Martin Seligman have long argued that shame plays a central role in how we respond to fear, risk, and moral threat.

wheels — a tool. They walked beside you, held the seat, gave you a push, and cheered when you made progress. Eventually, the training wheels came off. They rode next to you until you could keep your balance and ride on your own. *And then the thing that scared you became fun.*

And wasn't there a bit of "Don't be a baby!" from a sibling or a friend to get you back on the bike when you fell over? That was shame — and it's what pushed you past your fear.

Is that any different from the first time a great boss helped us step into leadership — guiding us through a tough performance review with someone who wasn't meeting the standard? They told us what to say, what to expect, and how to handle it. They helped us prepare, gave us a script, maybe even observed us the first time and stood by to back us up if needed. And wasn't part of the reason we pushed through the discomfort because we didn't want to let them down?

Unfortunately, the vast majority of managers in the workforce today don't realize it's their responsibility to train their subordinate leaders — mostly because no one ever trained them. But just because you don't have a leader helping you build courage doesn't mean you can't learn it on your own.

You can get training and tools for specific tasks like performance counseling from reputable leadership and management courses. And while they probably won't include a module on overcoming fear or anxiety, you can still inoculate yourself by taking baby steps — or what we call "confidence targets" in Special Forces. Start with low-risk conversations that have a high chance of success and build from there. Ask a senior manager or mentor you respect to help you prepare and give feedback along the way.

I've helped hundreds of people work through this process: trained them; given them tools; prepared them to act with courage in difficult situations; and occasionally instilled some "healthy" fear into them. So I am 100% certain it can be done.

"Fearless Leader" Isn't a Punchline - It's The Standard

But learning how to accomplish some difficult tasks, and thereby inoculate yourself against the fear and anxiety they bring, is just the beginning. That's basic training. Leading lions requires an entirely different level of fearlessness. Most people use "fearless leader" as a joke. That's because they've never met one.

Taking initiative and making things happen requires more courage than standing by and hoping for a favorable outcome. Leaders face situations every day where personal courage is essential: confronting disciplinary issues or disruptive behavior, driving innovation when change feels risky, speaking honestly to superiors about questionable decisions, deferring to subordinates with deeper technical knowledge, or letting go of top talent to serve a larger mission. Leadership requires the courage to make hard calls and the resolve to uphold standards when it matters most.

But even handling those situations will feel easy compared to what it takes to build and lead exceptionally high-performing, truly great teams. The foundational behaviors we're about to discuss are difficult because their consequences, especially the second and third order effects, often don't appear until much later. You'll need the courage and faith to act anyway, even when it doesn't seem worth the cost, and even when everyone around you says you're wrong for trying.

Prioritize Team Success Over Your Own

It's easy to settle into the routines of management, handle day-to-day challenges, and start operating on cruise control without ever pausing to think about the larger role you play as the leader. That might be fine for a normal team. But if you want to build an A-Team, your leadership has to be intentional. You'll need a clear command philosophy, something that tells your team what matters to you, and why.

There are many benefits to writing a command philosophy and sharing it with your team, but one of the most important advantages is that it forces you to pull yourself above the day-to-day noise and look down at your organization from the 5,000 or even 25,000-foot level. That elevated view helps you see how the machine actually runs, and where you need to focus to keep it running smoothly. It also creates just enough separation between you and the team, which is necessary if you're going to lead well. The leader is part of the team, but also apart from it.

Your job as the leader is to make sure the team accomplishes the mission. Sometimes that means stepping back and standing apart to ensure the work gets done. It's not about you — it's about the mission. When you lead with a mission- or purpose-based mindset, you focus on making sure the team wins, not you. Of course, if the team wins, you win, too. But it's critical to understand that the *team's success must come before your own.*

This takes a leap of faith — like throwing yourself out of an airplane and trusting a flimsy piece of cloth to open and carry you safely to the ground. The idea that we are separate from our team, and that the team takes priority, is a major mental shift for many leaders. That's because of what it really implies. But make no mistake, this isn't about turning yourself into a martyr or sacrificing yourself for the team. So take a breath, set the fear aside, and don't fixate on the potential pitfalls. I told you this would be uncomfortable for many of you, and it's going to get worse before it gets better. But look farther ahead. Think about the potential of building a truly extraordinary team that outperforms everyone else. And don't worry — we'll walk through every "what if" as we cover each behavior of this mindset.

Prioritizing team success over our own means training someone on the team to take our place. It means creating our successor. It means sending star performers to other departments for the good of the company, and to give our people better opportunities. It means constantly developing our team so that each member becomes better than us in every way. It means setting aside ego, freely admitting when we don't know something, and recognizing when someone else has more experience than we do. It means having the character, confidence, and courage to see the team as something bigger than ourselves, and understanding that we've been given the privilege to serve as its caretaker and leader.

Remember, our job as leaders is to work by, with, and through our teams. That means the team must succeed. And there's data to support this. A ten-year longitudinal study by Harvard Business School concluded, "The best managers are those who help their teams succeed."[45] One article on the

---

45 Gabarro, J. J., & Hill, L. A. (1994). Managing People and Organizations: A Longitudinal Study of Managerial Transitions. Harvard Business School Working Paper. (Referenced in various HBR summaries and leadership analyses; see also coverage in Forbes and Inc.)

study went further: "While exceptional executives led with a humble confidence that graciously extended care to others, second-best executives were inclined to manage perceptions, creating the illusion of collaboration while masking self-interested motives." We can't fake it. Our teams will know. And the only way to lead this way is to overcome our fear.

The First Redwood Principle

> Thinking about putting the team's success ahead of your own might seem counterproductive to your career. But consider what we can learn from the most successful life-form on Earth — the Giant Sequoias, also known as the Sierra Redwoods. In fact, the next nine most successful species combined still don't match the prosperity of these eternal titans. Many live over 2,000 years. The President — the oldest recorded Sequoia — is 3,240 years old and took root when Pharaohs still ruled Egypt. Ironically, the language from which The President takes its name, Latin (praesidentum), wouldn't be invented until it was already 500 years old.
>
> The oldest known redwood fossils date back more than 200 million years to the Jurassic period. And while there are older individual trees, nothing in history comes close to the immensity of the redwoods, which are, on average, ten times larger than a blue whale. The mass of the largest sequoia is 642 tons — roughly equivalent to 107 adult African savanna elephants, the world's largest land animal. And it wasn't just isolated giants. All the trees across a 2-million-acre stretch, an area half again as large

as the state of Delaware, lived for thousands of years and regularly reached the height of 30-story buildings before logging wiped out much of the old-growth population in the early 1900s.

But what is truly remarkable about these ancient behemoths is that, despite their size, they don't have taproots to anchor them. Their roots only reach about 12 feet into the ground — hardly enough to support trees that routinely grow over 250 feet tall and 30 feet in diameter. And yet, they have survived countless forest fires and natural disasters for thousands of years because of one thing: their ability to rely on each other. Their root systems are completely intertwined, creating an interdependent web that allows them to grow to unfathomable heights, become the largest living organisms on the planet, and outlast almost everything else on Earth. This is why they are known as the most successful lifeform in history.

In addition to their majesty and the awe they inspire, there's something remarkable hidden within the Sequoia groves. The oldest trees are never the largest. The "First Redwood" is never the tallest or the thickest. It does the heavy lifting. It creates the conditions for the rest to thrive. And yet — ironically and seemingly unjustly — it never reaches the same height as some of the trees it helped raise.

But is it really unfair? Think about it. Would the First Redwood have survived thousands of years or grown so large in isolation? Not a chance. With such a shallow root system and no taproot to anchor it, a lone Sequoia might, at best, reach only a quarter of its potential size and lifespan. On its own, it would have never come close to that kind of success.

For a time, the First Redwood is the tallest — the one that rises first while anchoring the others. But its real strength comes not from standing alone, but from making it possible for others to rise even higher. It becomes majestic, outlives its competition, weathers cataclysmic storms, and touches the sky because it anchors the team. It takes the risk that another redwood will grow taller.

So if the idea that "team success is more important than your own personal success" feels scary, take a lesson from a lifeform far more prosperous than we could ever hope to be. Be the First Redwood for your team. Don't fear the possibility that someone on your team might become more successful than you. Be confident in the fact that one of them will — and know that it won't matter. Because by creating the conditions for others to thrive, you'll achieve more than you ever could have on your own.

Understanding and believing this is the first step toward becoming a fearless leader.

Be the First Redwood.

Give Them All the Credit and Take All the Blame

As already mentioned, the success of the team is paramount. When they win, you win, even if it doesn't seem like it at the time. This goes far beyond the integrity issue we discussed in Chapter 2, where we covered not taking credit for someone else's work or implying you had more to do with a win than you really did. This is a full 180. You are going to give every shred of credit to your people, every time — even when it was entirely your work, your idea, and your effort.

Yes, there's a risk that others might see you as superfluous if all they hear is how great your team is. But after the second or third success, the truth becomes obvious. You're the one creating the environment where that kind of performance happens. You're the one leading.

Additionally, you are going to take all the blame anytime something doesn't go well — even when it's not your fault. Even if you gave explicit instructions to stop doing it the wrong way. This doesn't mean hiding mistakes or covering for someone. We treat mistakes as problems the team doesn't want to repeat, so they're discussed openly. But you still take the blame. Why? Because somewhere along the line, you failed to train someone, give clear guidance, provide enough motivation, supervise properly, cross-train the task, or catch something sooner. *My team. My fault. Always.*

Some refer to this as "extreme ownership," and if it helps you to think of taking full responsibility as extreme, that's fine. But in the special operations community, and much of the conventional military, *this isn't extreme. It's expected.* If you're the military leader and the team screws up for any reason, it's your fault. Full stop. One way or another, it's your fault. And God help you if you try to shift blame onto a team member. Your commander will crucify you. And if it happens again, *it's even more your fault* — because now you've failed to coach, correct, motivate, or remove the person who made the mistake twice.

If the real problem is that you have a team member who doesn't belong, then after the team discussion about the issue, you immediately write a Cooperative Performance Agreement (CPA — discussed in the next chapter). The CPA will either stop the mistakes or establish the first link in an iron-clad paper trail that any HR department can use to justify removing that person from your team. This doesn't mean you're passive. It doesn't mean people are walking over you or that you're covering for someone. It means you're taking responsibility for the failure — and acting on it. [46]

Are we splitting hairs here? Are we really just "saying" we'll take the blame and then letting everyone else know it was someone else's fault? The answer is no. But it doesn't matter *because it still works even if we're faking it.* We address mistakes as opportunities for the team to learn, but the person who made the mistake will still appreciate the fact that you made this issue about the *improper action* and *not the person* themselves. It's the difference between saying, "We didn't get the project done because Alex didn't do his part," and "We didn't get the project done because I didn't supervise my team well enough." But trust me, everyone knows what Alex did or didn't do.

Why do this? Because the payoff is huge. In the short term, you'll impress the hell out of your team and start building the kind of Fierce Trust needed to create something exceptional. And while others in the organization (including your boss)

---

[46] Some positions, like project managers, come with responsibility but no real authority. The PM is accountable for results and project completion, yet none of the team members are direct reports. Team members often expect the PM to cover for missed deadlines or incomplete work, and if the PM doesn't, they'll complain that the PM is the problem. This dynamic is especially difficult in technical fields like IT, where software engineers are in higher demand and often earn more than the PM. Responsibility without authority is one of the worst positions to be in and must be addressed openly with supervisors.

might initially believe some of your people are smarter or better than you, that's okay. If your actions are sincere, the second and third order effects will show up fast. And they will be significant.

First, your team will begin to flourish, and their motivation and trust in you will skyrocket. Knowing you have their back when they make a mistake or miss the mark gives them the confidence and mindset to push boundaries and attempt the impossible. They can't achieve the impossible until they attempt it—and you make that possible by giving them "top cover." Your consistent praise, especially when it costs you, drives them toward excellence, for themselves and for you. And because it's all about the team's success, if you do the work to remove a non-performer from the team, they'll respect you even more.

After you've consistently done this, your team will actively find ways to help you succeed. They won't give up the new team culture you've established—something that could easily unravel if a clueless executive misunderstands the real dynamic, replaces you, and things slide back to the way they were. And because your team knows you'll always give them the credit, the only way they can make you look good is by exceeding the standard in *everything*.

Ultimately, when the team is consistently successful, third-order effects kick in: it becomes obvious to everyone that you're an outstanding leader. And while you always give credit to the team, the *one thing that can't be attributed to them* is the fact that you're the one leading. If your team is consistently smashing records and exceeding standards, it means they're being led well—and that will land squarely on you.

There are additional third-order effects once everyone realizes it's your leadership that's making the difference. People will start treating you differently. Your boss's boss will begin to notice you. Colleagues from other sections or divisions may approach you about openings on your team. If you have a good boss, you might get extra resources and an expanded team to take on more challenging responsibilities. Some of your peers will even start asking for your advice.

However, if your boss is fearful, they may start looking for ways to sabotage you, worried that you'll replace them. Some of your peers may become jealous and try to undermine you or spread stories. You might also have one or two team members who resist the new culture and attempt to subvert the team's efforts—either through targeted inaction or by stirring up conflict, constantly arguing, or saying things like, "Who does she think she is?" In companies where it's difficult to fire people, those employees will pose ongoing challenges to your leadership and must be addressed quickly.

As you can see, the philosophy of "there is always enough credit to go around" takes real courage to sustain over time, especially for new leaders. But it's not that hard. It's not a foreign concept to you, because you've already seen that it can be done. This mindset is sometimes called an "abundance mentality," or you may have heard a version of one of my favorite sayings: "Nothing is impossible if you don't mind who gets the credit."

We've all seen outstanding leaders who never say the word "I." They talk about what the team accomplished, downplaying their own efforts while highlighting individual contributions. But really—despite what they say—*everyone* knows they're the reason the team is so successful, and everyone wants to work for them. You respect that, right?

Then let's start doing that now.

When I'm working with new clients, I can usually tell within the first five minutes what kind of leader they are just by listening to how they talk about their team. If I hear a lot of "me" and "I," along with reasons why any problems aren't their fault, I know we'll be starting with the basics. But if I hear more "we" and "our," I know we can move on to more advanced topics. I've observed and worked with leaders from hundreds of organizations over the past 35+ years, and I'm convinced—without a shadow of a doubt—that believing in and practicing the idea that "there's always enough credit to go around" is one of the most important and foundational things a leader can do to become wildly successful. Like any of the scary things we've discussed, though, it takes courage to practice it long enough to see the results for yourself.

Time Out - Idealistic and Impossible

Okay team, huddle up, take a knee, and let's talk about this. I originally planned to address it at the end of the chapter, but I can already hear the objections—so let's handle them now before we go any further.

This idea—that the mission and team take priority—isn't just scary. Some people, including authors of popular books, will tell you it's *the exact opposite* of what you should do to gain power. There are books out there right now that claim you should take credit for everything and always pass the blame. Most of us don't want to operate that way, but we've all seen people who focus only on themselves and still appear successful. They aren't leaders; they're managers, practicing the worst possible form of management: perception management. They don't care about doing a good job. They care about looking good and doing whatever it takes to reach the top. Instead of focusing their energy inward on the team—the real engine of success—they spend it outward, on anyone who might be useful to their climb up the ladder or their games in office politics. They're worried about the paint job and how the engine sounds when it's revved, not on the engine itself.

But it's a sad truth that perception management can be an effective way to gain personal power. It's a path to promotion—and sometimes even the CEO role—if the board fails to conduct due diligence. But ultimately, it's all smoke and mirrors. The fakers never achieve real success or happiness. Yes, some will have expensive cars and houses, but they live in constant fear of being found out. They might always shift the blame to others, but eventually it becomes clear they're the problem. That's why they never really let anyone get close to them at work, and why they tend to move around a lot—so whatever short-term success they've managed can be leveraged into the next position, before anyone realizes they were never more than a second-tier manager.

But the most important difference is that those who practice perception management never achieve the impossible—because that requires a team with Active Trust, and fakers can't build that. Think about any time you've heard of someone achieving the impossible; a closer look always reveals a team behind it. Even the most celebrated individual sports achievement in modern history, Roger Bannister's breaking of the "impossible" four-minute mile, was a team effort. Two of Bannister's friends, Chris Chataway and Chris Brasher, trained with him for an entire season to prepare and plan. Together, they choreographed the entire race. Bannister drafted behind his friends for most of it, with Brasher setting the pace for the first two laps and Chataway for the third and most of the fourth. When Chataway began to fade, Bannister surged and broke the record. He was never a front-runner, and they all knew he was strongest when coming from behind—so his team helped him do exactly that.

Fakers never achieve greatness. They might look good, they might have the trappings of success, but they never achieve the impossible, much less routinely.

I'm not talking about entrepreneurs with non-existent leadership skills who bulldoze their companies to stardom. They're not practicing perception management—they just don't care. They're trying to change the world. They're not chasing a posh car or a mansion; they're sleeping on couches and working out of garages. They have a vision and refuse to be held back by anything or anyone. They want to win, and because of that vision, people will follow them, at least for a while, to be part of something great. They are the anomaly.

Do you want to look good or win races? What gets watered grows. Your time and energy are limited. Will you spend them on a fancy paint job and new rims so the car looks good, or will you focus on the engine and win races? Are you in it to win it? Focusing on the team is the longer game, but if you win races, you'll look far better than someone who just makes sure the car looks fast. And despite what those other books might recommend, the research shows this approach works. [47]

How to Apply the FIT™ 5-Step Method

We just covered the education phase—identifying the fear, understanding how it works, and what it costs you. Now we move into training, tools, and a plan.

Part of training (Step 2) includes understanding what we're about to do before we do it. Like reading the instructions before assembly. The overall concept is simple: we start with confidence targets. These are low-stakes situations that expose you to manageable stress and help you build experience. It's just like riding a bike or learning to ski. You begin on the bunny hill, doing small things over and over until they feel natural. Then you take on the next challenge.

We're not trying to master anything yet—just to move. "Fake it till you make it." "Do it until it gets easier." Anything at all that moves us in the right direction because research shows *any* forward motion helps weaken fear. As I like to tell my clients, "Just get started getting started!"

Step 3 is building a plan, mentally preparing, and gathering your tools. Our tool can be something simple like writing

---

[47] Leaders who operate from an abundance mindset—by giving credit freely, developing others, and supporting talent mobility—have been shown to foster higher engagement, deeper trust, and stronger long-term performance. See: Grant, Adam M., and Justin M. Berg. "Prosocial Motivation at Work: When, Why, and How Making a Difference Makes a Difference." In The Oxford Handbook of Positive Organizational Scholarship, edited by Kim S. Cameron and Gretchen M. Spreitzer, 28–44. Oxford University Press, 2012.

down a core concept on a post-it-note and placing it where you'll see it every day—something like "Pass the Credit; Take the Blame," or "Good → Team; Bad → Me." Seeing it daily matters. Repetition builds readiness.

Here's how we execute (Step 4). We're mentally ready, we've been using our tool, and now we're waiting for the opportunity to try it. Being ready and waiting ensures we won't be caught off guard and forget and revert back to our old ways. The trigger is simple: it is when something good happens and someone congratulates you. Instead of saying "thanks," respond like Michael Jordan or Tom Brady—talk about how it was a team effort. That's it! Super simple! Just don't use the words "I" or "me." You don't need to single out individual team members yet; just keep the focus on the team. Once that feels easy, start highlighting one team member who did a great job—and do it in front of others, especially your boss. Skip any mention of your own role; it's already assumed. Give the team all the credit, and take all the blame.

Afterward, immediately reflect and analyze. Was it hard or easy? How did it feel—emotionally and in your body (heart rate, tension, breathing)? How did others respond? Did the feared outcome actually occur, and if so, what was the real impact? What worked, what didn't, and what would make the next attempt better, easier, or more effective? Rate your sense of control from 1 to 10 and record it.

Feed those insights straight back into **Education**—update what you know—then into new **Training, Tools**, and the next **Exposure**. Maybe the outcome suggests asking a mentor for fresh guidance (Training) or tweaking your language (Tool).

Finally, plan your next rep now, escalate the stakes slightly, and repeat. Document each cycle on an Enhanced Franklin Grid to establish a positive feedback loop. Rapid iteration is what turns a single success into lasting inoculation.

But you have to *do* it. The **Experience** part of the cycle demands that you do it again as soon as possible and incorporate your lessons learned. This is a paradigm shift—a new way of seeing the world—and no amount of reading or listening will change your mind. After you do this a few times, you'll see for yourself that it really works and you'll just *feel* it. You'll have that "a-ha!" moment, update your LOS, your default setting will change, and you'll never go back to doing things the old way again.

Do the same thing when something goes wrong. If the team starts arguing about what happened or who's to blame, stop them immediately by saying, "It's my responsibility." You don't need to explain why it's your fault—just say the words and own it. If your boss or senior leadership is upset and wants answers, tell them the same thing: "Something went wrong. We're not sure yet what the real issue is, but we're going to figure it out and make sure it doesn't happen again. Ultimately, it's my responsibility."

Don't try to explain the failure yet because the truth is, *you don't really know*. You might think you know and feel tempted to say, "Morgan just didn't get it right." But is that really the issue? Did Morgan miss the mark because she wasn't properly trained? Maybe she was trained, but the training didn't account for this particular situation—so the training is inadequate. Or maybe the system itself is outdated, built for an old reality that no longer applies. Bottom line: you're not sure.

And your boss will be far more impressed if you don't rush to judgment just to protect yourself.

Then go back to your team and run a proper After Action Review (AAR) to figure out what went wrong and how to fix it. The value of an AAR is that it gets to the heart of the issue and removes the sting of admitting something didn't go right. Everyone simply describes what they did and when. Start from the beginning, move forward through the timeline, and let each person explain their actions in order. Focus on fixing the problem—not assigning blame.

People should only speak for themselves and stick to the facts. They shouldn't say things like, "I couldn't do my part because Morgan didn't give me the information on time." Only allow "I" statements, and encourage them to think through the situation more carefully. Then you'll get clearer input, like: "I got the data at 10:30 and didn't have enough time to analyze it and write my section of the report, because it takes two hours to sort the data, another hour to analyze it, and another hour to write up the results." (We cover AARs in depth in Book Two.)

Don't let them blame each other. Instead, make it clear that it's ultimately your responsibility—for not organizing the effort better or spotting the issue in time to address it effectively.

Since Morgan supplies the initial data, she's first in the chain, so she speaks first. If she thought there was a structural or system issue, she could bring it up and help address the actual problem. More importantly, if the mistake really was hers, it's much easier for her to admit it herself than to have someone else call it out. This method short-circuits the usual defensiveness that automatically pops up in these situations.

The first time you conduct this process, some team members may be afraid to admit they made a mistake. They might dissemble or say something vague like, "Well, the computer took too long to boot up that morning," even when you know it didn't. If that happens, *it's still your fault.* Why? Because you haven't yet built enough trust on the team for someone to feel safe admitting they were just having a bad day.

Maybe you suspect Morgan was out late partying with friends and came in hungover and drowsy. Regardless, you treat the slow-booting computer as the potential problem and write it down as something to follow up on. After the AAR is complete and the team shifts to discussing next steps, assign Morgan the task of checking with IT to find out what went wrong with her computer and to develop a plan to ensure it doesn't happen again. Let her know she'll brief the team next time on the new procedures. Maybe she'll come to you later and admit the truth. If that happens, you can tell the team it was a one-time occurrence and there's no need to worry. That's not a lie. It was a one-time occurrence—because you can be sure Morgan won't make that mistake again.[48]

But even so, if Morgan says during the AAR, "I was distracted and I took longer than usual to compile the data," you still step in and say, "No, Morgan—it was my responsibility. I should have checked to make sure everything was on track and there weren't any issues." Take full responsibility. Own it.

This will be hard to do the first time, but it'll hit like a bomb. The team might know it was really Morgan's fault, but

---

[48] If she goes to IT and comes back with a false story, you have a more serious problem that you'll deal with separately and immediately because you can never tolerate integrity issues.

the fact that you take the hit—because you are the leader—will change your relationship with them instantly and permanently. Nothing says "I AM the MF'ing Leader" like taking full responsibility for a situation. If Morgan is a good person, she'll never make that mistake again and will be grateful you covered for her. If she's had performance issues in the past and this is part of a pattern, you'll handle it one-on-one, as discussed in the last chapter, to make sure it doesn't happen again and that appropriate consequences are in place.

The Hidden Costs of the "Know-It-All" Manager

We've already covered this in Chapters 2 and 3—knowing your strengths and weaknesses, building self-confidence, and developing active trust. But we need to go deeper, because this isn't just about leadership. It's about the company's bottom line.

Ask a new business owner, "What do you do?" and you'll almost always hear something like, "We can pretty much do everything in the area of X, and we serve everyone!" Seasoned entrepreneurs will shake their heads and smile—not just because they've heard it before, but because they've said it themselves. And they've learned how important it is to move past the mindset of "I'm good at everything." Every successful business eventually finds its niche. A very successful owner I'm familiar with has a laser-specific elevator pitch: "Our gym *only* trains and prepares *female* bodybuilders for *competition*, and we only take clients who have *already competed*." The better you are at something, the more specialized you become. Trying to be everything for everyone is a formula for failure.

Remember when I talked about the makeup of a Special Forces team? The strength of the team lies in the fact that everyone is an expert in one area—and no one expects anyone to know everything. In fact, the only thing a team leader is expected to be an expert in is operational planning and in knowing how to best leverage the team's strengths to ensure the best possible outcomes and mission success.

I'll ask again: was Einstein a great basketball player? Is LeBron James a great physicist? Does anybody care? We play to our strengths. Real experts are always willing to tell you what they're not good at and what they don't know—because they're confident in what they do know.

So, why is it that we feel the need to be an expert on everything? Why do we think that admitting we don't know something will make us look incompetent, lose credibility, get replaced, or seem like we're not in control?

Well, of course, it's because we're afraid that we might get replaced or not get promoted. And remember, this is *natural* and instinctive behavior - a survival instinct.

Many managers, especially new ones, don't feel secure in their position and worry they'll be fired or demoted if someone "uncovers the truth" about what they don't know. So they pretend to know everything or refuse to admit when someone else has a good—or even better—idea, and in doing so, they lower the team's performance. This same fear is why they'll take credit for and implement someone else's idea six months after it was first proposed, when it's often too late to get the full benefit.

We've all seen people who do this. It's irritating, and we treat it as an annoyance to work around. *But it's far worse than that.* Leaders who can't admit they don't know something, or that someone else might have a better idea, prioritize ego over performance. That means they've stopped looking for the best solutions—which *directly affects company performance.*

Admitting you don't know everything, or that someone else has a good, or even better idea, is a *necessary condition* for finding the best answers and becoming wildly successful. You can't build a great team, let alone achieve the impossible, if you're not taking advantage of every idea. The best ideas are critical to success—no matter where they come from.

I've mentioned before how terrible we are at identifying our own hypocrisy and faults. Some of the worst leaders I've ever seen will read this and think, "This isn't me, I would never do that!" Then they'll do it the very next day and not realize it. A great many second-tier executives have convinced themselves they are such strong leaders that this could *never* apply to them - so they'll never look at themselves critically.

So how do you know if this pertains to you? Pay attention to your inner voice the next few times you talk with someone. If you feel the urge to one-up them, this probably applies. If someone mentions their new car or a great vacation, do you feel the need to bring up yours—just to make sure people know it's better? Do you find yourself talking about your new boat or recent trips so others will think you're impressive? Could you walk into a party and say nothing about yourself for 30 minutes? And if there's a true expert in the room, do you feel compelled to prove you know just as much? If so, this likely pertains to you.

If you're in a leadership position, pay attention to how many ideas you truly listen to from the person that most annoys you. If you automatically dismiss them, then this probably applies. And if you've ever adopted someone else's idea later and passed it off as your own, it definitely applies. Watch how your high performers interact with you. If they prefer their own counsel and only come to you for approval, not insight or support, this probably applies.

If you're a senior leader, you *must* identify every know-it-all manager in your company and retrain them immediately. These people are literally holding you back from being more successful. Until you retrain or get rid of them, you're nowhere near peak effectiveness. If you're not relentlessly pursuing the best solutions and the most effective ways to operate at every level, you won't scale—and you won't become a great company.

How to Stop Sabotaging Your Own Success

How do we crush these fears and stop sabotaging ourselves, our teams, and our organizations? We fight fire with fire. We reframe the situation and counter the fear of not knowing everything with a greater fear: the fear of making poor decisions, missing the best outcomes, letting the team down, and falling short of our potential. And if a senior manager points out the problem, add one more to the list—the fear of ignoring what your boss just told you to fix.

We also need to dig deep and confront the perceived shame that someone might find out we're not fully qualified to lead if we admit we don't know something. Because what's truly shameful is getting passed over for promotion again and again—or being laughed at behind our backs because our team underperforms and no one can rely on us. We harness our fears and shame through peer pressure. Tell managers in other departments that your team is going to increase production by a bold, ambitious number by the end of the quarter. Now you're on the hook. You'll have to put your ego aside, get the team aligned, and use everything available to make it happen.

To be the best and most successful, your team must generate the best ideas and use the most effective methods. When the team wins, you win. So stop hobbling yourself and limiting your chances of success. You want the best? Start asking for it. Your top performers will be thrilled you're finally listening, and when it's time to implement one of their ideas, they'll make sure it succeeds. They're invested. They want to be heard again. And when it works, the team wins—and everyone sees you as a great leader.

How do you apply the FIT process? You've had the education. You're getting the training now. You've got the tools: a bigger fear and the plan you're making now. Next, think about when you'll have an opportunity to try this and be ready for it. Start with confidence targets. Ease into it by simply asking for the team's input the next time a decision needs to be made or new ideas are needed. Step four is to do it—"fake it till you make it," and "just do it until it gets easier." This will already feel easier now that you've committed to giving the credit to the team. Why? Because one of the biggest reasons we're afraid to acknowledge someone else's idea is the fear that we won't get the credit. But if you're giving all the credit to the team anyway, it *no longer matters whose idea it was* because you just care about winning.

When it comes to admitting we don't know something, it's simple: stop doing what we usually do—pretending to know, and saying something just to sound smart. Instead, stop talking. Listen. Ask questions. If it helps, the first few times, take on the mindset of "I actually know this, but I'm training the team and want to hear their thinking," and say, "Sarah, what do you think? Jim, how would you approach it?" Ask why they think it would work, and actually evaluate it—because in the end, it's still your decision. It doesn't matter how you do it, as long as you stop telling and start asking—and really listen to the answers.

Reframe the situation: you have more important things to do. As your team becomes more successful and that success is clearly tied to your leadership, it will get easier to say "I don't know" without anxiety. Eventually, you'll be *proud* to say, "Don't ask me. I pay Jim to be the expert on that." Because even if you know the answer, you'll have more important things to focus on than proving how smart you are. Do successful CEOs answer every question themselves? No. They have people for that. And now, so do you.

Remember to take a moment and reflect and analyze how it went. It probably felt good. If so, take a victory lap - even if it's just mental. Smile and tell yourself that you did a good job. Then think about how to do it even better the next time and annotate it on your Franklin Grid.

Admitting you don't know everything and acknowledging others' good ideas requires a paradigm shift. You have to just do it until it clicks—and then suddenly you'll understand that getting the best ideas, regardless of where they come from, is the *only* path to real success for your team and for your own career.

There is no success without a successor
Managers motivated by fear try to hold onto as much knowledge as possible because they see it as power. If they give

someone else the knowledge to do their job, they assume that person will eventually take it from them.

Leaders motivated by opportunity take the opposite approach. They make sure the entire team knows what they know so they can tap into everyone's input and get the best ideas and solutions. Start by following the recommendations in the communications chapter: be 100% honest and transparent with your team, unless there's a restriction. Share all that matters, but protect their time by not CC'ing them on things they don't need.

But now you're going even further. You're not just keeping them informed; you're giving them *everything* they need to take your job. It seems counterintuitive but you become irreplaceable to the company by working to replace yourself at every level.

Managers motivated by opportunity believe it's their responsibility to train their team to take over the leader's duties for many reasons. If you prioritize the team's success over your own, you know they need to be ready in case something happens to you. What if you get hit by a bus or end up in the hospital for a few weeks?

> One of the best CEOs I know recently took a two-week vacation with his family into a remote wilderness area with no internet access. I consider that the gold standard for leadership. If you can step away from a company with hundreds of employees for two full weeks and know the team will run it without you, it means you've done your job and trained them well.

> When I told him I considered that the gold standard and said I was proud of him, he laughed and said, "I am easily the weakest link in my company. Everyone else is way more talented than I am, and I know my place."
>
> After hearing that, no one should be surprised to learn that in the past five years this CEO has grown his company by 500 percent, acquired a much larger competitor, and increased profits exponentially.

Fear-based managers believe it would actually be a *great* thing if the team imploded without them. In their minds, a total collapse would prove to everyone that they were irreplaceable. They rarely delegate anything important because they're afraid someone else might do it better—and get noticed.

Opportunity-based leaders would be appalled if their section fell apart without them. They see that as a fundamental failure of leadership. They understand *there's no success without a successor,* and it's their responsibility to ensure that multiple people are always ready to step in and keep the mission on track, no matter the circumstances.

This idea is incredibly scary for many people. "Why would I train my competition if they might take my job or get the promotion I want? That would be stupid, right?" The truth is, bad things can happen, especially if you work for a bad manager. But the fear-based view is shortsighted in many ways, not least because it slows down *your* chances of moving up in the organization.

While holding onto knowledge might give you short-term job security, it also anchors you. You don't want to be known as the technical guru for a specific product or program, because that ties you to it forever. And if the company discontinues that program, you get discontinued, too. Instead, you want to be known as the person who builds amazing teams that achieve the impossible. But how can you prove that unless your team can succeed without you—so you're free to take on the next challenge? Ultimately, you should be able to lead a team doing work you don't personally know how to do, and still have the confidence to build and lead them well.

XOMO

> Will was a prior-service Mustang who had been assigned as a scout platoon leader in an armored cavalry regiment. He did well as a scout platoon leader and when he was promoted to 1LT, he was given the toughest job in the regiment, Executive Officer (XO) of the Headquarters and Headquarters Troop (HHT). The hard thing about the HHT XO job was that it was actually two full time jobs. The first was to do what all other troop or company level XO's would do (already twice as much work as a scout platoon leader). But the hardest part of the job was that the HHT XO was also the Squadron Motor Officer (MO).
>
> The Motor Officer position in a Cavalry squadron is incredibly important because every mission relies on vehicles and Cav Scouts routinely travel three times as far as normal motorized units. It is an important enough job that there is even a special school for it. But there wasn't time to send Will. Nonetheless, he was still responsible for ensuring that each and every one of the squadron's 124 old, beat-up vehicles was ready to deploy within 18 hours.

Will didn't grow up changing oil filters and timing belts like lots of teenage boys, so he absolutely believed he was NOT the right guy for the job because he had no technical knowledge.

On his first day Bill walked into an understaffed, constantly overworked, completely disgruntled squad of mechanics led by a crusty old Staff Sergeant who was pissed off because they made Will the XO four days before the longest road march the squadron had ever attempted – 450 miles with every vehicle, followed by a 28 day field exercise of constant operations, followed by another 450 mile road march home. To SSG Smith, Will wasn't just worthless, he was less than worthless because he was a drain on his time. He had to stop working to constantly explain things to Will who was continuously being asked by HQ about the "status" of everything.

Halfway through the first day, Will's only thought was "I won't survive this job, but until I get thrown out of the Army, how can I make these guys' lives less miserable." So he asked SSG Smith what was the most important thing that needed to be done that Will could actually do for him. SSG Smith was wasting time in meetings and walking back and forth to HQ, so Will told him he would go instead. SSG Smith laughed and started rattling off the parts he needed and 12 other tasks that needed to be done.

Today Will says: "I'm sure all the things he said are actually real words, but at the time it sounded like: "I need 25 zoooops and 25 zaaaaaaps for the globbering gickamuks, and we need to call the depot and request gobsmackers from the chief dunderhead."

It was like SSG Smith was speaking a foreign language so Will pulled out his pen and started writing it down. SSG Smith growled, grabbed the pen out of Will's hand, and wrote down each thing he needed on a separate 3x5 card. Will read it all back to make sure he pronounced everything correctly. SSG Smith laughed and said "good luck," over his shoulder as he walked back into the maintenance area.

Walking up to HQ, Will tried to memorize all of the cards, but the words were just too strange. So he chose the two he thought were most urgent and spent the 15 minutes memorizing just those two. When it was Will's turn to speak at the staff meeting he just rattled off what he had memorized on the card and amazingly, everyone in the room understood what he said.

The Squadron XO (a major) said SSG Smith had already asked for these same things and was told multiple times that he wouldn't get them. Will now understood why SSG Smith had laughed. He knew Will wouldn't be successful, but at least he'd be out of his hair and he could get some work done. The major waited and raised an eyebrow as if to say "is there anything else lieutenant?"

Will asked the major what would change his mind. He told Will he'd have to convince the colonel to call up to Regimental HQ and cash in a favor, which he wouldn't do.

But Will didn't give up because it was the *only* thing he could actually do to help. So after the meeting, he just kept at it. When people told him it couldn't be done, he'd reply with, "Oh, sorry, I'm brand new and I don't know anything. Please explain why this can't happen so I can understand in the future." And in a patronizing tone they'd patiently explain to the dumb lieutenant how things "really" worked and why he couldn't get what SSG Smith needed. He'd thank them and then immediately go to the failure point they'd identified and repeat the process.

After innumerable phone calls and meetings Will was able to get whatever it was he needed (to this day he's still not sure what it was or what it did) and to ensure it arrived on time, he used his own credit card to have UPS go pick it up and send it 2nd day air since expedited shipping wasn't authorized.

Exhausted, and sheepish that he'd only been able to accomplish one of the many things that SSG Smith needed, Will headed back to the motor pool. Everyone else had gone home, but the mechanics were still hard at work at 7 pm. Will found SSG Smith, handed him back the card he'd written out that morning, and said, "It will be here in 2 days." SSG Smith was silent but gave Will one of those flat looks that obviously meant "You're full of shit. You may think you've done this, but I'm sure you didn't get it right." So Will explained who he'd talked to, what they promised and that it was being sent 2nd day air to ensure it would be there on time.

SSG Smith silently looked at Will for what seemed like an entire minute, but finally broke the silence by saying, "Good job Sir" in a perfectly neutral voice and went back to working on a vehicle. Will said it was the best "sir" he's ever gotten because no one has any respect for a new lieutenant that hasn't proven their worth. Nonetheless, military courtesy must be maintained, so instead of "Sir" enlisted soldiers often use an officer's rank – or in the case of lieutenants the term "LT" (pronounced "el-tee"). They don't start calling you "Sir" until you prove yourself to them or hold the rank of captain or above.

It was the strangest job Will ever had because he had no clue what he was doing. But SSG Smith wouldn't let him fail because he knew Will would fight to get what the mechanics needed. So he'd write down what to say and Will would go to a meeting, pretend he knew exactly what he was talking about, and fight like hell to get it.

It took a full six months before Will even began to understand the job, but during that time something magical happened. Somehow the maintenance section, which had previously been referred to in official reports as "understaffed and dispirited" became "the envy of the squadron". And despite the fact that the motor section usually had less than 30% of their authorized mechanics, they maintained one of the highest Organizational Readiness rates ever (94%) during six months of extremely fast-paced, near constant operations and deployments.

In short, those mechanics did the "impossible." And Will took none of the credit because, as should be crystal clear by now, he had no clue what he was doing. The only thing he did was prioritize the team, find ways to get what they needed, and take care of them. And full of esprit-de-corps and confidence in their leader, those mechanics routinely worked past midnight without being asked to ensure vehicles were ready the next day for operations.

They had become a true team, proud of their ability to do so much, with so little, so often.

At some point the mechanics gave Will a new name. HHT Soldiers normally referred to Will as the XO (executive officer). But the motor section felt so strongly that Will was one of them that they added the Motor Officer (MO) portion of his job to the end of the XO and Will became known throughout the entire squadron as XOMO (pronounced Zo-Mo).

That is the power of true leadership. Will didn't actually have to know a single thing about the job (or to even know what the words meant) to be effective and accomplish the mission as long as he got his team what they needed and took care of them. He worked By, With, and Through his team, provided them with Purpose, Direction, Motivation, and Resources and created Fierce Trust. Those mechanics would have followed Will anywhere and done anything for him. And in the end, without ever taking any credit for *anything*, Will got credit for *everything*. He was rated as the top lieutenant in the Squadron, got glowing reviews and an early promotion.

And that's how the least qualified motor officer in the U.S. Army ended up being one of most successful HHT XO / MOs in the squadron's history.

So, how do you develop the courage to do this? It's no different from what we did before. You just do it. Your "confidence targets" will be training *different* team members on different parts of your job. That's how you fulfill your responsibility to make sure the team stays successful even if that bus hits you. Even in the worst-case scenario, if the company brings in someone brand new, your team will be able to keep things moving by showing that person how it all works.

But once you've taught a few people a few different parts of your job, your mindset will already start to shift. What began as a cautious move to protect yourself will start to feel like an opportunity to let go of tasks you don't need to hold onto. After you've spent time teaching a few people how to handle different parts of your job, you'll recognize who has real leadership potential, and instead of feeling threatened, you'll actually want to teach them more. As you continue developing them, you'll let them take on the tasks you've taught so they can get real experience. Some will be excited for the opportunity and will want to take those tasks off your plate permanently, which frees you up to focus on more important leadership tasks.

As the second- and third-order effects begin to show up, you'll have more motivated team members who can handle multiple tasks. That gives you the space to do your real job— supervising their work and focusing on goal setting, training, mentoring, performance agreements, and all the other critical functions that usually get neglected because they aren't urgent.

Here's the best part. Once you've taken care of all the important things and have the team running smoothly and efficiently, you can go to *your* boss and let her know you'd like to learn from her. Explain that you've created some space, so if there are things she wants to take off her list, she can hand them to you. When she asks why you have extra time, explain to her that you've trained your team on many of your functions for their own development, and they're now doing those tasks to build proficiency.

Even if your boss operates from fear, and you should be able to recognize that, she'll still appreciate the extra help. She might keep taking credit for the work you're doing, but over time it will become clear to everyone what's really going on. If she starts to feel threatened because you're learning too much, explain how she can benefit by supporting her boss and positioning herself for even bigger opportunities. If you're truly sincere in your desire to help, even the most jaded leaders will eventually come around and appreciate that you're making them look good.

You've started a virtuous cycle within your company that can't help but be noticed and recognized at some point, even though you never take the credit for anything.

Other Common Fear-Based LOS Managerial Problems
There are so many fear-based behaviors that block great leadership, we couldn't list them all if we tried. But we'll cover a few of the more common ones. By now, you should be able to use the FIT process to work through them—and I'll include a few suggestions along the way.

Doing things instead of leading; being a DOer and not a leader. The Paradox of the New Manager is this: people get promoted because they were good at something (X). But now that they've been promoted, they're not supposed to do X anymore. This is a common trap for new managers, especially those who've never received actual leadership training. No one has told them what they should be doing instead. Sure, the company might have a "management course," but that's not the same as learning how to lead.

I work with a very successful national restaurant chain that has a 30-day training program for their managers. However, their training consists of two weeks in the "back of the house" and another two weeks in the "front of the house," where they learn how to do all the jobs in the restaurant. They're still learning how to "do" things, which is undeniably helpful because it teaches them what everyone should be doing and what the standards are. They can fill out manning schedules and corporate "plan-a-grams" to address corporate goals, but they don't know how to convert those goals into weekly targets. They asked me to help train their managers to lead with a purpose—because it was something they'd never addressed before.

Even in the best companies, the new manager only "kind of" knows what to do. They've watched other managers in other jobs, but they don't know how to write an effective performance review, deal with personnel issues, or motivate their team. They do the best they can, but because they haven't received any leadership training—and because they assume other managers have—they're petrified that upper management will realize they made a mistake in promoting them. They're afraid someone will find out the truth: they don't actually know how to be a manager.

Additionally, managers are often afraid of being overshadowed by a high-performing team member who is visibly accomplishing results. Most management roles still include some direct responsibilities; sales managers continue to close deals, and accounting managers still handle key accounts. A fear-driven manager will often focus on those tasks because they provide one area where their competence can't be challenged. *It allows them to look good while failing.*

This is the wrong approach. In the tech world, there's a saying: "Make your best tech a manager and you lose your best tech—and still don't get a manager." In the wild, the pride leader rarely hunts; their job is to protect the pride's territory so the other lions can hunt. That's your job, too. Make hunters, create the conditions for their success, and let them do it. And don't be afraid to let the newbies try new things on their own—and fail. Failure is to be expected (if people are actually striving) and it's often the best teacher. So don't try to do it for them. Create the kind of environment where they can fail safely and figure it out for themselves.

You are no longer a do-er. Your job now is to ensure the right things get done—and done right. Green Berets are strategic assets. They're "force multipliers," which means even the youngest Green Beret can take a platoon or company of untrained freedom fighters and turn them into a competent fighting force. That Green Beret isn't doing most of the fighting anymore; he's responsible for employing the combat power of 40 to 120 fighters effectively. That's how you should think of yourself—as a combat multiplier.

Micromanagement is another symptom of the fear of being "discovered," but it also layers in additional fears: fear of personal failure, fear of not being seen as the leader, and fear that the team isn't up to the task. Micromanagers often believe that if a team member accomplishes something impressive, the credit still belongs to them—because it was their idea, and they gave precise instructions on how to do it. In their mind, the team only handled the "easy stuff" by executing a fully prescribed plan. They believe that they are the real star because they could have swapped in anyone and achieved the same result.

But ultimately, micromanagement always comes back to the same deep-seated fear: that someone will figure out the truth—that I'm not actually a good leader, no matter what I keep telling myself or the people around me.

Perception Management was discussed earlier in the chapter. It's what happens when we spend more time trying to look like successful bosses than actually helping our teams succeed. It's when our priorities flip—when we care more about *what we can report rather than how we can support*. Because reporting almost always creates extra work for the team, perception management turns the purpose of leadership upside down. Instead of supporting the team, the team ends up supporting our career.

This behavior is similar to "doing instead of leading," but with a twist: it often appears when we don't actually know how to do the jobs our teams are doing. This is common when leaders are promoted to senior roles that span multiple teams. They neither know how to lead nor how to perform the technical work themselves, so they generate lots of busywork to *look like they're in control*—rather than focusing on the mission.

Of course, there will always be some reporting requirements. But when we start inventing new reports that don't move the team closer to its mission or goals, it's probably fear-based. Perception management demands that we take credit when things go well and deflect blame when they don't—because it's ultimately about protecting personal power, not improving team performance.

To make sure our boss and other leaders see us as "managerial," we start scheduling meetings. Then more meetings. Then meetings to prepare for upcoming meetings, where the real focus is making the slides—and ourselves—look good rather than solving problems. We send a flood of emails, CC'ing our boss and their boss to show we're on top of everything. We email after hours to demonstrate how dedicated we are. And we require constant updates from our teams, interrupting their real work, just so we can build PowerPoint decks that prove how busy and essential we are.

Ironically, at this level managers often start using "we" instead of "I." But it's not because they've started giving credit to their teams. No, it's because they don't actually understand the work their teams are doing and they want to appear as part of the group that's still producing real results. The problem is, the only thing they're producing is more work and more stress. Instead of helping their teams, they are burdening them by demanding constant status updates, sending late-night messages that feel urgent, scheduling meetings that don't benefit anyone, treating everything like a top priority, and demanding that everything gets "done now!" Instead of protecting their teams from outside demands, they prioritize work for other departments so they look good to other managers—even if it puts their own people behind.

They start looking for ways to cut costs, even when senior leadership hasn't asked for it, because it gives them a sense of control. Rather than fighting for additional resources to help their teams succeed, they begin eliminating anything that isn't obviously essential—because it makes for a good bullet point on their next evaluation. At the same time, while trimming budgets and letting go of "expensive" personnel, they often assign even more work to the remaining team. The goal isn't impact; it's having something to point to and say, "Look what I've done."

Because looking like the boss is paramount, these managers start reading the latest business books and repeating trendy phrases to their teams. But they rarely take the lessons to heart or teach the material in any meaningful way. It's not about learning. It's about sounding like someone who belongs in senior leadership. They latch onto one or two popular ideas and try to tie everything the team does to that theme, turning it into the catchphrase of the quarter.

That's not to say these phrases should never be used. They can be helpful—but only if they're used with clarity and purpose. Don't lean on them as a crutch to sound intelligent or experienced. The same goes for rallying concepts and team slogans. Use them if they make sense, but make sure you actually understand what they mean and what it takes to apply them. Don't ask your team to "turn this quarter around with win-wins" unless you can explain what a real win-win looks like—and how to get there.

Stepping Into the Spotlight. A common fear when taking over a team in a high-stakes role is that you could be let go after the very first perceived mistake. So even if you want to follow the advice in this book, you may feel like you don't have time to build trust or let others see your long game.

The pressure to appear competent from day one becomes overwhelming. This is where all the previously discussed behaviors tend to converge. We take credit for wins, avoid blame when things go wrong, hide what we don't know, lean into tasks we're already good at, and demand constant status updates. We schedule meetings, generate reports, and send emails up the chain—not to advance the mission, but to make sure we look like we're doing the job. It's perception management under pressure, and it's driven by fear.

There is often some validity to this fear, but even in finance, where everyone is judged by the quarter, the first one is still a freebie *as a new manager*. A significant individual loss might get you fired—but not if you're executing your EPIC leader's plan.

Even when a leader is brought in to take over a failing department, there's still an expectation that they'll need some time to identify the problems, develop a plan, and execute it. The fear that we have to look excellent right away is usually in our own heads—unless we're dealing with a truly bad boss.

The best way to address this fear is to explain your plan to your boss. Chapter 1 of Book 2 includes a detailed 21-step approach for taking over a team. If you share just the first seven steps along with a rough timeline, it will be the best plan they've ever seen—and you'll get the time you need without the stress of worrying about being fired.

You can also tell your boss that things might look a little weird at first because you're going to take the blame for everything and give your team all the credit. Let them know you're assessing what everyone already knows, so there will be times when you'll say you don't know how to do something—just to see what the team comes up with. You can explain your plan to cross-train the team and build a real succession plan, and as part of that, you'll be permanently delegating some of your DO-ing tasks to free up time for the leadership work you're actually there to do.

If you're still worried, write up a strong Cooperative Performance Agreement (also in the next chapter) that clearly lays out expectations, timelines, and the metrics for success.

Melinda the Senior Level IT Manager

"Melinda" works for a Fortune 50 healthcare company that everyone knows. She was recently promoted to a more senior management role that oversees multiple departments. The position that Melinda took was unoccupied for almost two years, in large part because the smaller departments took care of themselves and accomplished their missions and tasks without any drama. But there was a "slot" for a senior manager and eventually it had to get filled. When Melinda took over she told her new teams how excited she was about her new opportunity.

One of the departments that reports to Melinda is an IT Configuration (Config) Team that handles front-end coding to integrate existing programs and systems and keep up with changes. Their job is straightforward so unless the team needs major resources, they just get things done, fix problems, and everyone is happy.

Melinda didn't waste any time making changes and immediately started asking all her sections for "status updates" and weekly (sometimes daily) PowerPoint presentations on what each department was doing. In order to demonstrate her worth and get other senior managers to like her, Melinda inserted herself into the flow of requests for the Config Team and began elevating the priority of less important tasks when asked for a favor. She made sure to CC her boss in the exchanges so he'd see what a good team player she was and that she was busy getting things done.

The Config team got behind on their real work because of all the new reporting requirements and false priorities. They asked to do a demonstration for Melinda so she could see for herself what the team does and reduce the number of reports; she refused. Instead she spent her time looking at the costs for each department to see what she could cut from the budget and said that the Config Team expenses were "too high" and set her sights on a highly paid contractor (Prabu).

While contractors are cheaper for the company overall, what's important for Melinda is that all contractor costs come directly from *her* budget whereas full time employees get benefits and bonuses from different pots of corporate money. And even though no one asked Melinda to reduce her budget, she decided to distinguish herself by cutting costs, and Prabu was by far the biggest expense on the IT team at 18% of total budget.

But Prabu was also the most knowledgeable and skilled person on the team. The other contractors on the team weren't U.S. based and didn't have the same experience, skill sets, or motivation as Prabu. He not only taught the other contractors how to do their jobs but often organized their efforts so that he could do the more difficult tasks.

Melinda didn't ask the Config Team Manager (Anya) how to cut costs in Config. So when Anya heard of the plan to get rid of Prabu, she objected. When it became apparent that Melinda was determined to cut costs, Anya instead recommended releasing two of the overseas-based contractors because they weren't as skilled as Prabu and time zone issues made it harder to communicate with them. But all Melissa saw was Prabu's big salary taking a chunk out of her budget.

This was a train wreck ready to happen. I want to stress again that everything was running smoothly for almost two years without Melinda, but once she took over, the constant reporting requirements, updates, meetings, and mis-prioritized tasks increased the workload tenfold.

Instead of taking care of her teams, Melinda had the teams taking care of her so she would look good in her new senior management role. Melinda created a maelstrom of stress in all her departments because everything became an urgent priority. Even though the Config Team followed procedures that had been established by higher authority for elevating routing tasks, Melinda didn't know how to do IT configuration, didn't care about the existing procedures, and didn't listen to her team. The metric for success appeared to be how many emails Melinda could CC her boss and peers each day so everyone could see how busy she was and all the things that she was doing for them. Emergencies were good for Melinda because she got to show how responsive she was and that she was leading the team through the "urgent" problems.

But Melinda was also wasting her boss' time because she was constantly sending him new reports and lots of emails. Instead of actually helping her teams be more efficient and effective, she was using their output as bullet points on her slides so she could show her boss what a good job she was doing.

When the IT team had problems that required Melinda's approval for resources, she didn't remove obstacles.

Instead, she scheduled more meetings. The Config Team eventually stopped asking for support altogether because it was too painful and now finds workarounds on their own. Melinda has only been on the job three months, but the pain and looming disaster have already pushed Anya to start looking for a way out.

Although Anya objected, Melinda fired Prabu, and problems began almost immediately. The remote contractors lacked the experience to handle the system's complexity. In the past, Anya had tried to bring in another senior tech to avoid making Prabu a single point of failure, but her requests were repeatedly denied. She even wrote a standard operating procedure to cover most tasks, but with so many programming permutations, it was impossible to account for every scenario. That is why having at least one experienced tech on the team was essential. Anya, a project manager rather than an IT technician, did not have the expertise to handle the mounting technical issues. A team that once ran smoothly was now consumed by crisis management. Anya took a better job before everything imploded - something she hadn't planned to do.

Melinda's role suddenly appeared more important than ever. She told her boss it was a good thing she arrived when she did because otherwise, the situation would have been much worse. She placed the blame on Anya, who couldn't defend herself. To solve the growing problems, Melinda plans to hire a less expensive replacement for Prabu. The move will ultimately cost the company more, but the hiring and training expenses come from HR's budget and will not reflect on Melinda's books.

This is a textbook case of looking good while failing. The trainwreck is inevitable, but Melinda will still be able to claim she cut costs in her first year as a senior manager, regardless of how much damage she leaves behind.

Senior executives, there's a big lesson here for you too. I *guarantee* you have a few Melindas in your organization right now. They are hard to spot if you only look at the reports. You *must* do your job and actually visit and speak with the people who are doing the work in your divisions. Rarely will anyone come out and say, "Please get rid of Melinda, she is ruining us!" Instead, they will demur. They'll hedge, hem and haw, and shuffle their feet. *That's* what you're looking for. And when you find that, you need to turn over every rock to find out exactly what is going on. Because Melinda is real (I changed her name to protect others), and she will continue to cause damage until you stop her and retrain her.

Board members, this goes for you too. If you aren't talking directly to lower-level managers, you are not conducting your due diligence. Some of the worst-run companies I know have CEOs who have convinced the board that everything is fine—or that any problems are not their fault. The number of companies with boards of directors oblivious to major issues within their organizations is astounding. If the only information you are getting comes from the C-suite, you are not doing your job as a board member.

Pay attention if the CEO always wants to schedule board meetings away from the company itself. Sure, it sounds great to have your board meeting in the Bahamas—but it's not to give you a nice vacation. It's a bribe to keep you happy and to stop you from asking questions that might ruin everyone's good time. It's to pull you away from company operations, where you might find information that conflicts with what the C-suite is presenting to you.

I don't spend a lot of time in this book discussing the specifics of senior management or corporate governance. But if you believe everything in that perfectly produced beautiful board packet is the truth - you're wrong! And you haven't done your job. You have an obligation to shareholders to turn over every rock and root out every Melinda and dissembling CEO that's out there.

This Makes Me Feel Uncomfortable
You might already know that you're trying to look busy, micromanaging, or doing too much instead of actually leading—and if that's the case, good for you. Remember, it's not your fault; we are all programmed with these default evolutionary responses. But after you address those behaviors using the FIT process, they'll start to fade on their own. You can also use an Enhanced Franklin Grid to guide and track your progress. In fact, there are enough leadership actions in this chapter to build three or four grids, and I suggest you do exactly that to help keep those fears in check. In the workbook, we've included three pre-filled Enhanced Franklin Grids on the leadership fears discussed in this chapter to get you started.

However, you may also be one of those people who genuinely believe you're showing strong leadership—and that none of this applies to you. So how do you know if you're fooling yourself? Start by asking if any of this makes you feel uncomfortable. If it does, follow that discomfort down the rabbit hole and strap in, because like most things related to character, it's going to take courage to face it head-on.

For many of us, confronting our fears and constraints triggers our fight-or-flight response. Parts of this book might annoy you—you might withdraw, avoid it, or put it down for a few days. Or you might feel resistant and combative. Maybe you're calling me a jerk right now and telling yourself I don't know what I'm talking about. That's perfectly normal. These reactions are automatic and largely outside our control, because the "threats" they respond to usually surface from the unconscious. Later, as those reactions rise into awareness, you'll likely feel that something just isn't right.

If you don't experience these feelings at least a few times while reading this book, you might be one of those managers who believes they're operating at the highest level—when in reality, it's just the opposite. It takes a lot of courage to confront long-held beliefs and perceived truths, especially knowing that the process might actually change you. It's always a pain in the butt to change out or update the operating system.

How do we deal with these feelings of defensiveness or withdrawal? Once again we turn to physical courage to give us the answer.

Go To The Sound of the Guns

Now we enter the realm of fabled courage where heroes emerge and legends are born. Firemen run into the fire, not away. Soldiers and Marines know they need to be where the big guns are because that's where decisive battles are won. Are they afraid? Absolutely! They will tell you the day they completely lose their fear is the day they will most likely die. Will there be some pain involved? Probably. But they go anyway. But they weren't always willing to head towards the danger, right? They had to learn to face their fears and overcome them for the good of others.

Courage—physical or psychological—is being afraid but not letting the fear stop you from doing what you need to do. And that's what you're going to do every time you start to get uncomfortable when confronting your perceptual or functional constraints,[49] whenever you feel triggered by anything in this book, or when someone tells you something you don't want to hear. You're not going to run and hide. You're not going to get angry at them. You're going to be ready when these challenges to your worldview arise and you're going to summon the courage to stick with the irritation, anger, or disbelief and look inside yourself to find out what is bothering you so much. You will choose to go down that rabbit hole and wrestle with whatever is living there until you come back up victorious. You will head towards the threat. You will go to the sound of the guns.

This is also a form of transformational learning, a way to shift your own paradigms. And the moment you can honestly identify the issue is the moment you break through the barriers and gain freedom from whatever limits and constraints you have accumulated. Some people are afraid of losing themselves in this process, but that won't happen. What you experience

---

49 Perceptual and Functional Constraints (a psychological term) limit and provide boundaries that influence our perception and interaction with the world. Scrutinizing and challenging these constraints means questioning and possibly disrupting the familiar and comfortable ways through which we typically perceive and engage with our surroundings. It means confronting our biases, reevaluating our beliefs, and venturing outside our comfort zones.

is *additive*, it doesn't take anything away; you will still have all your previous frames of reference to call upon. But you're no longer limited to doing things as you did before. Every time you choose to go towards the sound of the guns you will feel immense pride and a new source of personal power. Do this three or four times and you *will* be unstoppable.

Some of the most important principles Ray Dalio used to build the most successful hedge fund in history (and to become one of the richest men in the world) deal with this very subject. He believes "pain + reflection = progress." He writes about the need to find the truth and the mistake of avoiding pain, especially "when people confront the harsh reality of their own imperfections."[50] Instead, he advocates, "Go to the pain rather than avoid it," and to expect that the more ambitious the goal, the greater the pain. In other words, go to the sound of the guns.

TTP - Other Helpful Tactics, Techniques, and Procedures
To completely conquer a fear you'll need to face it and inoculate yourself using FIT. However, the following TTP (Tactics, Techniques, and Procedures) will help us execute the inoculation process and give you a place to start. There isn't room to list them all here, so you'll find three additional pages of TTPs in the workbook.

Get Started Getting Started! Just do anything, no matter how small, because movement abates fear. Now is good. There will never be enough time, and there will never be a right time. Just start moving in ANY direction, and you can make course corrections along the way. Even if you're running in

[50] Principles, by Ray Dalio, Pg 152-3, Simon and Schuster, New York, 2017

the wrong direction, it will give you the space to start thinking clearly again. But generally, when it's time to "just move," you should go to the sound of the guns. Your mind will kick into overdrive, scrambling to come up with a solution as you are sprinting to get there.

Reductio Ad Absurdum (reduce to absurdity) is a logic argument used to prove an idea can't possibly be true by showing that denial of the opposite would lead to a ridiculous conclusion. A mainstay of Greek philosophy, it is the basis for the Socratic method and has been used by Aristotle, Plato, Euclid, Archimedes and many others throughout history. A classic example was used to prove the earth isn't flat. The argument: "The earth cannot be flat because the earth is finite and therefore if it was flat people would ultimately find the edge and fall off." Pretty silly, right? Use it to your advantage.

A fear we've already discussed is that giving credit to others could diminish our own standing. We start by making a small assertion – that we aren't the dumbest or the worst person in the world. So if we've seen other leaders (not all of whom were better or smarter than we are) giving credit to their team and it hasn't hurt their career, why should it hurt ours? And if giving credit to others actually makes those other leaders look good and people want to work for them, why wouldn't that work for us? Isn't it absurd to think that we can't do something that other normal people can?

And while you're being absurd, take it to the next level and **Get Silly** because humor tempers fear. Give your fear a name like "Muffin, the puppy in a cup." How could you possibly be afraid of a puppy in a cup? Seriously. Try it now. Think of something super stressful that you're afraid of (like having to tell a team member that they're performing poorly) and rename "poor performance review" to "Niblet, puppy in a cup." It immediately changes the way you feel about it. There is a ton of research that shows **humor** reframes our perception of a fear or stressor and allows us to deal with it more effectively.

Ask yourself, "**What would I do if I wasn't afraid?**" and you will get some amazing answers. This is one of my favorites and I use it often. "What would I do if I knew I couldn't screw this up?" is another great confidence builder.

Change the Locus of your Focus. Stop thinking about yourself! Take the focus off of you. Why do firemen rush into buildings? Because they are focused on the team or someone else. Hyrum Smith, co-founder of Franklin Covey, asked a woman in one of his seminars if she'd cross a beam from the top of one building to another. She said no. He offered her a million dollars but added there was now wind and rain. She said no. He then told her to imagine he was holding her child over the edge on the other side and would drop him in 10 seconds, and she immediately shouted "Yes!" How does this apply to you? One example is to consider that constructive feedback is a gift. It may seem difficult, but ask yourself if it's better to let someone keep making mistakes until they get fired or is it kinder to give them some tough feedback now so they can improve before it's too late.

Conclusion

This was a long chapter because fear-based management is the invisible current in organizational culture, and it's what holds most people back from becoming truly great leaders.

Despite overwhelming evidence from more than two decades of research, most coaches, academics, business schools, leadership consultants, and professional journals still fail to connect poor leadership behaviors—like micromanagement—to their root cause: fear. As a result, many of us keep working on the symptoms instead of addressing the actual disease. A few things to remember:

- ◊ Being a new or untrained manager means carrying around a suitcase full of fears.

- ◊ Courage is not the lack of fear; courage is not letting fear control your actions.

- ◊ Fear is built into our basic operating system from birth and our body doesn't distinguish between physical and psychological fears. Unfortunately most psychological fight, flight, or freeze responses to psychological fear are counterproductive and must be retrained.

- ◊ Pretending those fears don't exist—or trying to ignore them—only makes things worse. The first step to becoming a great leader is to acknowledge and address those fears.

- ◊ Just like everyone else, Green Berets go through processes to master their fears. You can, too!

- ◊ This will hurt. And it won't be easy. But, as Ray Dalio says. "Pain + Reflection = Progress." He also says, "Evolve or Die" or, as we've been saying: Embrace the Suck.

- ◊ The best methods for overcoming psychological fear are the same as overcoming physical fear. If you learned how to ride a bike, you can learn to give away credit and take the blame.

◊ Stress and fear are closely related and, just like stress, we can inoculate ourselves to specific fears through Fear Inoculation Training: education, training and tools, exposure, experience, and, ultimately, inoculation.

Paradoxically, just being willing to face your fears already makes you more courageous. That willingness, however small, starts the cycle. It's a capacity that grows every time you choose to look at the thing that scares you instead of running. The more fears you face, the more confident you become. The more confident you become, the more courage you can access the next time it counts.

Congratulations! You've finished Part I of *The Green Beret Way*. You've started your own journey from being a fear-based manager to an opportunity-based leader. Well done. This book isn't an easy read like most leadership books, so just getting to this point shows real determination.

But now the hard part begins. In the introduction, I recommended that you read through the entire book first without stopping to do the exercises—because we want to read all the instructions before we try to use our new skills, remember? Well, now it's time to go back and do the work.

Start by taking the assessment at https://thegreenberetway.com/epic. Don't shortchange the process, and get as many people as you can to take it for you so you get accurate results. Use the instructions online and in the book to evaluate your results, and then build your personal Q-Course as laid out in

Chapter 3. After that, try using some EMP+ communication (if you haven't already) to get a feel for it and finally address any fears you identified in this chapter.

Why now? Because this is the point when Green Berets complete their individual training and move to their new teams where they learn the advanced skills required to operate at the highest levels. You want to be ready before you take on Part II, which is all about how to build and lead your own elite teams. Book Two introduces methodologies, processes, and advanced tools that rely on the foundation of Part I.

If you don't want to go back through the book again, you can use *The Green Beret Way Workbook* and simply open it up and follow the instructions. Every exercise from this book (and more) is included and arranged in the correct order. You don't need the workbook to succeed. It just makes the process easier.

In Book Two, we shift from the inner work of becoming a leader to the outer work of building and leading elite teams. You'll learn specific, concrete steps to take over any team and make it extraordinary—through intentional team design, training, personnel development, continuous improvement, and evolution. You'll also learn how to apply different leadership styles to unlock the full potential of each individual and the team as a whole.

We'll cover the most powerful problem-solving and decision-making process in the world—already used by some of the most successful companies—which ensures you make the best possible decisions. It's the same reason teams of Green Berets are never wiped out, despite always being first in and operating in the harshest environments.

You'll also learn advanced time management for individuals and teams, how to create and operationalize goals using a superior planning system, and how to build a leadership culture that enables your organization to routinely exceed expectations.

So move out Candidate, conduct your own assessment and complete your training, and we'll meet again soon in Book Two of *The Green Beret Way*.

ACKNOWLEDGEMENTS

Many people contributed to this book and I'd like to begin by thanking every client and company that has trusted me to train, advise, and assist your most precious resources. You gave me the opportunity to validate the ideas and methods in this book so that others may successfully use them in the future.

There are four people that I've worked for that were absolutely terrible leaders. In hindsight I realize that I learned more from them than I did from most leaders I worked with and I thank them for their lessons - which are still crystal clear. Their examples of "what not to do" feature prominently in the book.

I've also had the honor of working with some truly exceptional leaders whose lessons are showcased in vignettes. I'm forever grateful for their mentoring and modeling of what great leaders do. Most people won't recognize the names Rich Piscal, Mark Marchant, Norm Fuss, Bruce Parkman (Pacman), Hanshi Bill Dometrich, or John Koko—but those who've met them will quickly affirm they belong in this story.

I'd also like to thank all of the other leaders I've worked for - you've all been solid examples of "how to do it right" and I'm sure some of you became truly exceptional leaders.

Thanks to all my Green Beret brethren for (mostly) being a shining example of excellence for me to try to emulate - and for putting up with me when I wasn't at my best. I still owe apologies to some of you for not being the leader you deserved.

Thanks to Major General John Kirk Singlaub, U.S. Army Special Forces - one of the WWII Office of Strategic Services (OSS) Jedburghs and founding member of both the CIA and the Green Berets for his friendship and the hours he spent mentoring me. He was one of the giants upon whose shoulders the rest of us stood. He is greatly missed by our entire community.

Colonel David Hackworth (Hack) was the most highly decorated soldier in US Army history (91 awards and decorations), a soldier's soldier and one of our greatest, most outspoken, and controversial leaders; Robert Duvall's character in the movie *Apocalypse Now* is based on him. In later years he was known as a prolific writer with multiple best-selling books and his reporting for Newsweek. What is less known is the treasure trove of articles he wrote while still on active duty about leadership in an unconventional warfare environment and published in numerous professional journals such as *Army, Army Digest, Military Review,* and *Infantry Magazine.* Yet even those barely scratched the surface and I am forever grateful that he shared excerpts from his unpublished book *The Platoon Leaders Combat Guide*, and every copy of *The Pathfinder* - an unofficial mimeographed wartime newsletter he wrote and distributed to his battalion during the Vietnam War to help his subordinate commanders be more successful. While some of that work was later distilled into his bestselling book *About Face,* I cannot overestimate the profound impact that his generosity had on me while still a young captain. I neglected to thank him in my first book where his influence was just as profound.

The EPIC Leadership Training Program™ has four parts - of which this book is the first. The second, the EPIC

Acknowledgments

Leadership Assessment™, is a critical piece of the program and could not have been developed so quickly or expertly without the help of Shalom Smolik (psychometrician) and Matteo Salverio (Online Developer), both of whom are outright geniuses in their respective fields. Their work has ensured that we can offer the assessment free of charge so it can help the greatest number of people, and that is no easy feat. While the assessment has met every expectation and been an invaluable tool for helping people assess their true leadership traits, we are excited about the fact that our work on the assessment is sufficiently unique, significant, and valid that we are advancing the science in the field of organizational psychology and we expect to publish at least one peer-reviewed paper in the near future.

I'd also like to thank all the people who did beta testing for the assessment and took it over and over again until we could get it right.

This book would have taken years longer to publish without Antoinette Kuritz, who shepherded the project forward with surprising speed once it reached her hands. Gwyn Flowers made everything look great, and Alyscia McDermott ensured every "i" was dotted and every "t" crossed. Mindy Wells designed The Green Beret Way emblem, and I couldn't be happier. Stephen S. Power was instrumental in editing the first chapter and shaping the overall structure.

My assistants Caren Tavares and (formerly) Debi Anders were an enormous help by suggesting early ideas, proofreading, preparing chapters, and building out the workbook (part 3 of the program) while simultaneously providing back-end support and program management of the course itself (part 4).

Many people were kind enough to read early drafts of the chapters and *not* say nice things about them. The value of their gift is directly proportional to the discomfort I experienced as they pointed out a number of problems with the original versions. Thankfully they provided plenty of suggestions that made the book better. I'd like to thank Bobby Newman, Marty Johnson, LTC Howard (Dan) Hill, Special Forces Ret, Chief Warrant Officer 4 Bob Pennington, Special Forces, Ret, Aja Baliker, Marianne Chevalier, and Marci Bunn.

To my Harvard brethren for always supporting me (and each other) in all our crazy schemes. In particular Robert Bunn and Chadwick Pelletier have always been steadfast friends and pirates at heart.

And finally to my wife, Olya, for putting up with another book and my kids Rowan and Nicholas who motivate me every day.

Unfortunately I'm sure I've missed a few people, so if you helped and I neglected to mention you, I'm sorry. And thank you. Let's hope we are able to publish a second edition so I can make it up to you.

Continue your journey.

Read the first chapter for **FREE** *at*:

thegreenberetway.com/book2

www.ingramcontent.com/pod-product-compliance
Ingram Content Group UK Ltd.
Pitfield, Milton Keynes, MK11 3LW, UK
UKHW022236230426
12048UKWH00018BA/1300